New Highlight 3

Cornelsen

INHALT

Unit **6*** ist nur Pflichtstoff für den E-Kurs in Nordrhein-Westfalen.

1◉-2 Als Hörtext oder Song auf der Audio-CD vorhanden; die Track-Angaben beziehen sich auf die Vollfassung (Bestellnummer 344576): 1◉-2 = CD 1, Track 2.

W ◉ Zusätzliche Aufgaben auf der CD-ROM im Workbook

Kann dem Portfolio-Ordner hinzugefügt werden

Aufgaben:

○ leicht ◐ mittel ● schwierig

Interkulturell

Wiederholung

Begleitend zum Schülerbuch finden sich unter www.new-highlight.de interaktive Online-Übungen, die am Ende jeder Unit bearbeitet werden können.

* Fakultativ (wahlfreie Bestandteile des Lehrwerks)

Here and there

1 The Britain and Ireland Quiz

1 2

a) Look at the map on page 7 and listen. Write the answers (a or b) to quiz questions 1–10.

b) Compare your answers with a partner.

c) Listen again and check your answers.

1 3

2 More about Britain and Ireland

a) Work with a partner.
Look at the map and finish these sentences. Write *England, Scotland, Wales, Ireland.*

1 ... and ... have borders with England.
2 ... has a tunnel to France.
3 ... is famous for a special beer.
4 ... is the home of golf.
5 ... has an animal on its flag.
6 ... is famous for a musical instrument.
7 ... is the home of great football clubs like Manchester United.
8 ... produces lots of computers and software.
9 The most popular sport in ... is rugby.
10 In ... men sometimes wear special clothes – kilts.

b) Look at page 181 and check your answers.

3 Here in Germany: Finish the sentences.

1 Germany is in the ... of Europe.
2 The capital of Germany is ...
3 Germany has borders with the Czech Republic, ...
4 People in Germany come from lots of different countries: Turkey, ...
5 The German flag is ...
6 Germany's most popular sport is ...
7 Germany is the home of ....
8 Germany produces lots of ...
9 Germany is famous for ...
10 Germany has great music: bands like ...

Tip:
Look at the map of Europe at the back of the book.

Britain and Ireland

Unit 1

London scenes

A

B

E

F

1 London sounds

1◉4 **Listen. Match the four sounds with four pictures on pages 8 and 9.**

"One" is picture ... "Two" is picture ... "Three" is ... "Four" is ...

2 London scenes

1◉5 **a) Listen. Which four pictures (A–H) on pages 8 and 9 are the people talking about?**

b) Listen again. Match these names with the four pictures.

RIDLEY ROAD MARKET	PICCADILLY CIRCUS	WESTMINSTER BRIDGE	THE LONDON EYE

► W 3, 1

C

D

G

H

3 City words

a) What can you see in the pictures? Work in groups.

b) Can you see the things in the green box? In which pictures?

c) Make a network with the city words in the box.

> I can see a/an ...
> I can't see a/an ...

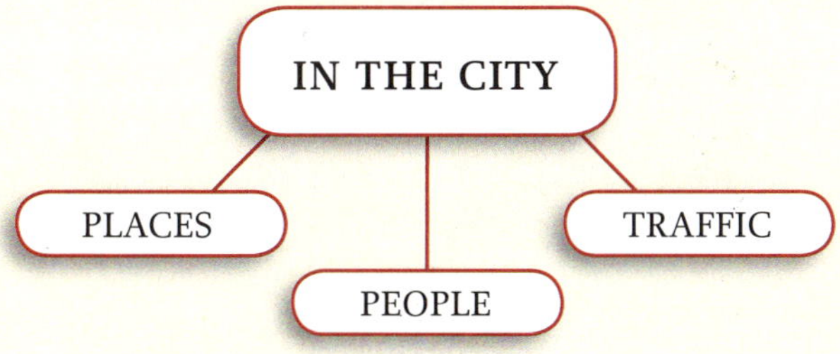

→ bike • child • boy • bridge • car • underground train • woman • park • motorbike • girl • man • restaurant • bus • shop • shopper • street • taxi • underground station

▸ W 3, 2–3

d) Now find more words for your network.

▸ Wordbank 1, p. 127

ASHA'S LONDON

Tip:
You can find out lots of things before you read a text. So always look at the title first.

1 Before you read:

a) Look at the title. Who's this page about?
b) Look at the texts. Are they letters, e-mails or postcards?
c) Who wrote the texts?

To Asha
From Per Li

Hi Asha,
How are you? How's London?
Is it very different from Singapore?
Is it very cold?
Do you have a new flat? Are you at your new school?
I have lots of questions. So please write soon.
I'm fine, but we all miss you here in Singapore.
Please send some photos.
Your friend,
Per Li

Here's a photo, so please don't forget me!

To Per Li
From Asha

Dear Per Li,
Thanks for your e-mail. Yes, London is very different from Singapore – it's bigger and colder! But there are lots of Asian people here. In fact, there are people from lots of different countries.
We're staying with my aunt at the moment. But we're looking for our own place. I'm starting at my new school next week and I'm feeling nervous. I don't have any friends yet.
Thanks for your photo, it's great.
I'm sending you some photos.
Lots of love,
Asha

I'm in Brick Lane. I'm eating some Asian food!

Look at mum and dad. They're standing near my aunt's house in Raleigh Road.

2 Read the e-mails and pick two titles.

- New in London
- New in Singapore
- Hello from Singapore
- Goodbye London

3 What's right?

1 Per Li is in Singapore/London.
2 Asha is from Singapore/London.
3 Per Li misses London/Asha.
4 London is colder/warmer than Singapore.
5 Asha is staying with her friend/aunt.
6 Asha is starting school/work next week.
7 Asha has/doesn't have friends in London.

► W 4, 4–5

4 SONGS

a) **Listen. What are all the songs about?**

1 6 b) **Talk to a partner.**

YOU	What do you think of the songs?
YOUR PARTNER	Song ... is great. / I like song ... / I love song ...
	Song ... is OK. / I don't like song ... / I hate song ...
	Song ... is my favourite. / All the songs are good / OK / terrible.

c) **Listen to the songs again. Then find out what the favourite in the class is.**

1 6 Who likes song 1 best? Who likes ...

PROJECT Learn about London

a) **What are places 1 and 2?** b) **Now find the names of places 3–6.**

c) **Now find out:**

1 How many people live in London?
2 What's the name of the big river in London?
3 Where does the English football team play?
4 When are the Olympics coming to London?
5 Where does the Queen live?
6 What famous people come from London?

Tip:
Find some books and brochures about London.
Or use the Internet. Go to this website:
www.new-highlight.de
Find the window for the webcode and put in:
NHL-3-11
First put in London. Then put in words like these:
pictures, people, river, football, Olympics, Queen.

You can use a dictionary.

d) **Work in groups. Make a London brochure.**

- **Find pictures.**
- **Write the names of the places.**
- **Write 3–4 sentences about London.**

e) **What can you see in your brochure? Tell the class.**

In our brochure you can see ...
It's very famous/old/new/big ...

► W 4, 6–7

1 **Before you read or listen:**

a) Where's Asha's new home?

b) What does she think of her new school?

2 **Look at the pictures in the story: Are these sentences right or wrong?**

1 Asha is at her new school.
2 She's very happy on the first day.
3 All the other pupils are friendly.
4 Asha is in a club.
5 It's a film club.
6 Asha is feeling happier in the last picture.

Tip:
Pictures often help you to understand better. Always look at the pictures before you read or listen.

Don't give up!

1⊙7

Scene 1: The classroom

It's Monday, Asha's first day at her new school. She's sitting in her classroom – 9PN.

LARA You're new.
ASHA Yes, it's my first day. I'm Asha.
LARA Hi, Asha. I'm Lara. Where was your last school?
ASHA In Singapore.
LARA Singapore? Is that in Africa?
ASHA No, it's in Asia.

Another girl is listening.

HOLLY Thousands of people come to London every year from Asia and Africa and other places. My dad says they take our jobs.
LARA That's stupid. Lots of English people have jobs in other countries. And London is an international city. Welcome to London, Asha.

Scene 2: The noticeboard

It's Friday and Asha is feeling lonely. She likes Lara, but Lara has other friends. Mr Nixon, the class teacher, is talking to Asha. They're standing next to the noticeboard.

MR NIXON Asha, can we have a chat?
ASHA Of course, Mr Nixon.
MR NIXON It isn't easy to find new friends. But don't give up. You should join a club.
ASHA OK, but which club? I don't like any sports.
MR NIXON Let's look at the noticeboard. There are some good clubs here. What about the music club?
ASHA The music club? Hmm ...!

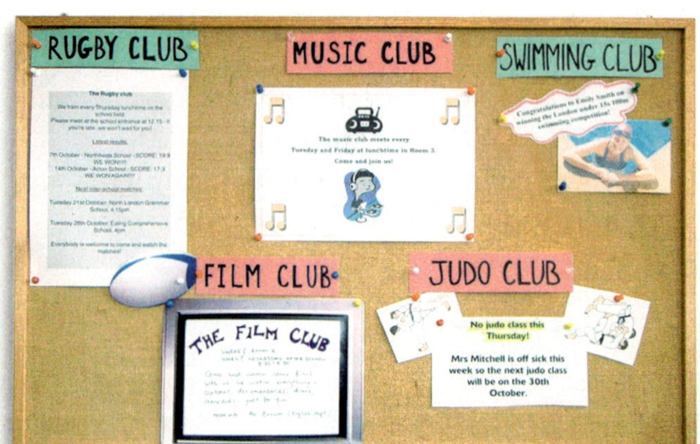

Scene 3: The music club

The music club meets every Tuesday and Friday at lunchtime. Asha is there today. Lara is there too. They're thinking about plans for their club.

LARA Listen! We need some ideas for the club.

But everybody is quiet. Then Asha speaks.

ASHA Let's start a school radio programme. There's one in my old school.

LARA A radio programme?

ASHA Yes. Every day at lunchtime they play music on the school intercom.

LARA Great idea! And we can read the school news.

HARRY Yes, like "Lara loves Luke Jackson" ...

LARA Don't be stupid!

ASHA I have another idea. My dad is a DJ. He can give us DJ lessons.

LUKE Great idea!

Scene 4: The radio programme

It's lunchtime on Monday – time for the first radio programme.

ASHA Hello and welcome to the *Music Club Radio Programme*. We have lots of things for you – great music, club news and school news. The first song is *Don't give up*. It's for Mr Nixon. He loves this song.

► W 5, 8–9

1 8

3 Listen to the radio programme:
a) Do you like it?
b) What clubs does Luke talk about?

4 Asha's school and your school: What's the same? What's different? Talk in your class about:
– clubs
– where pupils come from
– school radio

5 Finish Asha's e-mail.

To Per Li
From Asha

... Per Li,
Monday was my first ... at my new school. One girl in my class thinks Singapore is in .... But she's nice – her name is .... Another girl isn't very nice – her name is .... Mr Nixon is my class ... and he's OK. He thinks that I should ... a club. We looked at the .... One club looks interesting – the ... club.
Lots of ...,
Asha

6 Now you're Asha. Write an e-mail to Per Li about your new club.

To Per Li
From Asha

...,
I'm in .... We meet ....
We're starting .... We play ....
We read .... Dad is giving us ....
...,
...

► W 5, 10

1 Make six sentences. The words are all in the story on pages 12–13.

You	feel	a chat.
	have	a club.
	join	the news.
	play	music.
	read	lonely.
	give	a lesson.

2 New words These words are on pages 12–13 too.

a) Put two parts together and make a word.

1 notice	time
2 lunch	national
3 inter	room
4 class	board

b) Which words go together?

1 class	club
2 judo	news
3 radio	teacher
4 school	programme

c) Put in some of the words from a) and b).

1 London is an ... city. People from lots of countries live there.
2 I usually have a salad at ...
3 You can read about the school clubs on the ...
4 My favourite ... is *The Top Twenty*.

3 You're in England with your grandad. He doesn't understand. What can you say in German?

4 Some or any?

a) Put in *some* or *any*.

These sentences are on pages 10–14.

1 Please send ... photos. (p. 10)
2 I don't have ... friends yet. (p. 10)
3 I'm eating ... Asian food. (p. 10)
4 I don't like ... sports. (p. 12)
5 We need ... ideas. (p. 13)
6 I don't have ... postcards. (p. 14)

b) When do you use *any*? Look at these examples and make a rule.

– I don't have any money.
– She doesn't like any sports.
– We didn't eat any chocolate.

You usually use *any* in sentences with words like ...

► W 6, 11–13 ► W ⊙

1 Clubs

a) Do you know the names of these clubs?

b) Think of more clubs and make a network.

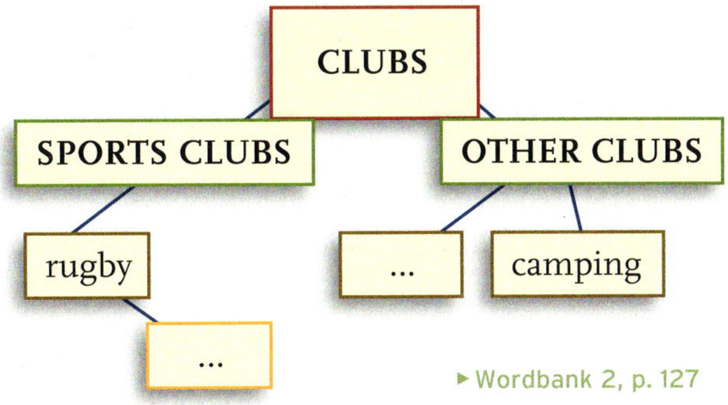

▸ Wordbank 2, p. 127

2 Word quiz

a) Ask your partner.

Can you think of ...

1 ... places that start with A? *Asia, ...*
2 ... clubs that start with c?
3 ... sports that start with b?
4 ... cities that start with S?
5 ... a subject that starts with m?
6 ... food that starts with s?

● b) Now make a quiz for your partner. Pick six things. Ask your partner.

Can you think of ...

→ clubs • sports • places • cities • a subject • food • fruit • animals • colours • days • months

... that start(s) with ...?

3 Small words

a) What word is missing?

	???	
1 Thanks		your e-mail.
2 It's time		the programme.
3 We're looking		a new flat.

b) And what word is missing here?

	??	
1 I'm		a new school.
2 She's looking		the noticeboard.
3 Our club meets		lunchtime.

c) And here?

	??	
1 Welcome		London.
2 He's talking		his parents.
3 Our house is next		the school.

4 Match the signs with the sentences.

You can use a dictionary.

1 This shop doesn't open on Sundays.
2 Buy two and you don't pay for the third.
3 Things are cheaper this week.
4 Please don't talk here.
5 Don't put posters here.

▸ W 7, 14–16 ▸ W ⦿

LISTENING Asking for help

1 A London tour

a) Look at the pictures. Where would you like to go in London?

1◉9 b) Listen. Where do Asha, her mum and her dad want to go first? And then?

1◉9 c) Listen again and look at the map. What's A? What's B? And what's C?

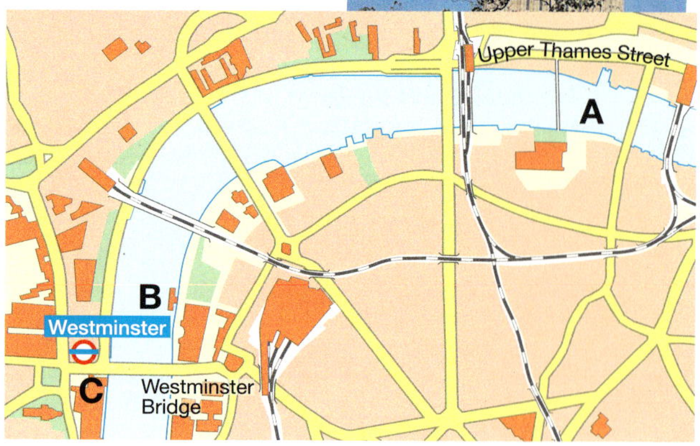

2 LISTEN FOR LANGUAGE What are the missing words?

1◉9

1 Excuse me, please. Can you ... me? – Yes, of course.

2 How do we ... there? – You can ... the tube to Westminster.

3 We ... to go to the London Eye. – ... across Westminster Bridge. The London Eye is on your left.

4 How do we ... to the Millennium Bridge? – ... along Upper Thames Street. Then ... right.

5 Sorry, which street did you ...? – Upper Thames Street.

3 PRONUNCIATION Be a word detective!

1◉10 a) Listen. How many words?

Tip: In English people sometimes don't say parts of words.

1◉11 b) Now listen again and repeat.

c) Say these words fast. Faster! What happens to the red letters?

help me • want to • get there • Thames Street • Westminster

▸ W 8, 17

SPEAKING Asking for information

1 At the London Eye

1 12 **a) Where does Asha want to go? Listen or read and find out.**

ASHA Excuse me, please. Where can we get tickets for the London Eye?
WOMAN You have to queue up here.
MUM And how much are the tickets, please?
WOMAN £12.50 for adults and £6.50 for children under 16.
MUM Sorry. Can you repeat that, please?
WOMAN Adults £12.50 and children £6.50.
DAD Oh, that's too expensive. Thanks.

b) Practise the dialogue in groups.

2 A boat tour on the River Thames

1 13 **a) Finish this dialogue.**

ASHA Excuse me, where can we ... tickets for the boat tour?
MAN You have to ... up here.
ASHA And ... much are the tickets, please?
MAN £...
ASHA Sorry. Can you ... that, please?
MAN They're £...
ASHA OK, thanks. Three tickets, please.

Tip:
In English you have to be very polite.
Start with "Excuse me".
People say "please" very often.
People say "sorry" too.
And "thanks" is very important.

b) Now act the dialogue with a partner.

3 ROLE PLAY

Partner A: You're new in London. You want to go to one of these places. Pick one. Ask Partner B.

OXFORD STREET

BUCKINGHAM PALACE

A Excuse me, please. How do I get to ...?
B ...
A Sorry. Can you repeat that, please?
B ...
A Thanks.

Partner B: You live in London. Look at page 124. Help Partner A.

4 INTERPRETING Some German people are in London. Can you help?

	POLICE OFFICER	YOU
1	You can take the tube to Westminster.	Er sagt, wir können mit der ...
2	Go along Kings Road.	Er sagt, wir sollen ...
3	Turn right at the bridge.	Er sagt, ...
4	You have to queue up here.	Er sagt, ...

▸W 8, 18–19 ▸W ⦿

READING Favourite stories

1 It was *Reading Week* in Asha's school. Asha read a famous story.

She wrote about it for the school website.
Before you read, look quickly at the text and find out:

a) What's the title of the story?
b) What city is the story about?
c) Does Asha think it's a good story?

OLIVER TWIST

Charles Dickens was a famous English writer. He wrote lots of books and he lived in London. In 1838 he wrote a very famous book – *Oliver Twist*.

Oliver Twist is a story about a boy. Oliver is an orphan – he has no mother or father. He lives in London. But it isn't a nice city in the story – it's always cold and dirty. The streets are dark and dangerous. The people are very poor. They have no money and they live in terrible houses. Oliver meets Fagin – a pickpocket. Fagin teaches Oliver how to steal things. So Oliver learns how to be a pickpocket too and he takes things from people in the streets.

This is an interesting story because you can see what life was like in London in 1838. It's very exciting and sometimes it's funny. But it isn't a very happy story – in fact, sometimes it's very sad. You should read it – or you can watch the film. It's great!

2 Who are they?

A

B

C

3 What are the paragraphs about?

Paragraph 1: – what the book is like
Paragraph 2: – the writer of the book
Paragraph 3: – the story

4 Read the text again and make notes about:

- Charles Dickens
- London
- Fagin
- the story

5 Words in the text: What are they in German?

a) Guess:

1 a writer (line 1)
2 an orphan (line 4)
3 poor (line 7)
4 a pickpocket (line 9)
5 sad (line 15)

Tip:
Some phrases in the text can help you:
WRITER: "He wrote lots of books ..."
ORPHAN: "He has no mother or father ..."
POOR: "They have no money ..."
PICKPOCKET: "He takes things from people in the streets ..."
SAD: "It isn't a very happy story ..."

b) Check your answers with a partner. Then check the words in the *Dictionary* (pages 151–165).

▸ W 9, 20

● 6 Work with a partner. Tell the story of Oliver Twist – in German.

WRITING About stories and books

1 Write Asha's notes about Oliver Twist.

TITLE ...
WRITER ...
WHERE ...
WHEN ...
WHO ...

STORY Oliver Twist lives in ...
He meets ...
He learns how to be a ...
WHAT IT'S LIKE ...

Tip:
When you tell the story of a book or a film, you often use the simple present.

▸ W 9, 21–22

2 Your favourite story or book

Write some notes about your favourite story.

Tip:
Use words from exercise 1 like: title, writer, where, ... And don't forget to say what the story/book is like.

3 A reading week

a) Look at the poster for reading week in Asha's class.
b) Work in groups. Plan posters for a reading week in your class.
c) Make the posters and put them in your classroom.

Class 9PN
Sponsored Reading Week

We're planning a reading week.
It's next week: October 8th to 12th.

We're reading lots of stories.
We're writing story notes for our school website.
You can help us: Please give us £1 for a story.
We want to buy more books for our school.

▸ W ⊙

THE LIFE OF A DJ

Every Wednesday, Thursday and Saturday Asha's dad works in a big club in London. He's a DJ. He works in youth clubs too. And sometimes he works in schools.

He always works at night, of course. So he goes to bed late and he usually gets up late too. He never goes to the club on Sundays. That's his free day so he often does something nice with his family.

Now it's Friday and Asha's dad has a special job. This evening he's working at Asha's school. The music club is having a Halloween party and lots of pupils are in the school. They're wearing funny clothes. There are ghosts, witches and Frankensteins everywhere! Some people are talking and laughing. Other people are dancing. At the moment Asha's dad is giving DJ lessons. Everybody is having fun.

1 Look at the sentences in the box.

Asha's dad works in a big club in London. • He's working at Asha's school. • The music club is having a Halloween party. • He works in youth clubs. • He goes to bed late. • They're wearing funny clothes. • Some people are talking and laughing. • He gets up late too. • Other people are dancing. • He never goes to the club on Sundays. • He does something nice with his family. • Asha's dad is giving DJ lessons.

a) Make two lists: **What happens every week?** (Simple present) — **What's happening now?** (Present progressive)

What happens every week? (Simple present)	What's happening now? (Present progressive)
Asha's dad works in a big club in London.	*He's working at Asha's school.*
...	...

b) Now find time phrases in the text for the two lists.

every Wednesday	*now*
...	...

2 WORD SEARCH Find the simple present forms on pages 10–17.

1 I ... lots of questions. (p. 10)
2 We all ... you here in Singapore. (p. 10)
3 Thousands of people ... to London every year (p. 12)
4 She ... Lara but Lara has other friends. (p. 12)
5 The music club ... every Tuesday and Friday. (p. 13)
6 They ... music on the school intercom. (p. 13)
7 You ... to queue up here. (p. 17)

3 WORD SEARCH Now find the present progressive forms on pages 10–20.

1 We're ... with my aunt at the moment. (p. 10)
2 I'm ... at my new school next week. (p. 10)
3 I'm ... nervous. (p. 10)
4 They're ... near my aunt's house. (p. 10)
5 She's ... in her classroom. (p. 12)
6 Mr Nixon is ... to Asha. (p. 12)
7 You're ... great music, Lara. (p. 20)

4 OVER TO YOU!

Make the sentences for the checkpoint and find more examples.

Tip: Write the checkpoint in your exercise book.

CHECKPOINT

Die Gegenwart

- Mit der einfachen Gegenwart *(simple present)* sagst du, ...
  Beispiel: *I play football every Monday.*
- Mit der *ing*-Form der Gegenwart *(present progressive)* sagst du, ...
  Beispiel: *I'm reading a book now.*

was jemand gerade tut oder plant.

was jemand immer wieder oder regelmäßig tut.

▸ Eine Übersicht über diese Regeln findest du auf der *Summary*-Seite 95.
▸ Extra Practice, pp. 92 ff.
▸ W 10–11

NACH DIESER UNIT KANN ICH ...

über eine Stadt sprechen.	▸ *London is very different from Singapore.*
Schulklubs und Arbeitsgemeinschaften benennen.	▸ *the music club, the film club, the judo club, ...*
sagen, was vorhanden ist.	▸ *We have some ice cream.*
sagen, was nicht vorhanden ist.	▸ *We don't have any milk.*
um Hilfe und Auskunft bitten.	▸ *Excuse me, please. Can you help me? How do we get to the London Eye?*
Wegbeschreibungen verstehen.	▸ *You can take the tube to Westminster. Go along Kings Road. Turn right at the bridge.*
sagen, was jemand immer wieder oder regelmäßig tut.	▸ *He always works at night. He goes to bed late.*
sagen, was jemand gerade tut.	▸ *At the moment Asha's dad is giving DJ lessons.*

Weitere Übungen: www.new-highlight.de

▸ W 12, Test yourself ▸ W ⦿
▸ Extra Reading, pp. 116–119

Unit 2

Scottish stories

1 **Films about Scotland**

1 14 **a) Listen. Put in the right words.**

Braveheart • DVD • TV • *Loch Ness*

1 Lauren and Callum watched ... on ...
2 Mum and Fiona watched ... on ...

b) Listen again. What are the films like?

exciting • funny • good • long • nice • romantic • sad • silly

Braveheart is a/an ... film.
Loch Ness is ...

► W 13, 1

2 AND YOU? Talk to a partner.

YOU	YOUR PARTNER
What films do you like?	I like exciting/funny/... films.
Did you watch a film yesterday?	Yes, I watched ... . / No, I didn't watch any films.
Where did you watch it?	I watched it on TV/on DVD/at the cinema.
Did you like it?	Yes, I liked it. It was great.
	No, I didn't like it. It was terrible!

▸ W 13, 2
▸ Wordbank 3, p. 128

A FILM FAN

1 About Fiona

a) Look at the pictures. Where does Fiona live?

b) Read the article. What does Fiona do in her free time?

EDINBURGH PEOPLE

FIONA MACDONALD (13)

Fiona, what do you think of our city?
I love it. There are so many great shops and cafes. I love the old streets and the history everywhere. Edinburgh Castle is my favourite place. I went there last weekend with my English friend Emma. Emma didn't know much Scottish history but she thought Edinburgh was great.

What do you do in your free time?
I play football in a girls' team. We practise every week in Holyrood Park. I love films too. I joined the school film club last year and I often watch films on TV or DVDs with my friends.

Do you have a favourite Scottish actor?
I think Ewan McGregor is very good. I liked him before he became famous.

Fiona thinks the capital has great shops.

Edinburgh Castle is Fiona's favourite place.

Fiona plays football in Holyrood Park.

2 Finish the sentences.

1 Fiona loves Edinburgh's ... and cafes and the ... streets.
2 In Edinburgh there's history ...
3 Fiona and Emma went to ...
4 Emma thought Edinburgh was ...

3 Information files

a) Put in information about Fiona.

Name: ....
Age: ....
From: ....
Sports: ....
Interests: ....

b) Make your file.

c) Put everybody's files in a box. Pick a file. Read it to the class but don't say the name. Ask: Who is it?

► W 14, 3–4

4 **Read the star file. Do you know Ewan McGregor's films?**

STAR FILE

NAME:	*Ewan McGregor*
JOB:	Actor
BORN:	In 1971
FROM:	Crieff in Scotland
INTERESTS:	Motorbikes, music
BEST FILMS:	• *Star Wars,* Ewan played Obi-Wan Kenobi • *Stormbreaker,* Ewan was Ian Rider. Great film – but Ian died too early! • *Moulin Rouge,* Ewan sang lots of songs!
OTHER:	Married, two children

5 **Write an article about Ewan McGregor for your school magazine.**

Ewan McGregor is an ... . He was born in ... and he's from ... . He's interested in ... and ... . His three best films are ..., ... and ... . He's ... and he has ... .

▸W 14, 5

6 ***Your Song* from *Moulin Rouge***

1 ◉ 15

a) Listen: Is the song about films, history or love?

b) What do you think of the song? Tell the class.

The song is great/OK/terrible/... . I like/don't like the music/the words/the singer.

My gift is my song
And this one's for you
And you can tell everybody
That this is your song
It may be quite simple
Now that it's done

Hope you don't mind
I hope you don't mind
That I put down in words
How wonderful life is
Now you're in the world

by Elton John/Bernie Taupin

PROJECT Your star file

a) Work with a partner or in a group. Pick another actor.

b) Write the headings in the star file in exercise 4: Name, Job, Born, ...

c) Find information for the headings. Look on the Internet or in magazines.

d) Find photos.

e) Write your star file. Use notes.

f) Tell the class about your star:

Our file is about ...
He/She is an ...
He/She was born in ...
...

Tip:
Look at the star file in exercise 4 again.

Tip:
Use complete sentences. Exercise 5 can help you.

1 What happened?

a) Look at the pictures. How does Fiona feel in the first picture? And in the last picture?

a frightened **b** jealous **c** happy

b) Read the story. Check your answers to exercise 1.

FILM COMPETITION

Are you a 13-year-old girl? Would you like to be in a new film with Ewan McGregor? Come and meet us on Saturday.

Best friends?

1 16

It was the last lesson of the day. Fiona looked at her feet and listened to the other pupils in the class.
"Who won the competition?" asked Cameron. "Lauren? Wow, great!"
"Congratulations, Lauren!" Lucy shouted.
Lauren was Fiona's best friend. And now she was in Ewan McGregor's new film. Fiona wanted to be happy for her friend, but she wasn't. Lauren always won everything. She was good at so many things. She was the best pupil in the class and she was a great football and tennis player too. Usually it wasn't a problem for Fiona because Lauren was a good friend. But Fiona wanted to be in that film!
After the lesson Fiona left the room fast. She didn't want to talk to Lauren and she walked home alone. Her mum wasn't there so she went to her room.
"Why did Lauren win the film competition? Why did they pick her and not me?" Fiona thought. She looked at the posters of Ewan McGregor in her bedroom and she started to cry. She felt sad and lonely.
She checked her mobile. There was a text message from Lauren:

Fiona waited a minute. Then she sent a message back.

Fiona's mum came home. "What's wrong?" she asked when she saw Fiona. "Did you have a bad day at school?" Fiona told her about the film.
"Well, I know this isn't much fun," her mum said. "But Lauren is your best friend. You have to talk to her."
Fiona knew that she was right.

Fiona walked to Lauren's house. Her brother Callum came to the door.
"Sorry, Fiona, she isn't here."
"Oh! Bye then."
"Hey, wait!" said Callum. "What did you think of Lauren's news? Lauren says she can take a friend. I wanted to go – I think Ewan McGregor is cool. But she wants to invite you. She says you're a big fan."
Fiona smiled. "Yeah, he's the best!"

She looked at Callum. She didn't talk to Lauren's brother very often. But he was nice. Very nice.

"You can watch Ewan McGregor's films at the *Filmhouse* this week. Er ..." Fiona stopped and looked embarrassed. Now Callum smiled.
"Yeah, I went there yesterday. ... What are you doing on Saturday afternoon?"

2 Right or wrong?

1 Lauren and Fiona were best friends.
2 Fiona said "congratulations" to Lauren in the classroom.
3 Fiona was the best pupil in the class.
4 Fiona didn't phone Lauren.
5 Fiona's mum helped her.
6 Fiona didn't like Callum.

3 Put the sentences in the right order.

1 d, 2 ..., 3 ..., ...

a So Lauren sent her a text message.
b At Lauren's house she talked to Callum.
c Fiona talked to her mum.
d Lauren won the competition.
e After school Fiona didn't wait for Lauren.
f Then Fiona went to Lauren's house.

4 What happened later?

a) Match 1–4 with a–d.

a Thanks. Were you angry about the film?
b That's good. You're my best friend.
c Yes, I was. I'm sorry. But it's OK now.
d Congratulations, Lauren!

● **b) Write sentences for 5 and 6.**

► W 15, 6–8

WORDPOWER

1 How do they feel?

a) Match the words in the box with the pictures.

These words are in the story on pages 26–27.

angry • embarrassed • jealous • lonely • frightened • sad

● **b) Finish the sentences.**

1 I feel lonely when ...
2 I feel angry when ...
3 I feel jealous when ...
4 I feel frightened when ...
5 I feel sad when ...
6 I feel embarrassed when ...

people hurt animals • my parents drive fast • children cry • my friends have new clothes • I speak in class • my parents aren't at home • I'm in a plane • my mum reads my e-mails • my sister takes my mobile • I watch horror films

▸ Wordbank 4, p. 128

2 ODD WORD OUT

1 cinema, school, competition, park
2 romantic, silly, actor, great
3 smile, cry, castle, laugh
4 city, married, capital, town
5 sang, felt, sent, problem

3 Finish the sentences.

Look at exercise 2 again.

1 Who won the film ...?
2 She's an ... in films and on TV.
3 Edinburgh has a famous old ...
4 She isn't ... . She lives alone.
5 I have a ... with my homework. Can you help me?

4 WORD SEARCH *Much* or *many*?

a) Put in *much* or *many*.

These sentences are on pages 24–27.

1 There are so ... great shops. (p. 24)
2 Emma didn't know ... Scottish history. (p. 24)
3 She was good at so ... things. (p. 26)
4 I don't have ... time today. (p. 26)
5 This isn't ... fun. (p. 27)

b) When do we use *much*? When do we use *many*? Read the examples. Make a rule.

How many people live in Scotland?
How much time do you have?

Wir verwenden ... bei Dingen, die man zählen kann.
Wir verwenden ... bei Dingen, die man nicht zählen kann.

▸ W 16, 9–11 ▸ W ⦿

MAKING NOTES

Tip:
Make notes about the most important information.
You can use symbols:
= is/are ≠ isn't/aren't
+ and
=> so

1 **Look at the photo. Would you like to try this sport?**

2 **Read the brochure. Use the underlined information and finish the notes.**

All about Scotland

Scotland ≠ part of England
languages: ____________
money: ____________
sports: ____________

All about Scotland

Is Scotland part of England?
No! It's part of Britain. Scotland is a different country with its own history.

What languages do Scottish people speak?
Everybody speaks English, of course. And some Scottish people speak Scots or Gaelic.

What money does Scotland use?
Like England and Wales, Scotland uses the pound. But Scottish money looks different from English money.

What sports are popular in Scotland?
Football, rugby and golf are very popular. Scotland has its own football and rugby teams and the teams play in international competitions. Scotland has its own special sports competition too: the Highland Games.

Tossing the caber[1] at the Highland Games

1) Tossing the caber ['tɒsɪŋ ðə 'keɪbə] Baumstammwerfen

▸ W 17, 12–13

PROJECT Scotland quiz

a) Go to www.new-highlight.de and put in the webcode NHL-3-29. Make notes about:
- Scottish names
- famous Scottish people
- special days in Scotland

b) Then work in two teams:
- Write five quiz questions about Scotland. Check them with your teacher.
- Ask another team your questions.

▸ W ⊙

LISTENING Likes and dislikes

1 Look at the picture. Where are Fiona and Callum? What does Callum have? What does Fiona have?

2 Fiona and Callum

1 17

a) Write 1–5 in your exercise book. Listen to the CD. Who likes what? (✔)

	Fiona	Callum
1 films about history	✔	✔
2 romantic films		
3 playing football		
4 football matches on TV		
5 Ronaldinho		

b) Now listen again and check.

3 Listen for language.

1 18

a) Fiona is talking to Lauren. Listen to the CD. Pick the right words.

1 Callum likes/doesn't like Fiona.
2 Callum hates/loves computers.
3 Fiona likes/can't stand computer games.
4 Callum doesn't like/loves fast food.
5 Fiona likes/isn't keen on hamburgers.
6 Callum loves/hates rap music.

▸ W 18, 14

b) Listen again and check.

4 PRONUNCIATION

1 19

a) Write sentences 1–5 in your exercise book. Listen. Which words do Lauren and Fiona stress? Underline them.

1 Callum likes you.
2 You hate computer games.
3 I can't stand them!
4 He hates rap music.
5 I love rap!

b) Listen again and repeat the sentences in a).

Tip:
We can stress words. This tells other people *how much* we like or don't like something.

5 AND YOU? Do you like these things? Talk to a partner.

I love ...	playing football.
I like ...	football on TV.
I'm not keen on ...	computer games.
I don't like ...	hamburgers.
I can't stand ...	rap music.
I hate ...	school.

SPEAKING Making arrangements

1 Fiona and Lauren

1 20 **a) Listen or read the dialogue. When are the girls going swimming?**

LAUREN Would you like to go swimming on Saturday?
FIONA I'm afraid I'm visiting my grandma then.
LAUREN What about Sunday morning?
FIONA That's fine. Why don't we meet at the swimming pool at 10 o'clock?
LAUREN Great!

b) Practise the dialogue with a partner.

2 Fiona and her mum

1 21 **a) Finish this dialogue.**

MUM You need new trainers. Would you ... go shopping after school tomorrow?
FIONA ... I'm going to Lauren's house then.
MUM ... Wednesday?
FIONA That's fine. ... meet at the shopping centre at 4 o'clock?
MUM ...!

b) Now act the dialogue with a partner.

3 ROLE PLAY Weekend plans

Partner A: You don't have any plans for the weekend. You want to play football with Partner B. Phone him/her and find a day, a place and a time.

A Hi, ... Would you like to ... on ...?
B ...
A What about ...?
B ...
A Great! Bye.

Partner B: Look at page 124. Make an arrangement with Partner A.

4 INTERPRETING You're watching a DVD in English. Tell your dad in German what they're saying.

Er schlägt vor, ...
Sie sagt, ...

Er will wissen, ...
Der andere Junge sagt, ...

▸W 18, 15–16 ▸W

READING A letter in a magazine

1 **Look at the picture. What do you think – how did the girl feel?**

2 **Read the letter. What was the special day? What did the people eat?**

We asked you for stories about special days. Our star letter is from Emma White.

Star letter

Dear Hi Magazine,

I want to tell you my story about Burns Night. On January 25th people in Scotland have parties on the birthday of Robert Burns (Scotland's most famous poet). Last year my friend Fiona from Edinburgh invited me to her house. People always eat haggis on Burns Night. I was the guest, so I took the haggis into the room. I didn't see a chair and I fell. Of course I dropped the haggis! Everybody was very quiet and Fiona's uncle looked angry. I was very embarrassed. Then Fiona started to laugh – and everybody laughed! Fiona's dad phoned for some pizza – not very traditional food! Later people read poems and sang *Auld Lang Syne*. It was a fantastic evening – but I don't want to see a haggis again!

Emma White (13), Birmingham

And here are the words of that famous song. Don't try and understand it. Sing it!

1 22

AULD LANG SYNE

Should old acquaintance be forgot
And never brought to mind?
Should old acquaintance be forgot
For the sake of auld lang syne?

For auld lang syne, my dear
For auld lang syne,
We'll take a cup of kindness yet
For the sake of auld lang syne.

3 **Read Emma's letter again and answer the questions.**

1 Who? ...
2 When? ...
3 Where? ...
4 What? She dropped ...

Tip:
Find out the most important information in a story:
Look for the answers to these questions:
Who? When? Where? What?

4 New words

a) Find these words in Emma's letter. What are they in German?

1 guest (line 6)
2 uncle (line 8)
3 traditional (line 12)
4 fantastic (line 14)

Tip:
Think of German words that look or sound like these words.

● b) Now guess these words in German. Then check in the *Dictionary* (pages 151–165).

1 address
2 electricity
3 machine
4 price

WRITING A letter to a magazine

Hi Magazine wants your stories about special days. Write us a letter and tell us your story!

1 Match the special days with the pictures.

→ birthday • carnival • wedding day • Halloween

1 
2 
3 
4 

2 A special day

a) Read Fiona's notes. Did she have a good day?

1 Special day?	my cousin's wedding day
2 When was it?	August
3 Where was it?	Glasgow
4 Who was with you?	parents and the family
5 What did you do?	danced all night
6 What was it like?	great

b) Finish Fiona's letter. Use the notes in 2a.

Dear *Hi Magazine*,

I want to tell you about .... It was in ..., in .... My ... were with me. We .... It was a ... day!

Fiona MacDonald (13), Edinburgh

● ## 3 Pick a special day.

Write your letter to *Hi Magazine*. The letter in exercise 2b can help you.

Tip:
Before you write:
- collect ideas
- make notes
- organize your ideas

▸W 19, 17–18 ▸W ⦿

THE STORY OF GREYFRIARS BOBBY

1

John Gray lived in Edinburgh and was a police officer.
He had a police dog.
The dog's name was Bobby.

2

Bobby loved John Gray.
But John Gray became ill and then he died.

3

Bobby stayed with John Gray.
He sat on his grave for 14 years and waited.

4

He only left when he needed food – at 1 o'clock every day.

5

When Bobby died, Edinburgh didn't want to forget him. You can see his statue in the capital.

6

And you can watch his story on DVD. Disney made a film about Bobby's life in 1961.

1 Finish the lists.
The simple past forms are in the story.

verb	simple past
live	lived
love	...
die	...
stay	...
wait	...
need	...
be	was
have	...
become	...
sit	...
leave	...
make	...

2 OVER TO YOU!
Finish the checkpoint. Put in examples.

CHECKPOINT

Simple past (1)
Mit dem *simple past* sagst du, was in der Vergangenheit geschah/geschehen ist. Damit kannst du Geschichten erzählen.
Regelmäßige Verben enden auf ...
Beispiele:
watch – watched, ...
Unregelmäßige Verben haben besondere Vergangenheitsformen.
Beispiele:
go – went, ...

▸ List of irregular verbs p. 180–181.

3 WORD SEARCH
Find these words in the unit.

1 Emma ... ... much Scottish history. (p. 24)
2 She ... ... to talk to Lauren. (p. 26)
3 Sorry I ... ... 4 U. (p. 26)
4 She ... ... to Lauren's brother very often. (p. 27)
5 I ... ... a chair and I fell. (p. 32)

4 WORD SEARCH
Now find these words in the unit.

1 ... you ... a film this month? (p. 23)
2 Why ... Lauren ... the film competition? (p. 26)
3 Why ... they ... her and not me? (p. 26)
4 ... you ... a bad day at school? (p. 27)
5 What ... you ... of Lauren's news? (p. 27)

5 OVER TO YOU!
Finish the checkpoint.

Tip:
Write the checkpoint in your exercise book.

CHECKPOINT

Simple past (2): did/didn't

Mit ... fragst du, was geschehen ist.

Mit ... sagst du, was nicht geschehen ist.

Beispiele: ...

▸ Eine Übersicht über diese Regeln findest du auf der *Summary*-Seite 99.
▸ Extra Practice, pp. 96 ff.
▸ W 20–21

NACH DIESER UNIT KANN ICH ...

über Filme sprechen.	▸ *I like funny films.* *My favourite actor is Ewan McGregor.*
Gefühle äußern.	▸ *I feel sad/happy/jealous/embarrassed.*
nach Mengen fragen.	▸ *How many people live in Scotland?* *How much money do you have?*
über Vergangenes sprechen.	▸ *Emma went to Edinburgh Castle last weekend.* *We didn't win the match yesterday.*
Vorlieben und Abneigungen ausdrücken.	▸ *Do you like ...?* ✔ *I like / I love football.* ✗ *I don't like / I'm not keen on / I can't stand football.*
Absprachen treffen.	▸ *Would you like to go swimming?* *What about Saturday?* *Why don't we meet at ten o'clock?* *That's fine. / I'm afraid I'm meeting Thomas then.*
von einem besonderen Tag erzählen.	▸ *I want to tell you about my cousin's wedding day. It was in August. We danced all night.*

Weitere Übungen: www.new-highlight.de
▸ W 22, Test yourself ▸ W 23–24, Portfolio ▸ W ⊙
▸ Extra Reading, p. 122

Unit 3

Wild Wales

1 A village tour

1 23 **a) Listen to the tour. It starts at A. But where does it finish – at B, C, D or E?**

b) Listen again. Work with a partner and find out what the places (1–8) are.

a shop • a bridge • a car park • a hotel • an ice cream shop • a cafe • a post office • a school

2 A dream street

a) Work with a partner. Draw a map of your dream street.
You can put in cafes, shops, a swimming pool, ... and make labels for your map.

b) Talk to the class about your dream street.

This is ... That's ... On the right you can see ...
On the left there's ... It's next to ...

► W 25, 1–3

MY BLOG

1 Look at the text and the pictures quickly and find out:

a) Where's Aled's house – in a town, in the mountains or near the sea?

b) Where can you find a blog – on the Internet, in a magazine or in a book?

Welcome to my blog.

I'm Aled Thomas. I'm 14 and I'm from Wales. I live near Beddgelert. It's a village in the mountains. We can see Snowdon from our house, that's the biggest mountain in Wales. It's nice here. But it's very quiet and lonely in winter.

Mum and dad have a mountain bike business – *Beddgelert Beics*. That's the Welsh word for bikes. They hire bikes to tourists in spring, summer and autumn. Sometimes I help. Dad drives a taxi too.

I can speak two languages. Dad is Welsh and mum is English so we have to speak English at home. But I speak Welsh with my Welsh friends. Most lessons at school are in Welsh – but not the English lessons! I go to school in Porthmadog – a town seven miles from here.

My favourite hobby is mountain boarding. That's great in summer, but in winter you can't do anything here. There's no cinema in Beddgelert and we don't have a TV. Mum and dad say it's a waste of time. But I have a computer! So I can do lots of blogging.

That's our house!

This is my summer hobby.

My winter hobby is blogging.

2 Aled's blog: What does he write about? Pick five things.

Beddgelert • brothers and sisters • mountain bikes • languages • pets • school clubs • hobbies • TV • computer games

3 Find out:

– What's the name of a mountain in Wales?
– What are Aled's hobbies?
– Where's Aled's mum from?
– Where's Aled's dad from?
– What languages can Aled speak?

▸W 26, 4

4 What do you think?

Talk about these things in your class:

1 Beddgelert looks/doesn't look nice.
2 A mountain bike business – I think that's interesting/boring!
3 Aled's house looks nice/lonely.
4 Two languages – that's great/terrible!
5 Mountain boarding looks exciting/boring.
6 No TV – I think that's great/terrible!
7 Blogging is/isn't a waste of time.

5 Your blog: Write some sentences for your blog.

Look at Aled's blog for some ideas.

Welcome to ...
I'm ...
I'm from ...
It's a village/town in ...
It's ... here.
I can speak ... ▸ Wordbank 5, p. 129
My hobbies are ... ▸ Wordbank 6, p. 129

▸ W 26, 5

PROJECT Find out about Wales

a) Pick a topic. Topic 1: The people Topic 2: The country

b) Work in groups. Look at the questions for your topic.
Use the Internet. Go to www.new-highlight.de and put in the webcode NHL-3-39.
Find the information and make notes.

Topic 1: The people

1 How many people live in Wales?
2 How many people speak Welsh?
3 What music groups come from Wales?
4 What film stars come from Wales?
5 What sports do Welsh people like?
6 What are the Welsh symbols?

Topic 2: The country

1 Is Wales a big or a small country?
2 What country is Wales' neighbour?
3 What's the biggest city in Wales?
4 What's the weather like in Wales?
5 Are there lots of mountains in Wales?
6 What sea is near Wales?

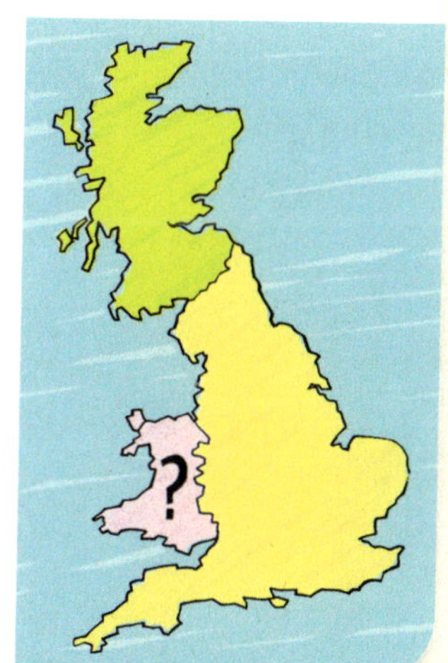

c) You're going to talk to the class about your topic.
- **Draw pictures or maps.**
- **Make a plan in your group.**
- **Who's going to talk?**
- **Now talk to the class. You have two minutes.**

You can use these phrases:

We found out about ...
We learned that ...
Do you know that ...?
Please look at the map ...
You can see ...
In this picture you can see ...

1 Before you read or listen – do you remember:

– Who lives in the mountains?
– Who drives a taxi?
– Who has no TV?
– Who thinks that TV is a waste of time?

Tip:
Not sure? Look at Aled's blog again.

Parents are a pain!

1 ⊙ 24

"Aled, hurry up! It's late! We have to go!" Aled's dad ran to the taxi. They went to five houses in the area to pick up other children. Then they went to Beddgelert. The children waited there for the bus to Porthmadog.

At school Aled met his best friend, Danny. Danny had a new mobile phone. He was sending texts. Aled watched. He couldn't send texts because he didn't have a mobile. "Mobiles aren't safe," his parents always said. "Parents are a pain!" Aled thought.

In the break some pupils in Aled's class were talking about TV. "Did you watch *Frightened* yesterday?" a girl asked. "Yes, it was great," Danny answered. "Poor Aled. He can't watch TV. He doesn't have a TV!" one boy said and laughed. Aled said nothing. "Parents are a pain!" he thought.

After school some pupils were talking about their plans for the evening. Some wanted to go to the cinema in Porthmadog. Some wanted to go to the sports centre. "I can't come," Aled said. "I have to go home." "Poor Aled. He has to go back to the mountains," one girl said. Everybody laughed. "You don't have to go home. You can stay at our house," Danny said. "Mum and dad are going to Bangor. And tomorrow is Saturday."

Aled phoned his mum on Danny's mobile. "We're going to the swimming pool at the sports centre. Can I stay at Danny's house? Please, please!" Aled's mum said OK. But Aled had to be back at Danny's house before 10 o'clock. Aled said OK.

Aled and Danny didn't go to the swimming pool. They didn't go to the sports centre or the cinema. They took the bus to Caernarfon, 16 miles from Porthmadog. They walked along the streets and went to lots of shops. Then they met Danny's cousin. He was older. He had some cider. The three boys went to the old castle in the town centre.
"My parents are strict. They say that I mustn't drink alcohol," Aled said.
"Parents are a pain!" Danny answered.
"You don't have to do everything they say."

That evening Aled's father was in Caernarfon. He was in his taxi near the castle. Suddenly he saw Aled and Danny. "I know those boys!" he thought. He was very angry.
"Oh, no! It's dad! He has seen us!" Aled said. Aled was in big trouble!

Aled was grounded for a month. He couldn't stay with Danny in Porthmadog.
"And you have to work hard every weekend for a month," Aled's dad said.
"Oh no!" Aled thought.
"We're going to make a mountain board track near the house," his mum said and smiled.
That wasn't so bad. Now Aled could invite his friends for mountain board weekends.
"Parents are a pain – but not always," Aled thought.

2 Finish these sentences about page 40.

1 Aled went to school and met ...
2 Danny was sending ...
3 But Aled didn't have ...
4 Some pupils were talking about ...
5 But Aled didn't have ...
6 After school Aled phoned ...
7 He wanted to stay at ...

3 Now use these notes and write sentences about page 41.

1 boys – take bus – Caernarfon
2 go – shops 3 meet – cousin
4 have – cider 5 go – old castle
6 Aled's father – see – boys
7 Aled – in trouble
8 grounded – month

Tip:
Use the simple past.

4 Aled and you: What's the same? What's different?

1 Aled can speak Welsh and English. I can speak ...
2 Aled lives in the mountains. I ...
3 Aled's house isn't near a big town. My house ...
4 Aled doesn't have a TV. We ...
5 Beddgelert doesn't have a cinema. Our town/village ...
6 Aled goes to school by taxi and bus. I ...
7 Aled doesn't have a mobile. I ...
8 Aled has a blog. I ...
9 Aled's parents are strict. My ...

► W 27, 6–8

WORDPOWER

1 Words in the story

a) Find the partners.

They're all in the story on pages 40–41.

1 early – *late*
2 don't have to – ...
3 worst
4 could
5 dangerous
6 can
7 after
8 younger
9 new
10 nothing

b) Put in some answers from a).

1 It's 10 o'clock. You're ... for school.
2 Danny is Aled's ... friend.
3 I ... meet you yesterday. I was grounded.
4 Grandad says, "Motorbikes aren't ... ."
5 I'm ... than my sister. She's only ten.

2 Who's saying what? Match the sentences with the pictures.

1

a) I'm in big trouble now!
b) You're grounded!
c) You can stay at our house.
d) Mobile phones aren't safe.
e) You mustn't drink alcohol!
f) You have to be back before 10 o'clock.

2

3

4

5

6

3 *This, that, these* or *those*

a) Look at the sentences.

I like this mobile. I don't like that mobile.

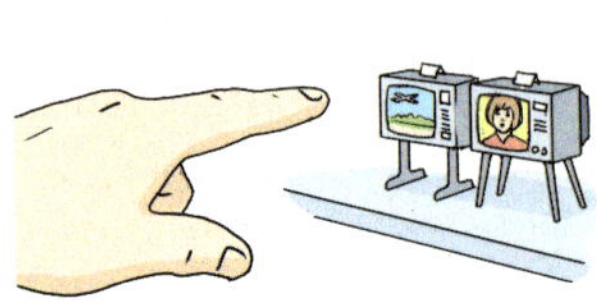

I like these TVs. I don't like those TVs.

b) Pick the right word.

1 I like this/these postcard.
2 But I don't like that/those postcards!
3 Can I borrow this/these pens, please?
4 I know that/those boy. It's Aled!

5 This is/That's my new girlfriend.
6 This is/That's Julia.

►W 28, 9–11 ►W ◉

1 The year

a) What are the four seasons of the year?

1 

2 

3 

4 

b) What's your favourite season?

c) What are the 12 months of the year?

Tip:
The German-English dictionary on page 166–178 can help you.

d) What are the dates?

1 Christmas?
2 Halloween?
3 Your birthday?
4 The next holidays?

▸ W 29, 12

2 Hobbies and sports

Draw this network in your exercise book and put in these words.

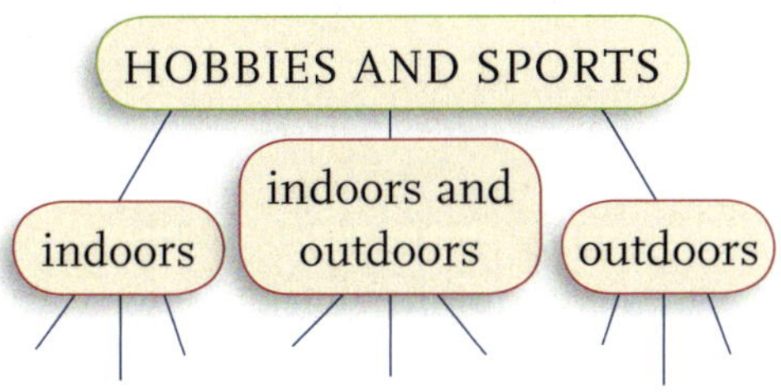

→ badminton • basketball • canoeing • computer games • cycling • dancing • films • fishing • horse riding • hockey • jogging • letterboxing • motorbikes • mountain biking • mountain boarding • music • pets • photos • quad riding • rugby • shopping • skiing • squash • Trikke riding • TV • walking

▸ Wordbank 6, p. 129 ▸ W 29, 13

3 Small words: Put in *near* or *in*.

1 Aled lives ... Beddgelert.
2 Beddgelert is ... the Welsh mountains.
3 There's an ice cream shop ... the village.
4 There's a good mountain biking track ... Aled's house.
5 Aled goes to school ... Porthmadog.
6 Lots of his lessons are ... Welsh.
7 Porthmadog is a town ... the sea.
8 The weather isn't very nice ... winter.

4 Pick A or B and tell your partner what it says in German.

You can use a dictionary.

Tip:
You don't have to translate every word.

A

WALKERS!

- You shouldn't leave the tracks.
- You should wear good walking shoes.
- You should always bring a map.
- Don't forget a good jacket.
- Please take your litter home.

B

PLAN YOUR DAY.

You should tell a friend where you're going and when you're coming back. You should always check the weather before you go into the mountains.

▸ W ⦿

LISTENING About mobiles

A

B

C

D

E

1⊙25

1 Look at the pictures and listen. Put the pictures in the right order.

"One" is picture ...

2 Mobiles, ringtones and text messages.

a) Match the sentences 1–5 with the answers A–E.

1 Can I borrow your mobile?
2 I like your new mobile.
3 That's text bullying!
4 Turn off that mobile, please.
5 That's your ringtone!

A Oh, it's mum: "Come home. You're late."
B Sorry, Ms Brown.
C Thanks. I got it for my birthday. It's a flip phone.
D Yes, some people send terrible text messages.
E OK. But I don't have much credit – only £1.20.

1⊙25

b) Listen again and check.

3 PRONUNCIATION

1⊙26

a) Look at these words. Listen and repeat.

Tip: You stress the **first** part of these words.

mobile	mountain	
credit	tourist	birthday
ringtone	lesson	Christmas
message	autumn	thirty

1⊙27

b) Now look at these words. Listen and repeat.

Tip: You stress the **second** part of these words.

today	forget	
July	arrive	outdoors
afraid	police	became
goodbye	thirteen	excuse

1⊙28

c) Listen. What do you hear?

1 That's 17/70 euros, please.
2 Mike is 14/40.
3 It's Friday, December 13th/30th.
4 Please read the story on page 19/90.
5 16/60 people came to my party.
6 Mum, can I borrow £15/£50 please?
7 I live at 18/80 High Street in Beddgelert.

● **4 You and mobiles: Talk to a partner.**

Do you have a mobile phone?
Should everybody have a mobile?
Do you send lots of text messages?
When are mobiles good?
Can you bring your mobile to school?
Do you have text bullying at your school?
What do you think of text bullying?

▸ W 30, 14

SPEAKING About your things

1 A new MP3 player

1 29 **a) Who has a new MP3 player? Listen or read and find out.**

ALED Is that a new MP3 player?
DANNY Yes, it is. We bought it last week.
ALED It's nice. How many songs can it hold?
DANNY About five hundred!
ALED Wow! Was it expensive?
DANNY No, it was on special offer – £79.
ALED Oh, that's OK. Can I try it?
DANNY Sure!

b) Practise the dialogue with a partner.

2 Aled has a new mountain bike.

1 30 **a) Finish this dialogue.**

DANNY ... a new mountain bike?
ALED Yes, it is. We ... on Saturday.
DANNY It's nice. ... gears does it have?
ALED Twenty-one.
DANNY ... expensive?
ALED No, ...
DANNY Oh, that's OK. Can ...?
ALED ...!

b) Act the dialogue with a partner.

▸ W 30, 15

3 ROLE PLAY

Partner A: Pick one thing and ask Partner B about it.
Partner B: Look at page 125 and answer Partner A's questions.

mobile phone

mountain board

DVD player

Partner A	Partner B
Is that a new ...?	– ...
It's nice/great/...	– ...
Was it expensive?	– ...
Can I look at it/try it?	– ...

4 INTERPRETING You're with your younger sister. You meet a young English boy. Your sister doesn't understand. Can you help?

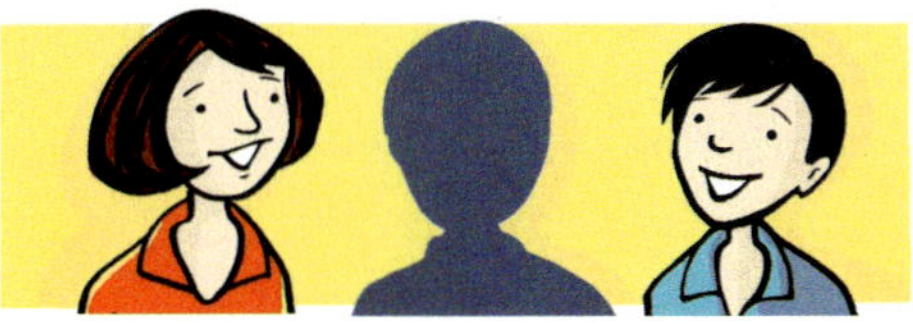

ENGLISH BOY	YOU
1 What are your hobbies?	Er fragt, was deine ...
2 I love mountain boarding.	Er sagt, er ...
3 I don't have a mobile.	Er sagt, ...
4 Can I look at your mobile?	Er fragt, ...

▸ W 30, 16 ▸ W

READING A poem

1 Look quickly at the poem – or listen – and find out: Where's the poet from?

1 31

I think I would cry
If they made me say goodbye
To the beautiful[1] land[2] of Wales.

With the mountains so high[3],
Crystal[4] streams running by,
All this in beautiful Wales.

Welsh rugby is a treat[5],
It's a great place to meet,
At the Millennium Stadium[6] in Wales.

Castle and leek,
The language we speak,
You can tell that we come from Wales.

This country is great!
Don't leave it too late,
To visit my beautiful Wales!

John Humphries (11)

2 Words in the poem

a) Guess what they are in German.

1 beautiful
= schön/hässlich

Do you think the poet likes Wales?

2 land
= Stadt/Land

Some words are like German words.

3 high
= hoch/klein

Hills are small, but mountains are ...

4 crystal
= verschmutzt/kristallklar

Crystal is like German.

5 treat
= Genuss/Grauen

Do you think the poet likes rugby?

6 stadium
= Stadt/Stadion

The Welsh rugby team plays there.

b) Check your answers with a partner. Then check the words in a dictionary.

3 Now find these things in the poem.

1

2

3

4

4 Which is the right title for the poem?

- My terrible Wales
- My beautiful Wales
- I'm going to Wales
- I'm leaving Wales

5 Which words rhyme in the poem?

Tip: Look at the next line in the poem.

1 Which word rhymes with *cry*?
2 Which word rhymes with *high*?
3 Which word rhymes with *treat*?
4 Which word rhymes with *leek*?
5 Which word rhymes with *great*?

▸ W 31, 17

WRITING Poems

1 A summary: Pick the right words and write a summary of the poem on page 46.

This poem is about **a**.	**a**	Welsh	Wales	rugby
The poet thinks that Wales is **b**.	**b**	terrible	cold	nice
There are **c** mountains there.	**c**	high	small	green
And the **d** are clean.	**d**	towns	mountains	rivers
Rugby is **e** in Wales.	**e**	fun	boring	bad
Castles, the leek and the Welsh **f** are important in Wales.	**f**	people	food	language
You should **g** Wales soon.	**g**	leave	come to	read about
The poet **h** his country.	**h**	likes	hates	doesn't know

2 Write a poem about your village, town or area.

Tip 3:
Think of things that you like to do in your town or area.
Examples:
- Shopping
- Walking
- Cycling
- ...

Tip 4:
Think of a nice place in your town or area. Examples:
- the park
- the town centre
- Parkcafe
- ...

My beautiful (1)
I think I would cry
If they made me say goodbye
To my beautiful (1).
With the (2),
All this in beautiful (1).

(3) is a treat,
It's a great place to meet,
In (4) in (1).

This (5) is great!
You shouldn't wait
To visit my beautiful (1)!

Tip 1:
Write the name of your city, town, village or area.

Tip 2:
Write:
- parks and streets
- mountains and hills
- rivers and fields
- ...

Tip 5:
Write:
- city
- town
- village
- area

3 Another poem

1⊙32

a) Read the poem. Find a title for the poem. What words rhyme?

Do you like my new ringtone,
And my super new flip phone?
What about my mountain bike?
You can try it if you like!
My laptop and MP3,
My mum bought these things for me.
But what I need in the end,
Is to find a good friend!

Hannah (14)

b) Write a summary of the poem.

Tip:
Think about these things:
- What's the poem about?
- What things does the poet have?
- What doesn't she have?
- How do you think the poet is feeling?

▸W 31, 18 ▸W ⊙

A BROCHURE

Beddgelert Mountain Board Centre

Fun for everybody – from 6 to 99!

The newest sport in Wales!

Prices:	1 hour	3 hours	Day
	£7	£17	£30

We have boards and safety gear.

Be careful!
Always use safety gear.

a helmet

protectors

Are you a skateboarder? Or a snowboarder?
- Yes? Then mountain boarding is easy.
- No? That's OK. We give lessons.

How to find us:
By car: Drive to Beddgelert.
Then take the Caernarfon road.
Follow the signs.
We're one mile from the village.
By bus: Take the bus to Beddgelert and phone us. We can pick you up.

We're open all year.

September–June	Sat & Sun 9.00–5.00
July–August	Every day 9.00–7.00

Phone: 012766 089 343

1 **Aled's new mountain board centre:**
Three sentences on the right are wrong.
Which sentences are wrong?
Correct them.

1 You have to be six or older.
2 You don't have to bring your own board.
3 You can hire a board for one hour.
4 You have to be careful.
5 You don't have to use safety gear.
6 You have to be a skateboarder.
7 You can get to Beddgelert by bus.
8 You can't ride mountain boards in the winter.

2 Phrase search:
Find the phrases on pages 38–48.

1 Wir müssen Englisch sprechen. (p. 38)
2 Wir müssen gehen! (p. 40)
3 Ich muss nach Hause. (p. 40)
4 Er muss zurück in die Berge! (p. 40)
5 Du brauchst nicht nach Hause zu gehen. (p. 40)
6 Du brauchst nicht alles zu tun, was sie dir sagen! (p. 41)
7 Du musst sechs oder älter sein. (p. 48)
8 Du musst vorsichtig sein. (p. 48)

3 Phrase search:
Now find these phrases on pages 38–48.

1 Ich kann zwei Sprachen sprechen. (p. 38)
2 Du kannst hier nichts machen. (p. 38)
3 Er darf nicht fernsehen. (p. 40)
4 Ich kann nicht kommen. (p. 40)
5 Du kannst bei uns übernachten. (p. 40)
6 Darf ich bei Danny übernachten? (p. 40)
7 Kann ich mir dein Handy ausleihen? (p. 44)
8 Du kannst mit dem Bus nach Beddgelert fahren. (p. 48)
9 Du kannst im Winter nicht Mountainboard fahren. (p. 48)

4 OVER TO YOU!
Finish the sentences for the checkpoint.

Tip:
Write the checkpoint in your exercise book.

CHECKPOINT

Die Hilfsverben *can/can't* und *have to/don't have to*
Mit ... sagst du, was jemand tun kann oder darf.
Mit ... sagst du, was jemand nicht tun kann oder nicht darf.
Mit ... sagst du, was jemand tun muss.
Mit ... sagst du, was jemand nicht zu tun braucht.

► Eine Übersicht über diese Regeln findest du auf der *Summary*-Seite 103.
► Extra Practice, pp. 100 ff.
► W 32–33

NACH DIESER UNIT KANN ICH ...

einen Ort beschreiben.	► *On the right you can see the post office.*
ein eigenes *Blog* gestalten.	► *Welcome to my blog. I'm Aled. I'm 13. I ...*
über Freizeitaktivitäten sprechen.	► *What are your hobbies?* *– Mountain boarding, horse riding, dancing, ...*
über Handys, MP3-Player etc. sprechen.	► *I like your new mobile. / It's a flip phone. / Is that a new MP3 player?*
sagen, was jemand tun kann/darf bzw. nicht tun kann/darf.	► *You can stay at our house.* *He can't watch TV.*
sagen, was jemand tun muss oder nicht zu tun braucht.	► *We have to go!* *You don't have to go home.*

Weitere Übungen: www.new-highlight.de

► W 34, Test yourself ► W ⊙
► Extra Reading, pp. 120–121

Unit **4**

Northern lights

A
Blackpool funfair. It has the fastest roller coaster in the world!

B
Blackpool in the north of England

C

1 A Blackpool trip

a) Before you listen: Look at the photos. Find the things in the box.

I can see ... in photo ...

electronic games • lights • the sea • the sun • trams • a fast food restaurant

2 1 **b) Imagine you're in Blackpool. Close your eyes and listen.**

c) Did you like the trip?

– Yes, I had fun.
– No, it was boring. I didn't like ...

2 1 **d) Listen again. Put the photos in the right order.**

Photo B, photo ...

2 AND YOU? Would you like to go to Blackpool? Talk to your partner.

– I'd like to go to Blackpool because I like funfairs/chips/...
– I wouldn't like to go there because I hate bad weather/funfairs/...
– Blackpool looks exciting/boring/...

D

Blackpool Tower and the pier

E

Lots of amusement arcades

F

Chips with everything

G

It's easy to get everywhere

3 Electricity

a) Look at the photos again. Which things use electricity? Make a list.

lights, ...

b) What other things use electricity? Write them in your list.

computers, ...

c) Imagine you have no electricity at home for two hours. What can't you do?

You can't	listen to make play use watch	the computer. games. a DVD player. lunch. music. TV.

▸ W 35, 1–3 ▸ Wordbank 7, p. 130

IT'S ELECTRIC!

1 Look quickly at the photos and the first part of the newspaper article.

a) What's the name of the boy in the photo? How old is he?
b) Why was he in the newspaper?
c) What are the Blackpool Illuminations?

Blackpool Illuminations Prize Winner

Tim Roberts (14) has won first prize in the Blackpool Illuminations quiz. Tim answered all the questions about Blackpool's famous light show. So he wins one hundred pounds. Congratulations, Tim!
Tim says he goes to the Blackpool Illuminations every year. He loves the games area with all the new electronic games. Will he be there this year?
"Yes, I'll be there with my brother and my dad," said Tim. "And I'm sure we won't be bored! It's always a great show – and it's free! What will I do with the prize money? Well, I think I'll buy some new computer games."

Did you know ...?

- Blackpool's light show started in 1879 with eight lights. Today the show has a million lights and uses lots of new technology.
- The electricity for the show is expensive: fifty thousand pounds!
- More than three and a half million visitors come to see the lights.
- This year the lights will be on for sixty-six nights from September 1st to November 5th.

2 Read the article. Pick the right words.

1 Tim always/sometimes goes to the Blackpool light show.
2 He likes/doesn't like the games area.
3 He'll be at the show with his friend/his family.
4 Visitors pay lots of money/nothing for the light show.
5 Tim thinks he'll buy a computer/computer games with his prize money.

3 Pick the right numbers.

→ 66 • 100 • 50,000 • 1,000,000 • 3,500,000

1 Tim's prize was ... pounds.
2 Today the light show has ... lights.
3 The electricity for the light show is expensive: ... pounds.
4 ... visitors come to see the lights.
5 The lights will be on for ... nights.

▸W 36, 4–5

4 Look at the picture of Tim's room. What can you see? Do you have all these things in your room?

5 How is Tim wasting energy? Finish the sentences.

1 The ... is on, but it isn't cold and the window is open.
2 The ... is on, but Tim isn't watching it.
3 The ... are on, but Tim doesn't need them.
4 The ... is on, but his phone is charged up.
5 The ... is on, but Tim isn't using it.

6 And how is Tim wasting energy here? Tell the class.

He's going ...

The radiator is on but Tim is wearing ...

7 How can Tim save energy, save money and help the environment?

Look at exercises 5 and 6.

1 He should turn off the ... when he ...
2 He should go by ... instead of by ...
3 He should wear ... in winter instead of ...
4 He should close ... in winter.

8 Do you save energy? Talk with a partner.

I	usually sometimes never	turn off go by wear	...

► W 36, 6

PROJECT A poster about energy

Work in small groups and make a poster.

a) Find a good title for your poster.

b) WHY should you save energy?

(help ..., save ...)

HOW can you save energy?

(turn off ..., use ..., wear ..., close)

Use the ideas on this page or your own ideas. You can use a dictionary.

c) Make your poster. Find photos.

d) Present your poster to the class.

The title of our poster is ...
Why you should save energy: ...
You can save energy like this: Turn off ...

e) Who has the best poster?

1 Look at the pictures. What do you think?

a The two boys in the first picture are friends/brothers.

b The two boys in the first picture are having/aren't having fun.

c It's a warm/cold day.

d Something nice/terrible happens.

The dare

2◎2

Tim was in his room with his brother Dan.
"I'm bored," said Tim. "What can we do?"
"I don't know," said Dan. "Oh, listen, Tim. Remember we talked about the gang? I asked Leo. He said you can be in the gang if you want."
Tim thought about it. Did he want to be in the gang? He didn't know. Dan was in the gang. And the gang was cool. Nobody knew what the gang did – but everybody wanted to be in it.
"Er ... you have to do a test," Dan said.
"What? Do a dare?" Tim asked him.
"Yeah," said Dan. "It won't be dangerous. But you can say no. I won't tell your friends."
"It's OK. I'll do it," answered Tim.

The gang met at the funfair. Tim loved the funfair but he didn't have any money – and Leo had other plans.
'"Let's walk," said Leo.
It was Leo's gang. Everybody did what he said. The six boys walked along the pier. It was very cold and wet. They stopped at the railings and looked at the sea.
"Nice day for swimming," said Leo and he laughed. Tim didn't laugh.
Leo put his hand on Tim's arm.
"Listen, Tim, climb down to the sea and back again and you can join us." Tim looked down.
"Frightened?" Leo laughed again.
"I can do it," Tim said. "Watch me!"
"I'll come with you, Tim," said Dan suddenly.
"No, Dan," said Tim. "It's OK."
But Dan took off his jacket.

Tim started to climb down. Then Dan followed. The railings were wet. Tim looked down and saw the sea. He closed his eyes.

"Are you OK, Tim?" shouted Dan. He was worried.

"Yes," Tim shouted back. "I'm fine. I'll be careful."

He started to climb down again. Suddenly his foot slipped ... but his hands were on the railings.

"Well," Tim said and tried to smile. "I won't do that again! I'm not keen on swimming."

He looked at Dan ... but Dan wasn't there.

"Dan!" he screamed. His face was white. "Dan!"

Then Tim jumped.

2 What happened? Put in the right words.

→ funfair • sea • gang • pier • dare

1 Tim wanted to be in the ...
2 Tim had to do a ...
3 First the boys went to the ...
4 Then they walked along the ...
5 Tim had to climb down to the ...

3 And then? Pick the right boy.

1 Tim/Dan closed his eyes.
2 So Tim/Dan was worried.
3 Then Tim/Dan slipped.
4 Suddenly Tim/Dan wasn't there.
5 Tim/Dan screamed.
6 Then Tim/Dan jumped.

4 Pick the best ending.

A The water was very cold. Where was Dan? Tim swam to the beach. And then he saw his brother. Dan was on the rocks. His eyes were closed.
"I'll get help, Dan," Tim shouted.
He started to run.

B The water was cold but it was OK. Tim looked for Dan. Suddenly there was a hand on his foot and Dan's head came out of the water.
"Hey, Tim," he said and he laughed.
"Nice day for swimming!"

I think A/B is the best ending.

● 5 Talk about the story.

a	I think	Tim Dan Leo	was	brave stupid frightened nice	when he	climbed jumped saw said	...

b I think dares are exciting/fun/stupid/boring/dangerous/...

▸ W 37, 7–8

WORDPOWER

1 Electric things: Match the words with the pictures.

amusement arcade • charger • funfair • radiator • roller coaster

1

2

3

4

5

2 Big numbers

a) Match the numbers with the right words.

1 115
2 5,600
3 30,000
4 590
5 100,000

Tip: The list of numbers on page 179 can help you.

a five hundred and ninety
b five thousand six hundred
c one hundred thousand
d one hundred and fifteen
e thirty thousand

b) How many pupils are in your school?

3 Find the verbs.

These verbs are in the story on pages 54–55.

1

t_ _ _ o_ _

2

c _ _ _ b

3

s _ _ p

4

s _ _ _ _ m

5

j _ _ p

4 WORD SEARCH

a) Find the right word.

These sentences are on pages 53–54.

1 The lights are on, but Tim doesn't need ... . (p. 53)
2 The TV is on, but Tim isn't watching ... . (p. 53)
3 "You have to do a test," Dan said. "What? Do a dare?" Tim asked ... . (p. 54)
4 "You can join ... ." (p. 54)
5 "I can do it. Watch ...!" (p. 54)
6 "I'll come with ..., Tim," said Dan. (p. 54)

b) Put in the missing words.

me • you • him • her • it • us • them

1 The amusement arcades in Blackpool are great. I love ...!
2 We can't use this DVD player. Can you help ..., please?
3 Where's my mobile? I can't find ...
4 Tim wasn't at school. I'll phone ...
5 You're funny. I like ...
6 That's my sister. Do you know ...?
7 Please send ... an e-mail.

▸W 38, 9–11 ▸W ⊙

SHORT TALKS

1 Something special

a) First look at the pictures. What are Lucy's and Ryan's special things?

2◎3 **b) Listen to the CD and finish the sentences.**

Lucy is talking about her ...
It's blue and ...
It's important because she loves ...

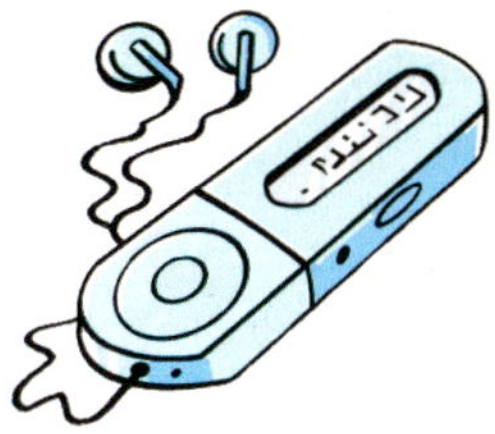

Ryan is talking about his ...
It's red and ...
It's important because it has the names of all the ... on it.

2 A good START and a good ENDING are important. Listen to Lucy and Ryan again. Who says these phrases?

START

1 I want to tell you about ...
2 I'm going to talk about ...

ENDING

1 So that's why it's special.
2 So to finish, I'd like to say ...

3 Put in the right words. Then listen to Ryan's talk and check.

2◎3

so • secondly • and • thirdly • because • ~~firstly~~

1 *Firstly*, it's special ... it's very hard to get the team's names.
2 ..., I love Manchester United ... I watch all their matches.
3 And ..., all my friends like Manchester United ... they think my bag is cool.

4 Your talk: Something special

a) Make notes:

- **What are you going to talk about?**
- **What's it like?** big/small/old/new/white/nice/expensive/...
- **Why is it important?** It was a present from ... / I bought it with ... / I love ... / I often wear ... / I play ... / ...

b) Organize your notes.

- Think how to say your notes in complete sentences.
- Use the phrases in exercises 2 and 3.

c) Present your talk to the class. Use these tips.

Tip:
Make notes.
Organize your notes.
Present your talk.

Tip:
Look at people in the class.
Use complete sentences.
Use pictures/the board/music/...

Tip:
Don't talk too fast.
Don't read out your notes.
Smile!

► W 39, 12–13 ► W ◎

LISTENING Instructions

1 At the station

a) Look at the photos. What are they?

a drinks machine • an Internet kiosk • a ticket machine

1

2
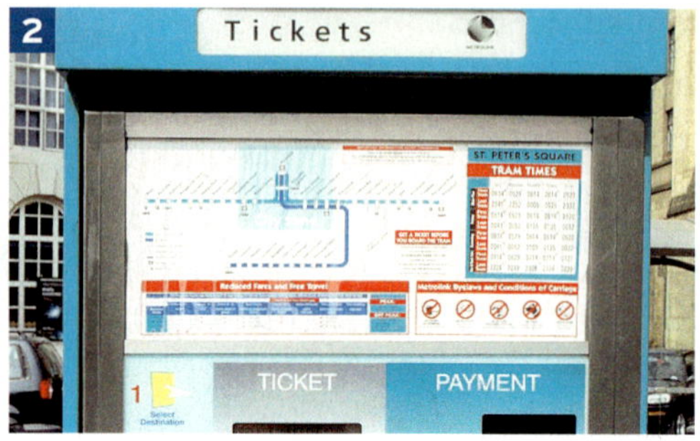

3
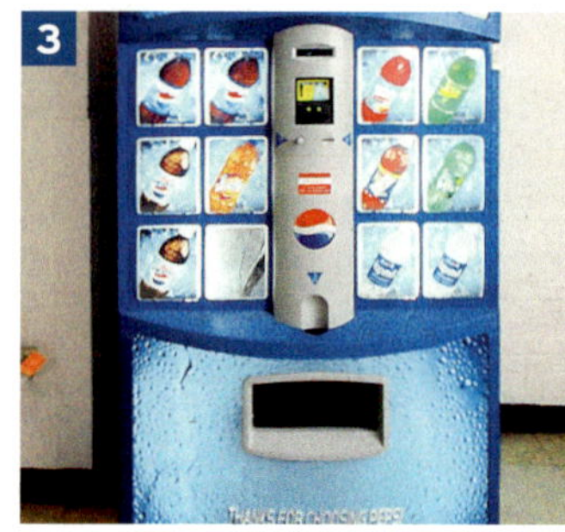

b) Tim is helping a tourist. Listen. Pick the right photo.

2 4

c) Put the instructions in the right order. Then listen again and check.

2 4

1 ..., 2 ..., 3 ..., 4 ...

A Then pick the right ticket.
B First pick where you want to go.
C And now take your ticket.
D Then put the money in the machine.

d) You're waiting at the ticket machine with your mum and you hear Tim's instructions. Tell your mum in German how to use the ticket machine.

Er sagt, zuerst muss man ...
Und dann ...

2 PRONUNCIATION [s] and [z]

a) Listen to these words. Repeat them.

2 5

Sound 1:
[s]: looks it's thanks that's
Sound 2:
[z]: excuse me use easy pounds

b) Listen to these sentences from an advert. When do you hear [s]? Say "Sound 1". When do you hear [z]? Say "Sound 2". Then repeat the word.

2 6

c) Now listen to these sentences. Repeat them.

2 7

She sells seashells on the seashore.

I scream.
You scream.
We all scream
for ice cream.

Tip:
First say the sentences slowly.
Then say them fast.

3 An instructions game

a) With your class, make a list of machines: in the street, at school or at home.

b) Pick a machine and write instructions for it. You can use a dictionary.

c) Now read your instructions. The class guesses the machine.

Put in some money/the DVD/...
Pick the game/programme/
a drink/where you want to go/
language/...
Take your drink/...
Push the (start/green/red) button.

▸W 40, 14

SPEAKING Offers

1 At Tim's house

2 8

a) Look at the picture. What's Tim offering his friend?

TIM I'll make lunch. Would you like a sandwich?
JAMIE Yes, please.
TIM Chicken or ham?
JAMIE Ham, please.
TIM What about a drink?
JAMIE Do you have apple juice?
TIM No, sorry.
JAMIE What about orange juice?
TIM Sure, no problem. I'll get it.

b) Practise the dialogue with a partner.

2 At grandad's house: Finish the dialogue. Then act it with a partner.

2 9

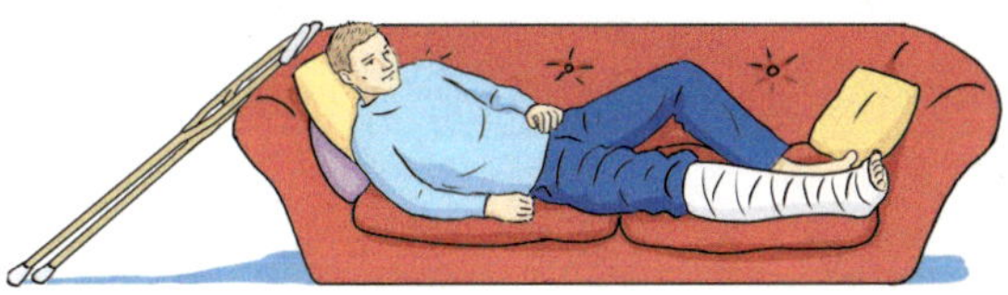

GRANDAD I'll make lunch. ... a sandwich?
DAN Yes, ...
GRANDAD Cheese or salad?
DAN ..., please.
GRANDAD What about a drink?
DAN Do you have cola?
GRANDAD No, sorry.
DAN ... milk?
GRANDAD Sure, ... I'll get it.

3 ROLE PLAY

Partner A: You're at Partner B's house.
Partner B: Look at page 125.

B ...?
A Yes, ...
B ...?
A ..., please.
B ...?
A Do you have cola/water/milk/orange juice/tea?
B ...
(A What about ...?
B ...)

▸ Wordbank 8, p. 130

4 INTERPRETING

You and your friend are in an amusement arcade in England. A girl speaks to you, but your friend doesn't understand her. Help him.

GIRL	YOU
I'll help you with this game.	Sie möchte ...
I'll show you another good game.	Sie ...
I'll play this game with you.	Sie ...
I'll meet you here tomorrow.	...

▸ W 40, 15–16 ▸ W

READING An exhibition brochure

1 Look at the brochure about an exhibition. What's the exhibition about?

a) new technology in Blackpool
b) a famous TV programme

Tip:
- Look at the pictures and the title.
- Read the description on the left.

Doctor Who is the world's longest-running science fiction TV programme. Visit this great exhibition and come face to face with some of the doctor's most frightening enemies.

See the collection of over 150 monsters, interactive displays and **Doctor Who** video clips.

Go into the Tardis, Doctor Who's famous time machine.

10 a.m. – 6 p.m.
Mon – Sun
Adults £6, Children £4
Family ticket:
2 children £18
3 children £22

On the Central Promenade
near the Tower and Central Pier.
Tel. 01253/299982

Doctor Who Exhibition
Blackpool

It's out of this world!

2 You want to go to the exhibition. Find out:

1. Where is it? Look for *on/near*.
2. When is it open? Look for *a.m.* and *p.m.*
3. How much is it? Look for *£*.
4. What's the telephone number? Look for *Tel*.
5. Can you watch *Doctor Who* programmes? Look for *video*.

Telephone numbers
You write: 01204
You say:
"oh" [əʊ] – one – two – "oh" [əʊ] – four.

3 Look at the underlined words and phrases in these sentences from the brochure. What are they in German?

1 ... the world's longest-running TV programme. You know *run*.
2 ... Doctor Who's famous time machine. You know *time* and *machine*.
3 ... come face to face with some of the Doctor's most frightening enemies. You know *face* and *frightened*.
4 See the collection of over 150 monsters. You know *collect*.

Tip:
- Think of words in English that look like these words.
- Look at the other words in the sentence.

▸ W 41, 17

WRITING A brochure

1 Blackpool Tower brochure: Answer the questions.

1 What is it?
2 Where is it?
3 When is it open?
4 How much is it?
5 What's the phone number?
6 Is there a website address?

2 Your brochure

a) First collect ideas with your class about interesting things in your area.

a castle, a funfair, a museum, a park, ...

b) Pick an idea for your brochure. Make notes. Use the questions in exercise 1.

c) Find out more information.

What makes this place special?
What can you do there?

d) Make your brochure.
Use your notes from 2b and 2c.
Use the phrases in the Blackpool Tower brochure.
Find photos (Internet, magazines).

e) You can put your brochure in your portfolio or send it to your Tourist Information Office. They can use it for English visitors.

▸ W 41, 18 ▸ W ⦿

QUESTIONNAIRE

1 Are you a technology freak?

a) Do the questionnaire. Write your answers. (1 a, 2 ...)

1 Are you interested in HOW things work?
- **a** Yes, very interested.
- **b** Sometimes.
- **c** No!

2 Your friend is going to a technology exhibition. What do you say?
- **a** "That won't be very interesting! I won't come with you, thanks!"
- **b** "That'll be interesting. I'll come too."
- **c** "Mmm, that'll be interesting. Bye!"

3 What do you think of mobile phones?
- **a** It's good to have a mobile – but it isn't the most important thing in my life.
- **b** I can't live without my mobile.
- **c** I don't need a mobile.

4 Your friend tells you about a problem with her computer. What do you say?
- **a** "Er, I'll look on the Internet."
- **b** "Sorry, I have no idea."
- **c** "I'll help you. No problem."

5 What would you like for your birthday?
- **a** I need a new, expensive, very cool MP3 player.
- **b** I think I'll get some DVDs.
- **c** I'm sure my parents will buy me some clothes.

b) How many points do you have? Look at the green box.

13–15 Yes, you're a technology freak! Do you think your mobile and your computer are more important than your friends and family?

9–12 You think technology is important but there are more important things in your life.

5–8 You think technology isn't important. But can you live without it in the modern world?

c) Talk about your points with your class.

I have ... points. I think ...

Your points:

1a:3 1b:2 1c:1 2a:1 2b:3 2c:2
3a:2 3b:3 3c:1 4a:2 4b:1 4c:3
5a:3 5b:2 5c:1.

2 WORD SEARCH
Find these words in the unit.

1 I ... there with my brother and my dad. (p. 52)
2 I think I ... some new computer games. (p. 52)
3 The lights ... on for sixty-six nights. (p. 52)
4 "I ... with you Tim," said Dan. (p. 54)
5 I ... lunch. (p. 59)
6 "Mmm, that ... interesting. Bye!" (p. 62)
7 I'm sure my parents ... me some clothes. (p. 62)

3 WORD SEARCH
Now find these words in the unit.

1 I'm sure we ... bored. (p. 52)
2 It ... dangerous. (p. 54)
3 You can say no. I ... your friends. (p. 54)
4 That ... very interesting! (p. 62)

4 WORD SEARCH
Find these words too.

1 ... he ... there this year? (p. 52)
2 What ... I ... with the prize money? (p. 52)

5 OVER TO YOU! Pick the right words and write examples.

Tip:
Write the checkpoint in your exercise book.

CHECKPOINT

Will ('ll)* und *won't

- Wenn du voraussagen willst, was in der Zukunft geschehen wird, benutzt du ... oder ... .
  Beispiele: ...
- Wenn du voraussagen willst, was in der Zukunft nicht geschehen wird, benutzt du ... .
  Beispiele: ...
- Fragen mit *will* werden durch die Wortstellung angezeigt.
  Beispiele: ...

► Eine Übersicht über diese Regeln findest du auf der *Summary*-Seite 107.
► Extra Practice, pp. 104 ff.
► W 42–43

NACH DIESER UNIT KANN ICH ...

über Technologie im Haushalt sprechen.	► *The TV is on.*
über das Energiesparen sprechen.	► *Turn off the lights when you aren't using them.*
etwas voraussagen.	► *I'm sure my parents will buy me some clothes.*
spontan Hilfe anbieten und Entscheidungen treffen.	► *I'll get help.* *I won't come with you, thanks.*
Anweisungen verstehen.	► *Put the money in the machine.* *Push the green button.*
Essen und Trinken anbieten.	► *Would you like a drink/a sandwich?* *What about ...?*

Weitere Übungen: www.new-highlight.de

► W 44, Test yourself ► W 45–46, Portfolio ► W ⦿
► Extra Reading, p. 123

Dubliners

This is me in the centre of Dublin.

This is me at my athletics club. I train here every week.

This is me with my family – and our dog.

This is me with my friends. We often go to the sea.

1 Liam's photos

a) Listen. Liam is talking about three photos on page 64. Which photos? 2 10

b) Listen again. 2 10

1 Santry is ...	Liam's mum.
2 Anna is ...	Liam's sister.
3 Tess is ...	Liam's friends.
4 Benjy is ...	Liam's club.
5 Alex and Kieran are ...	Liam's dog.

2 Your photos

Put some photos of you, your family or your friends in your exercise book. Write notes about the photos. Then talk to your partner about your photos.

E

We have a big family – six kids.
I'm the oldest.

F

This is our mobile home.

G

I sometimes go to the shopping centre with my sister.

H

Dad has ponies.

3 Gina's photos

2 11 **a) Listen. Gina is talking about three photos on page 65. Which photos?**

b) What's right? Make notes. Check your answers with a partner. Then listen and check.

1 Gina's ~~friends~~ are Martina and Rose.
2 She lives in a ~~big~~ mobile home.
3 Gina's ~~mum~~ buys and sells ponies.
4 Gina and her friends ride the ~~quads~~.

4 SONG *Our house* by Madness

2 12 **a) Which family words do you hear? Listen to the song and make notes.**

b) Listen again. Who are the people in these two pictures?

▸W 47, 1–3

From *Dublin Kidz*

1 Look quickly at the article. What do you think *Dublin Kidz* is?
– A sports magazine? – A teen magazine? – A TV magazine?

Teen Dreams

Dublin Kidz, April 16

Are teenagers happy? What's important for them? What are their dreams for the future? *Dublin Kidz* talked to two teenagers in Dublin about these things.

***Liam O'Brien** (15) lives in Dublin with his mum and his sister (10). Liam's dad died two years ago.*

"When dad died, my world changed. But my friends were great and they helped me. Friends are very important. Then I joined an athletics club. Now athletics are very important to me – I love the high jump. I came third in the *Dublin Games* last summer. I hope that I'll come first this summer.

And my future? Well, I hope that I'll find a nice girlfriend. And if I get a good job, I'll buy a cool car and I'll travel to lots of places. Maybe I'll be an athletics trainer."

***Gina Ward** (16) lives in Dublin too. Gina's family are travellers. They don't stay in the same place for very long.*

"The family is very important for travellers. If somebody has a problem, the others will help.

Our mobile home is OK, but I'd like to live in a house. Dad says that if he gets a job, we'll buy a house. I'd like that! I like school and I work hard there. I like athletics and I love running. I want to run for Ireland!

My future? If I finish school, I'll get a good job and I'll have a nice big house – and a big family."

2 What's important for Liam and Gina? Match the notes with the names.

Liam

Gina

friends
running
athletics
the family
a nice house
the high jump

3 Future dreams: Make sentences.

Liam wants to ...	be an ...	finish ...
	get a ...	find a ...
	run for ...	come first in ...
Gina wants to ...	travel to ...	live in a ...
	have a ...	buy a ...

▸W 48, 4–5

4 Write six sentences about your dreams.

MY DREAMS
- I think I'll ...
- Maybe I'll ...
- I hope I'll ...
- I'm sure I'll ...
- I'm sure I won't ...
- I hope I won't ...

live ... • have ... • run ... • get ... • buy ... • meet ... • find ... • be ... • drive ... • go ... • visit ... • leave ...

▸ Wordbank 9, p. 131
▸ W 48, 6

PROJECT A teen survey

Find out about teenagers at your school. Do this survey.

a) Groups: Make groups of four or five pupils. Pick a chairperson.

b) The questionnaire:
1 Pick some questions for your questionnaire.

What are your hobbies?
What's important for you?
What are your favourite subjects?
What are your dreams?
What makes you happy?
What makes you angry?
What's your favourite season?
What's your favourite TV programme?
What sports would you like to do/try?
...

Tip:
You need about three to six questions for your questionnaire.
Write your questionnaire like this:

2 Write your questionnaire on a computer.

3 Then give your questionnaire to another class.

c) The results: Talk to the class about the results of your questionnaire.

We gave our questionnaire to Class 9a.
Here are the results:

10 pupils think money is important.
17 pupils think friends are important.
21 pupils think family is important.
5 pupils want to be famous.
23 pupils want to get a good job.
Nobody ...

A teen survey
Group C

1) What's important for you?
family ☐ friends ☐ TV ☐
money ☐ school ☐ food ☐

2) What are your dreams? – I hope I'll ...
be famous ☐ get a good job ☐
have a family ☐ travel ☐

3) What things do you hate?

1 Before you read or listen: What do you think will happen in the story?

- Liam and Gina will/won't train together.
- Liam and Gina will/won't be friends.
- Gina will/won't leave her home in Dublin.

Tip:
Look at the pictures and guess. Then listen to or read the story and check your answers.

Two worlds?

2 13

It was Saturday morning. Liam was at the athletics club.
The door opened and a girl came in. She was shy and she looked nice.
"Can I help you?" Liam asked.
"Er, yes, er ... I'd like to ... er ... join the club."

Gina Ward joined the club. She went there every Saturday. She was a good runner – she was very fast. "If Gina trains hard, she'll get on the athletics team for the *Dublin Games*," her trainer said.

Liam liked Gina and Gina liked Liam. They met at the club every Saturday. They often talked and sometimes they trained together in the club gym or on the track.

One Saturday Liam invited Gina to his house. "My parents are very strict," she answered. "If I don't go home now, they'll worry." "Oh, please, Gina," Liam said. Gina said OK and they took the bus to Weston Road.

Liam's house was big and modern. There was expensive furniture. Everything was very nice. Later, when they were at the bus stop, Gina said, "Liam, we're from two different worlds."
"What do you mean?" Liam asked.
"You live in a big house, on a nice road, in a quiet suburb. I'm a traveller. I live in a mobile home. Don't you understand? We're different!" Gina answered.
"Houses aren't important! People are important. And we're good friends," Liam said. Gina took his hand.
"That's the problem," she thought. "We're more than good friends."
But she said nothing.

The next Saturday Gina didn't come to the club. Liam sent her a text message, but he got no answer.
"The *Dublin Games* are on June 2nd. Gina must train. But if she doesn't train every week, she won't get on the team," the trainer said to Liam.
"Maybe she's ill," Liam thought.

Liam found Gina's address in the club. He took the bus and went to the other side of the city. He walked along a busy road. There were lots of cars, buses – and ponies! Kids were playing in the road.
"Excuse me," Liam said to some kids.
"Where does Gina Ward live?"
One boy walked to Gina's mobile home with him. But it was closed.
A man was watching. "They aren't here," he said to Liam.
"Where are they?" Liam asked.
"They've moved back to England."

Liam was devastated. Why did Gina leave? Why didn't she say goodbye? Were they really from two different worlds?
But a week later Liam got an e-mail.

Hi Liam,
I had no time to say goodbye. And I was too sad.
I'm sorry. Dad got a job in Manchester.
We have a house now – and a computer too.
I'll be in Dublin from June 1st to June 4th.
I'll come and watch you in the *Dublin Games*.
Please send me an e-mail soon.
Love, Gina

2 Who ...

1 ... was shy?
2 ... was a good runner?
3 ... trained together?
4 ... lived in a quiet suburb?
5 ... lived near a busy road?
6 ... took Liam's hand?
7 ... didn't come to the club?
8 ... sent a text message?
9 ... left Dublin?
10 ... got an e-mail?

3 Gina and Liam

a) They were the same because:

1 They lived in ...
2 They liked ...
3 They were in the same ...
4 They went there every ...

b) They were different because:

1 Gina lived in a mobile home, but Liam ...
2 Liam did the high jump – Gina was a ...
3 Liam stayed in Dublin, but Gina ...

● 4 Dear diary: Pick a) or b) and write some sentences (60–75 words).

a) Imagine that you're Liam. Write about Gina's first morning in the club.

Dear diary,
This morning I was at the ...

b) Imagine that you're Gina. Write about your afternoon at Liam's house.

Dear diary,
Today I went to Liam's ...

▸W 49, 7–8

WORDPOWER

1 Use the words in the box and finish the sentences.
They're all in the story on pages 68–69.

busy • devastated • different • fast • modern • ill • shy • strict

1

Gina is very ...

2

And she's very ...

3

Gina's parents are ...

4

The road was very ...

5

Liam was ...

6
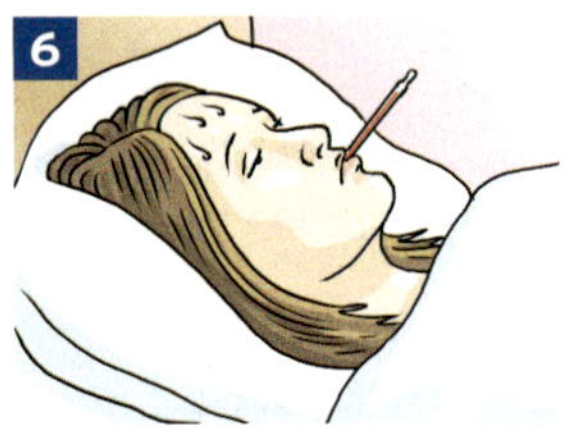
Maybe Gina is ...

7
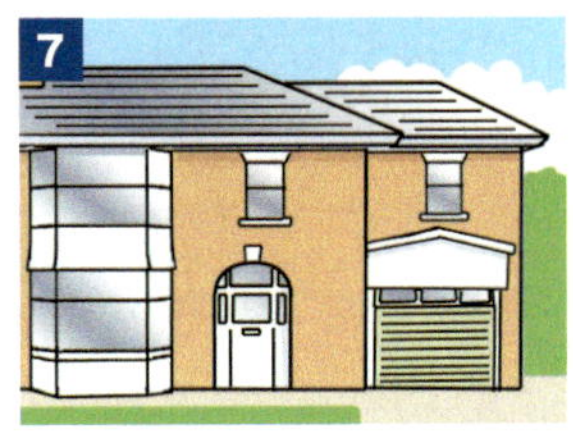
Liam's house is ...

8

We're ...!

2 SENTENCE SEARCH
They're all in the story on pages 68–69.

1 Kann ich dir helfen?
2 Ich möchte dem Verein beitreten.
3 Was meinst du damit?
4 Wir sind gute Freunde.
5 Gina muss trainieren.
6 Vielleicht ist sie krank.
7 Sie wird nicht in die Mannschaft kommen.
8 Es tut mir leid.

3 WORDS IN THIS UNIT

a) What's what?

A gym / A trainer / Athletics / A suburb

1 ... is sports like running, the high jump.
2 ... is a room where you do athletics.
3 ... is a part of a city.
4 ... is somebody who trains a team.

b) What are these words?

1 ... are people who live in Dublin.
2 ... is things like tables and chairs.
3 A ... is somebody who's 13, 14, 15, 16 ...
4 ... is another word for "children".
5 A ... is where you find lots of shops.

4 WORD SEARCH

a) Find the right words.

1 I came ... in the *Dublin Games*. (p. 66)
2 I hope that I'll come ... . (p. 66)
3 The *Dublin Games* are on June ... . (p. 69)
4 I'll be in Dublin from June ... to June ... . (p. 69)

b) Finish this list in your exercise book.

first	1st
second	...
...	3rd
fourth	...
...	5th
sixth	...

...	7th
eighth	...
...	9th
tenth	...
...	11th
twelfth	...

▸W 50, 9–11 ▸W ⊙

Tip:
The list on page 179 can help you.

1 You can make nouns from verbs.

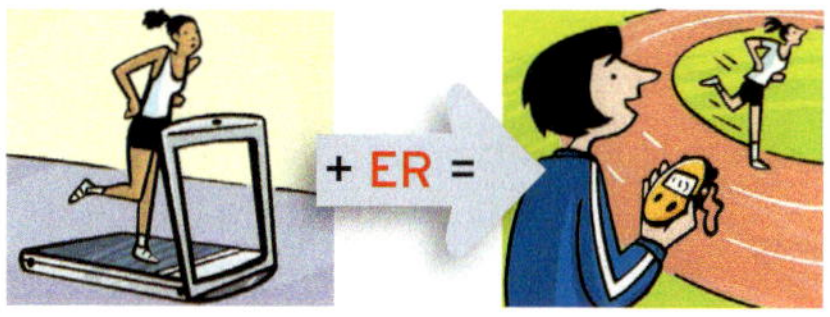

train trainer

Some words need another letter.

travel

traveller

a) Make nouns from these verbs:

climb • help • play • present • read • send • sing • walk • work

b) Now make nouns from these verbs:

blog • run • swim • win

2 Verbs

a) What are the right verbs for these phrases? Put in *have*, *live*, *get* and *work*.

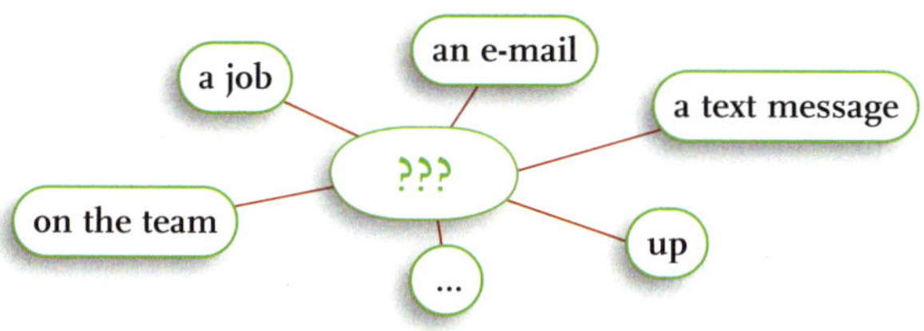

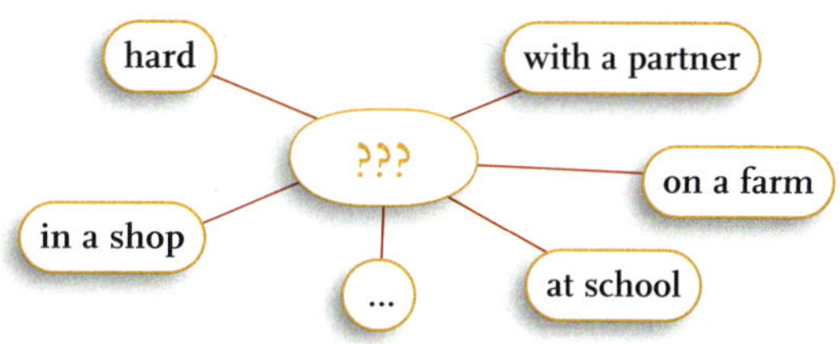

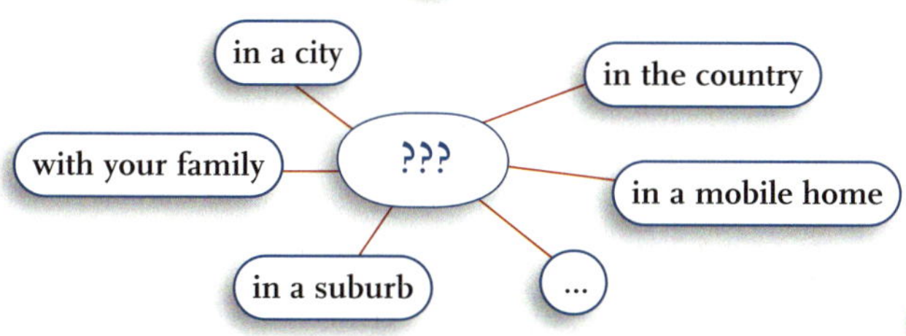

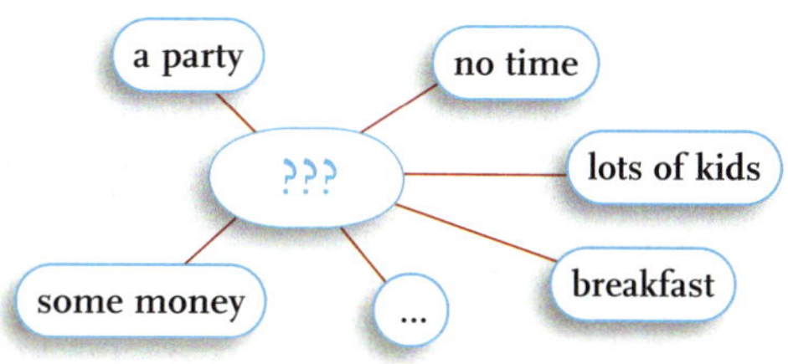

b) Make four sentences about your partner's future. What does she/he answer?

YOU				YOUR PARTNER
I think I'm sure	you'll you won't	have live get work	a fast car • lots of kids • in the country • in a big city • a good job • get on the school team • in a department store • in a factory	– Yes, I will. – No, I won't. – Maybe!

3 SAY IT IN GERMAN

Look at the advert. Tell a partner what it says.

You can use a dictionary.

THE DUBLIN ATHLETICS CLUB

Get fit! Get healthy! Have fun!

You can train all year in our modern gym. If you want to try a new sport, our professional athletics trainers will help you: Running: 100 m, 200 m, 400 m and 5000 m. High jump, long jump, hurdles, discus, shot-put, javelin, pole vault.

JOIN THE DUBLIN ATHLETICS CLUB TODAY!

▸ Wordbank 10, p. 131 ▸ W 51, 12–13 ▸ W ⦿

LISTENING I agree!

2 14

1 What topic are the teenagers talking about? Listen.

2 Listen for language.

a) Write the sentences in the right order.

A I told my teacher. You should always tell somebody!

D What did you do?

C I think you're right. If you tell somebody, you can get help.

B I think bullying is terrible!

E That's true. And last year I had a problem in my old school. Some pupils didn't talk to me.

F I agree. There are lots of bullies at this school.

► W 52, 14

b) Now listen again and check.

2 14

3 PRONUNCIATION *th*-words

a) Listen and repeat these words.

2 15

[θ] think, thanks, Thursday, three, bathroom

[ð] this, that, these, those, brother

b) Listen and repeat.

2 16

thing – then
through – they
maths – mother
healthy – other
thought – there
birthday – brother
nothing – weather
something – father

c) Now try this tongue twister.

2 17

Whether the weather is fine, or whether the weather is not,
Whether the weather is cold, or whether the weather is hot,
We'll get the weather, whatever the weather, whether we like it or not!

SPEAKING I don't agree!

1 In the club: Gina is back for the *Dublin Games*.

2 18 **a) What are the teenagers talking about? Listen or read and find out.**

GINA We aren't welcome in lots of places.
CIARA Oh, I don't agree! Most people have no problem with travellers.
LIAM That isn't true! If you're a traveller, you can't get a job.
SHANE I don't think you're right! There are two travellers in my mum's shop.
GINA Great! But it isn't always like that.

b) Practise the dialogue with partners.

2 More dialogues

a) Put in the missing words or phrases.

1 Parents should be stricter!
– I don't ...! I think parents shouldn't be too strict.

2 Teenagers have an easy life.
– That isn't ...! Teenagers have lots of problems.

3 Mobile phones aren't safe.
– I don't think you're ...! Mobiles are fine.

4 Athletics is boring.
– ...! I love athletics.

5 Spiders are terrible! – ...! Spiders are nice.

b) Act the dialogues with a partner.

▸ W 52, 15

3 ROLE PLAY

Partner A: Pick some sentences and tell Partner B what you think.
Partner B: Do you agree with Partner A? Say what you think. The lists on page 126 can help.

There are/aren't bullies in our class. • Bullying is/isn't a terrible thing.
There is/isn't bullying in our school. • You should/shouldn't tell somebody about a bully.
Girls are/aren't worse bullies than boys. • You should/shouldn't talk to a bully.

4 INTERPRETING You and your friend are with Gina and Liam in Dublin. But your friend can't speak English. Tell him what they're saying – in German.

LIAM Dublin is a great city!
GINA That's true. But Manchester is better.
LIAM I don't agree. Manchester is terrible!
GINA Don't be stupid! You've never been to Manchester!

YOU Liam sagt, dass ...
Gina meint, ...
Liam findet, ...
Gina ...

▸ W

READING An advert

1 **Read the advert for holidays in Ireland.**
Which area would you like to visit – the West, Northern Ireland or Dublin?

HOLIDAYS IN IRELAND

Come to the West.
You'll find mountains, lonely roads and the sea! It's special! Visit Europe's highest cliffs – the Cliffs of Moher. Go surfing in the Atlantic. See beautiful beaches. Visit old castles. Listen to great music in the villages and towns. Look for whales on the coast.

Come to Northern Ireland.
The Giant's Causeway is amazing – about 37,000 volcanic rocks in the sea. People say that a giant wanted to walk to Scotland to visit his girlfriend, so he put these steps in the sea.

Come to Dublin.
Visit the Saint Patrick's Day Festival (17th March). It's a big party. There's a parade, music, dancing in the streets and lots of fun for the family. Green is the colour of Ireland, so don't forget to wear something green. And if you're lucky, you'll see the "little people"!

2 **Read the advert again. Where in Ireland can you see these things?**

1

2

3

3 **Words in the advert**

a) Match the pictures (a–h) with the words (1–8).

1 cliffs	**5** volcanic rocks
2 go surfing	**6** a giant
3 whales	**7** a parade
4 the coast	**8** the "little people"

b) What are the words in German?
Check your answers in a dictionary.

a

b

c

d

e

f

g

h

► W 53, 16

WRITING A picture story

1 **Talk about the pictures 1–6 in your class. What can you see? What's happening in the pictures?**

Tip:
Write the story in the *simple past*.
Think of names for the boy and girl.

2 **Work with a partner. Write sentences for pictures 1–4.**

WHO? the Müllers
WHERE? from Bielefeld
WHAT? plan – quiet holiday – Ireland – parents happy – kids not happy

WHEN? on the first day of the holiday
WHERE? in Dublin – city centre
WHAT? lots of people – exciting – not quiet – happy – not happy

WHEN? on the second day
WHERE? in the West – at the sea
WHAT? see – lots of birds – sheep – whale – everybody happy

WHEN? two days later
WHERE? at the Cliffs of Moher
WHAT? walk on cliffs – shout – frightened

● **3** **Finish the story.**

Tip:
First, make notes for pictures 5 and 6.
Use the question words: *When? Where? Who? What?* Say how the people felt.

▸W 53, 17 ▸W ⦿

HOLIDAY TIPS

A

B

C

D

E

F

Hurling – the most exciting game in the world!

1 Match the photos (A–F) with these holiday tips (1–6).

1 If you go to Dingle, you'll hear about Fungi. He's a dolphin. He's very friendly.
2 If you visit the Cliffs of Moher, you'll see the highest cliffs in Europe.
3 If you go to Ireland, you should watch a hurling game. It's an Irish sport.
4 If you have time in Dublin, you should go on a Viking boat tour. It's wild!
5 If you travel to Limerick, you shouldn't miss Bunratty Castle. It's beautiful.
6 If you see signs in Irish, you won't understand them. But they're usually in English too.

2 WORD SEARCH

a) Find the words on pages 66–76.

1 If I ... a good job, I'll buy a cool car. (p. 66)
2 If somebody ... a problem, the others will help. (p. 66)
3 If he ... a job, we'll buy a house. (p. 66)
4 If Gina ... hard, she'll get on the athletics team. (p. 68)
5 If you ... to try a new sport, our trainers will help you. (p. 71)
6 If you ... signs in Irish, you won't understand them. (p. 76)

b) Find these words on pages 66–76.

1 If I finish school, I ... ... a good job. (p. 66)
2 If I don't go home now, they ... . (p. 68)
3 If she doesn't train every week, she ... ... on the team. (p. 69)
4 And if you're lucky, you ... ... the "little people"! (p. 74)
5 If you go to Dingle, you ... ... about Fungi. (p. 76)
6 If you visit the Cliffs of Moher, you ... ... the highest cliffs in Europe. (p. 76)

3 WORD SEARCH Now find these words on pages 72–76.

1 If you tell somebody, you ... get help. (p. 72)
2 If you're a traveller, you ... get a job. (p. 73)
3 If you go to Ireland, you ... watch a hurling game. (p. 76)
4 If you travel to Limerick, you ... miss Bunratty Castle. (p. 76)

4 OVER TO YOU! Draw this table in your exercise book.

Put in:
– *will/won't*
– *can/can't*
– *should/shouldn't*
– simple present

CHECKPOINT

***If*-Sätze**

Nebensatz	Hauptsatz
If + ...	... + verb

► Eine Übersicht über diese Regeln findest du auf der *Summary*-Seite 111.
► Extra Practice, pp. 108 ff.
► W 54–55

NACH DIESER UNIT KANN ICH ...

über Zukunftspläne und Träume sprechen.	► *I think I'll be a trainer. I hope I'll be famous.*
eine Umfrage durchführen.	► *In our survey, ten pupils think money is important.*
eine Geschichte schreiben.	► *On the first day ... / Two days later ... / ...*
Zustimmung und Ablehnung ausdrücken.	► *I agree. / That's true. / I think you're right. I don't agree. / That isn't true. / I don't think you're right.*
sagen, was passiert wenn ...	► *If I get a good job, I'll buy a cool car. If you have time in Dublin, you should go on a Viking tour.*

Weitere Übungen: www.new-highlight.de ► W 56, Test yourself ► W 57–58, Portfolio ► W ⦿

Unit 6*

Cornish holidays

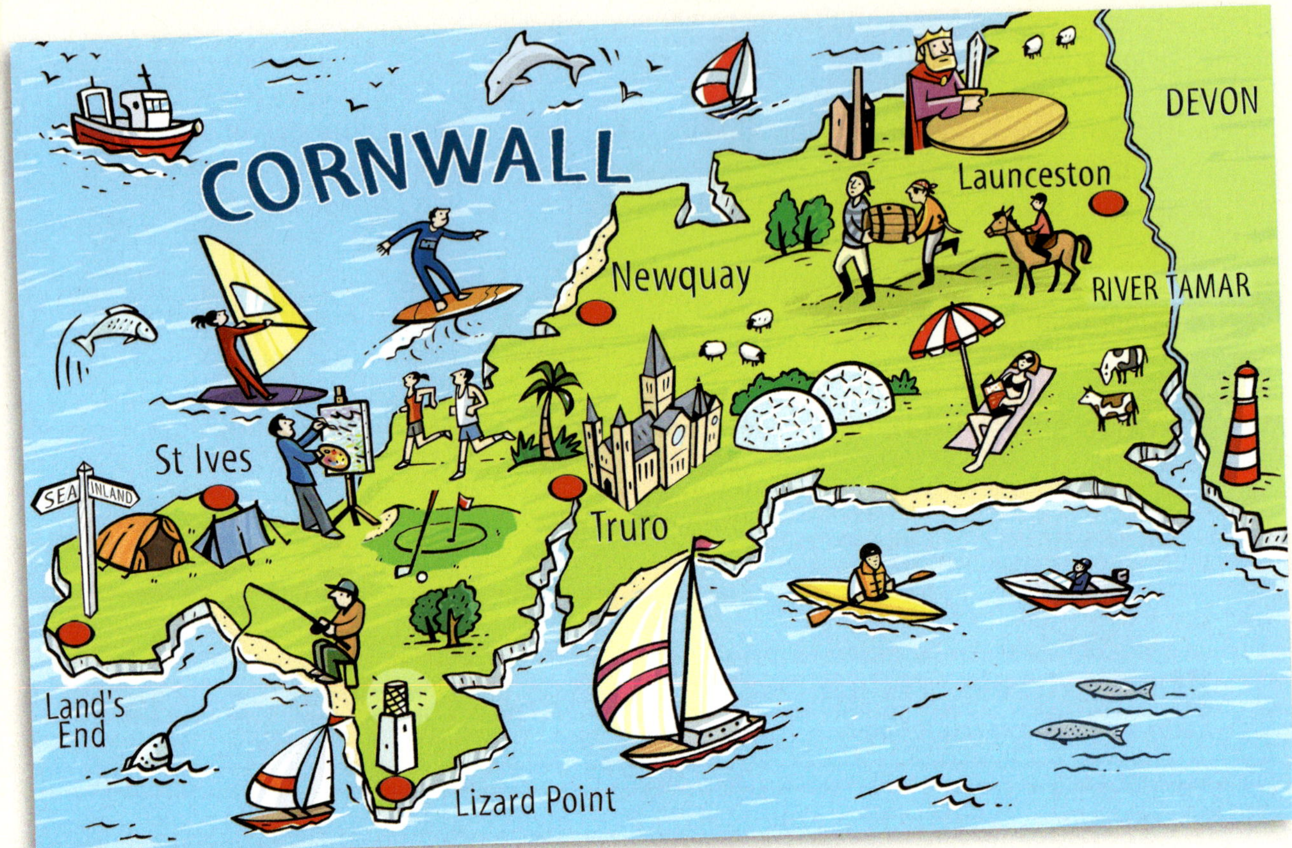

1 In Cornwall

a) Look at the postcard. Pick the right words.

1 Cornwall is in the south-east/south-west of England.
2 Land's End/Truro is the furthest place west in England.
3 Cornwall has sea/mountains on three sides.
4 In Cornwall you can/can't do lots of outdoor activities.

Tip:
You can check on the map on page 7.

b) Work with a partner. Which of these activities can you see on the map?
I can see ... here.

camping • canoeing • fishing • golf • horse riding • jogging • mountain biking • painting • sailing • shopping • sunbathing • surfing • volleyball • windsurfing

c) On the map find: Newquay, Lizard Point and Launceston. Where are they?
... is in the north/... of Cornwall.
What activities can you do in these places?
You can go ... in/at ...

*Unit 6 ist nur Pflichtstoff für den E-Kurs in Nordrhein-Westfalen.

NEWQUAY

A

B

C

D

2 In Newquay

Listen to the dialogues.
2 19 **Match them with the photos.**

Dialogue 1: Photo ...
Dialogue 2: ...
...

3 AND YOU? Look at photo D again.

a) Do you know people with tattoos? Tell your class.

My big sister/brother/... has a tattoo.
It's a fish/sun/... . It's on her/his arm/...

b) Talk about tattoos with your class.

I think tattoos look terrible/cool/interesting/beautiful/...
They're OK for boys/girls/teenagers/...
I don't like big/... tattoos.
One is fine, but not lots of tattoos.
Sticker tattoos are OK, real tattoos are stupid.
I'd like to have ...

I agree. / That's true. / I think you're right.
I don't agree. / That isn't true. / I don't think you're right.

▸ W 59, 1–4 ▸ Wordbank 11, 12, p. 132

At Pauline's cafe

1 Look at the pictures. Find out:

1 Where's Matt working?
2 What can you eat there?

2 Read the dialogue. Why does Matt's mum need help?

2 20

MUM Listen, Matt, it's great that you can help me when Sue's ill. But do you have to wear those clothes? They look terrible.

MATT Oh, Mum, give me a break. All my friends wear clothes like this!

MUM And your hair ...

MATT What's wrong with my hair?

MUM This is a cafe. If there's hair in the food, we'll have a big problem.

MATT Oh, I hadn't thought of that. OK, ... Mum, before Sue got ill, I had made an arrangement with Jake for Saturday afternoon. We're meeting in town to sell our pictures. And I'd like to go surfing on Sunday with Luke.

MUM That's OK. If you can help me in the morning, your dad can work in the afternoon. And I hope Sue will be back at the cafe soon.

3 Right or wrong?

1 Matt's mum doesn't like his clothes.
2 Matt's friends don't like his clothes.
3 Matt's hair is a problem in the cafe.
4 Matt wants to meet Jake on Sunday.
5 Matt doesn't have to work all day at the weekend.

4 AND YOU? Talk with your class.

a) How do you help your parents?
I help at home / in the garden / in their shop / with the car / with the shopping / ...
Do you like helping them?

b) What problems do you have with your parents?
Problems with my clothes / food / friends / ...
I don't have any problems.

► W 60, 5

5 **The cafe's Cornish pasties are very popular. Make them with your class.**

Cornish pasties

1 Make the pastry: Mix the butter, the flour and some salt with your hands.

2 Put in the water and mix the pastry into a ball.

3 Roll out the pastry.

4 Cut round a small plate four times.

5 Cut the beef, potatoes, carrot and onion.

6 Mix the beef and vegetables and salt and pepper. Put in the centre of the pastry.

7 Put some water on the sides of the pastry. Make four pasties.

8 Bake for 20 minutes at 220° C, then 20 minutes at 160° C.

6 **Explain in German: What's a Cornish pasty? How do you make it?**

Tip: The pictures can help you.

PROJECT Your English cafe

a) Work in small groups.

b) Find a name for your cafe.

c) What's your cafe like?

It's modern/...

d) What's in the cafe?

There are posters, magazines, ...

e) Go to www.new-highlight.de, find the window for the webcode and put in NHL-3-81.

f) Look at the cafe menus and information there.

g) Make a menu for your cafe: things for breakfast and lunch, and drinks. Find photos or draw pictures.

h) Present your cafe and menu to the class.

▸ W 60, 6–7

1 Look at the pictures. Finish the sentences.

Picture 1:

a Matt is working in the ...

b He's talking to a ...

Picture 2:

c Matt and his friend are sitting in the ...

d They're selling ...

Picture 3:

e The boy and girl from the cafe are standing near a ...

f ... is shouting.

Too young

2 21

It was Saturday. Matt was busy in the cafe. At about 12 o'clock he noticed a family at table 3. They were waiting with the menu.
"Sorry," Matt said. "It's self-service."
"Can you say that again?" said the girl. She was about 13. She looked bored.
"What about "please"?" thought Matt.
"It's self-service," he said. "Pick your food and pay over there and don't forget your cutlery."
"Cutlery? What does that mean?" the girl asked.
"Oh, sorry," said Matt. "Knives, forks and spoons."
"Thank you," the boy said. He was older than his sister. "This is our first trip to England."
"OK," said Matt. "Where are you from?"
"Germany," said the boy.

When Matt took the plates of hot food to table 3, he noticed the German boy's T-shirt.
"Hey, you're wearing a *Lemon Jelly* T-shirt," Matt said. "That's my favourite band."
"I'm a big fan of their music," said the boy.
"Should I ask him if he'd like to go to the beach party later?" Matt thought. But the cafe was busy. Before Matt found time to talk to the boy, the family had gone.

In town Matt sat in the street with his friend Jake. They painted pictures and in summer made lots of money from tourists.

They hadn't been there long when Matt saw the German boy and girl from the cafe. The girl was near the tattoo shop and her brother was shouting.

"Hi again," Matt said to them. "I'm Matt. Can I help?"
"Hello," said the boy and smiled.
"I'm Moritz ... and that's Leni. She's stupid – she wants to get a tattoo."
"Lass mich in Ruhe!" Leni said. She went into the shop. Moritz looked nervous but Matt smiled.
A short time after she had gone in, Leni came out. "Ach, es ist sowieso zu teuer. Ich gehe lieber einkaufen."
She went and looked in a shop window.
"I didn't understand that," said Matt. "What did she say?"
"Oh, er ... she says it's too expensive. She's going shopping."
Matt tried not to smile. "OK. Do you want to go to a party later? At the beach? There'll be music. I'm sure they'll play *Lemon Jelly*."
"Yes, great," said Moritz. "I love the beach, we don't live near the sea at home. Can Leni come too?"
"Sure. Let's meet at 6 o'clock at the cafe. See you later."

Matt went back to Jake. "That girl wanted to get a tattoo."
"Too young," said Jake. "You have to be 18. Does she know that?"
Matt laughed. "I think she knows now."

2 Put the sentences in the right order.

a) But she didn't get a tattoo.
b) At lunch a German family needed help.
c) Later Matt saw the boy and girl again.
d) Matt worked in the cafe in the morning.
e) The girl wanted to get a tattoo.
f) After lunch the family left the cafe.

3 What are they like?

Work with a partner. Write about Moritz, Leni and Matt.

→ short/long/blonde/brown hair • nice • friendly • not friendly • wild • shy • silly • funny • frightened • interesting • ...

He/She has ... hair.
He's/She's ... and he's/she's ... too.

4 In Britain

a) Put in the right words.

→ sea • please • eighteen • self-service • sorry

1 In Britain people always say "..." when they ask for something.
2 In Britain many cafes are ... but somebody usually brings hot food to your table.
3 People in Britain often say "..."
4 In Britain a lot of people live near the ...
5 In Britain you have to be ... to get a real tattoo.

b) Write five sentences about Germany like the sentences in exercise 4 a.

► W 61, 8–10

WORDPOWER

1 WORD LINK 1

a) Match the words and make phrases.

These phrases are in the story on pages 82–83.

1	go	a	lots of money
2	paint	b	pictures
3	make	c	a tattoo
4	say	d	a big fan
5	be	e	to a party
6	get	f	"sorry"

b) AND YOU? Pick the right words.

1 I like/don't like going to parties.
2 I sometimes/never paint pictures.
3 I want/don't want to make lots of money.
4 I often say/don't say "sorry".
5 I'm/I'm not a big fan of a band or singer.
6 I want/don't want to get a tattoo.

2 Say it in English.

These sentences are in the story too.

1 Kannst du das nochmal sagen?
2 Was bedeutet das?
3 Kann ich helfen?
4 Das habe ich nicht verstanden.
5 Was hat sie gesagt?
6 Bis später.

3 In a cafe

Find the words for the pictures.

These words are on pages 80–83.

1 I'll have a  of orange juice, please.

2 Can you give me the  and , please?

3 I can't cut my food with this .

4 Can I have a  of tea, please?

5 I need a  for my tea.

6 Excuse me, this  is dirty.

7 That's a big  of chips!

4 Word groups

a) Work with a partner or in a small group. Make lists. Who has the most words?

1 food: apples, ...
2 drinks: cola, ...
3 clothes: T-shirt, ...
4 shops: clothes shop, ...

b) WORD LINK 2

Find verbs for these words.

BREAD

COLA

A SHOP

CLOTHES

bake • borrow • buy • cut • drink • eat • go into • go to • hate • leave • like • look for • make • take off • wear • ...

► W 62, 11–13 ► W ⊙

Interpreting (German → English)

1 In Newquay: Moritz is in a clothes shop with his mum. Her English isn't very good. Read the dialogue with two partners. What does his mum want to do?

2 ◉ 22

MUTTER Ich würde gern die Jeans aus dem Schaufenster anprobieren.
MORITZ My mum would like to try on the jeans in the window.
ASSISTANT No problem. What size does she take?
MORITZ Welche Grösse hast du?
MUTTER Normalerweise Größe 40.
MORITZ Size 40.
ASSISTANT OK, here you are.
MUTTER Wo ist die Umkleidekabine?
MORITZ Where's the ... er, place ..., er, the place where you can try on clothes?
ASSISTANT The changing room? Over there.

2 In the clothes shop

a) Read the dialogue in exercise 1 again with a partner.
Use these phrases instead of the words in blue.

→
- die Jacke da drüben
- Größe 36
- der Spiegel
- the thing where you can see yourself
- mirror

3 Words: How can you explain these words in English?
Kasse, Bäckerei, Reiseführer, Regenjacke, Konfitüre.

Tip:
You don't know a word? Try to explain it.

It's a kind of book/food/...

It's a place where you can pay for/buy/...

You use it/wear it/... when ...

It's something to eat/wear/...

● 4 On holiday in England: Practise the dialogue with two partners.

DAD Frag mal, ob sie Badeschuhe haben. Ich habe meine zu Hause vergessen.
YOU Badeschuhe? Er, excuse me, my dad is looking for something to ... . You ... them when ...
ASSISTANT Ah, yes, flip-flops. What size?
YOU Welche Größe hast du?
DAD 44. Aber ich würde die Badeschuhe gerne anprobieren.
YOU ... . He'd like to ...

► W 63, 14–16 ► W ◉

LISTENING Conversations with visitors

1 Look at the photo. What's happening?

2 Questions for visitors

a) Put in the words from the box.

think • where • long • like • from

1 Where are you ...?
2 How ... are you staying here?
3 ... are you staying?
4 What do you ... of the food here?
5 Do you ... Newquay?

2 ◉ 23 **b) Listen to the conversation and check.**

2 ◉ 23 **c) Listen again. Pick the right answers.**

1 Leni and Moritz are from ...
a the south-west of Germany.
b the north of Germany.
c the north-west of Germany.

2 Leni and Moritz are staying for ...
a a week.
b two weeks.
c three weeks.

3 Leni and Moritz are staying in ...
a a bed and breakfast.
b a hotel.
c a mobile home.

4 Leni and Moritz think English food ...
a is better than German food.
b is very different from German food.
c isn't much different from German food.

5 Leni and Moritz ...
a love Newquay.
b think Newquay isn't bad.
c don't like Newquay much.

▸ W 64, 17

3 PRONUNCATION [d] and [t]

2 ◉ 24 **a) Listen and repeat.**

1 [d] bed, food, bread, wild, found, bad, road
2 [t] meet, great, pet, rat, put, that, aunt, chat

2 ◉ 25 **b) Listen. Which word do you hear?**

1	a feed	b feet	4	a bored	b bought
2	a sad	b sat	5	a could	b cut
3	a ride	b right	6	a spend	b spent

c) Say the words in 3b).

SPEAKING Helping visitors

1 In Newquay

2 26 **a) Look at the photos. Listen to or read the dialogues. What are the visitors looking for?**

VISITOR Excuse me, where's the tourist office, please?
MATT It's on Marcus Hill, near the library. It's a big building. You can't miss it.
VISITOR Thanks.
MATT You're welcome.

VISITOR Excuse me, where can I buy a book about the town, please?
MATT There's a bookshop in Gover Lane, opposite the pasty shop.
VISITOR Thanks.
MATT You're welcome.

b) Practise the dialogues with a partner.

2 In your town

Practise new dialogues with a partner. Think of your town or use the map of the town here.

VISITOR Excuse me, where's the post office/station/park/..., please?
YOU It's in ..., near/behind/... the station/church/swimming pool/... . You can't miss it.

VISITOR Excuse me, where can I buy some T-shirts/DVDs/ice cream/..., please?
YOU There's a clothes shop/DVD shop/... in ...

3 Role play

Partner A: You're in your town. An English tourist (Partner B) wants your help. Help Partner B. Then find out about him/her. Use the questions in exercise 2 on page 86.

Partner B: Look at page 126.

▸W 64, 18 ▸W

READING Museum information

1 Before you read: What do you think? Which of these things are right?

In the past, smugglers ...

- **a** needed money
- **b** worked at night
- **c** took things in or out of a country
- **d** used boats
- **e** drove cars
- **f** did dangerous things

2 Now read the information and check.

Cornwall's smugglers

In the 18th and 19th century, there were lots of smugglers in Cornwall. People were poor and they could make lots of money from smuggling goods like alcohol and tea. The taxes on these things in Britain were very high but in France alcohol and tea were cheap. So Cornish men and women went to France in boats and bought these goods there.

After they had landed on the beach in Cornwall, the smugglers put the goods in caves there. Later, they took the goods to an inn or another place. Smuggling was very dangerous because the King's men waited on the beaches. They wanted to stop smuggling. There were often fights and sometimes people died.

Lots of ships crashed on the rocks in Cornwall. Then everybody ran down to the beach. Often they didn't help the people on the ship, they just took everything – before the King's men came.

3 Find the words in the text. Pick the right German word.

1. goods: Leute Waren Tiere
2. taxes: Steuern Probleme Ideen
3. in caves: in Höhlen in Zimmern in Geschäften
4. fights: Liebesgeschichten Kämpfe Grüße
5. crashed: segelten begannen zerschellten

Tip:
- Look at the other words in the sentence and the sentences near the word.
- Look at the pictures.
- Compare with a partner. Then check your answers in the *Dictionary*.

4 Are the sentences about the text right or wrong?

1. Poor people in Cornwall got money from smuggling.
2. Taxes on alcohol and tea in France were very high.
3. Smugglers were always men.
4. The smugglers put the goods in caves.
5. The King's men wanted to help the smugglers.
6. People from the villages often took things from ships on the rocks.

▸W 65, 19

WRITING A holiday e-mail

1 Moritz's holiday e-mail: Read Moritz's e-mail to a friend in the USA. Which things in the box does he write about?

beach party • restaurants • shopping • smuggling • sunbathing • surfing

Hi Tyler,

I'm writing from an Internet cafe in Britain today. I'm on holiday in Cornwall in the south-west of England. It's a great place. There are lots of beaches for surfing and sunbathing and some good shops too. I've bought a cool T-shirt and a great CD.

Cornwall is famous for its history of smuggling. We went to a smuggling museum yesterday. It was very interesting.

Tomorrow I'm doing a surfing course. I'll tell you about it next time!

Hope you're OK.

Moritz

2 Your holiday e-mail: Imagine you're on holiday in England, Scotland, Wales or Ireland or another place. Send a friend an e-mail in English and write about your holiday.

Tip:
Think about your last holiday or look in Units 1–5.

Tip:
Look at exercise 1 again for help.

Hi ...,

I'm writing from .... I'm on holiday in ....
It's a ... place. There is/are ... here. I've bought ....

... is famous for .... We went to ... yesterday and it was .... Tomorrow I'm ....

Hope you're OK. Write soon.

...

▸W 65, 20 ▸W ⦿

GOODBYE

1 Read the story. What did Matt give Leni?

2 27

Moritz and Leni had spent two great weeks in Newquay, but now they were at the airport. It was time to go home. The two kids felt sad because they had loved their holiday by the sea.

"Where's Matt?" said Moritz.
Before they left, Matt had said he wanted to say goodbye at the airport. But Matt hadn't come and now it was time to go to the plane. Suddenly somebody shouted: "Wait!" It was Matt.
"Sorry," he said. "I hadn't forgotten but mum was ill, so I was in the cafe ...
Hey, we're going to the Netherlands in October! Mum says we can visit you."
"Great!" said Moritz.
"I have something for you," Matt said and gave Moritz a bag and Leni a small present. Moritz looked in the bag.
"Cornish pasties!" he said. "Mmm, thanks. What did you get, Leni?"
Leni opened the present. It was some beautiful small pictures, "Tattoos for under 18s," said the note with them. Leni looked at Matt and started to laugh.

2 WORD SEARCH
Find these words in the unit.

1 Before Sue got ill, I ... ... an arrangement with Jake. (p. 80)
2 Before Matt found time to talk to the boy, the family ... . (p. 82)
3 A short time after she ... ... in, Leni came out. (p. 83)
4 Moritz and Leni ... ... two great weeks in Newquay, but now they were at the airport. (p. 90)
5 The two kids felt sad because they ... ... their holiday by the sea. (p. 90)
6 Before they left, Matt ... ... he wanted to say goodbye at the airport. (p. 90)

3 WORD SEARCH
Now find these words in the unit.

1 I … … of that. (p. 80)
2 They … … there long when Matt saw the German boy and girl from the cafe. (p. 83)
3 But Matt … … and now it was time to go to the plane. (p. 90)
4 I … … but Mum was ill. (p. 90)

4 OVER TO YOU!
Finish the checkpoint. Put in the right words and find examples.

Tip:
Write the checkpoint with the right words in your exercise book.

CHECKPOINT

Past perfect
- Wenn zwei Handlungen in der Vergangenheit passieren, steht die frühere Handlung im *past perfect*.
- Das *past perfect* wird gebildet mit … und dem *past participle* (Partizip Perfekt).
- Beispiele: …

Remember
You make some past participles with *-ed*.
You have to learn others.

► Eine Übersicht über diese Regeln findest du auf der *Summary*-Seite 115.
► Extra Practice, pp. 112 ff.
► W 66–67

NACH DIESER UNIT KANN ICH …

meine Meinung zu Tattoos äußern.	► *I think tattoos look terrible.*
Einkaufsdialoge führen.	► *How much is that jacket?*
zwischen Deutsch und Englisch vermitteln.	► *She wants to try on the jeans in the window.*
Gespräche mit Touristen führen.	► *How long are you staying here?* *What do you think of English food?*
Auskunft erteilen.	► *There's a good bookshop in Gover Lane.*
eine E-Mail über Urlaubserlebnisse schreiben.	► *Yesterday we went shopping.* *Tomorrow we're going surfing.*
von Handlungen in der Vergangenheit berichten.	► *After we had finished lunch, we went to the beach.*

Weitere Übungen: www.new-highlight.de

► W 68, Test yourself ► W
► Extra Reading, p. 123

EXTRA PRACTICE

1 An interview with Asha for the school radio programme

a) Match the answers with the questions.

LARA	ASHA
Hi, Asha. Welcome to our radio programme.	Hi, Lara.
1 Where are you from?	a Yes, I do. I like music and books.
2 Where do you live in London?	b Yes, it's great. I love big cities.
3 Do you like London?	c I'm from Singapore.
4 What do you think of our school?	d I love hip hop and rock.
5 Do you have any hobbies?	e It's OK. But we get too much homework.
6 What music do you like?	f I **hate** country music!
7 What about country music?	g We live in a flat in Mark Street.

b) Now finish this text about Asha for the school magazine.

Asha is new at our school. She's/isn't from Singapore. But she lives/doesn't live there. She lives/doesn't live in London. Her parents have/don't have a flat in Mark Street. Asha likes/doesn't like London. She says/doesn't say that school is terrible. She thinks/doesn't think that it's OK. Asha loves/doesn't like hip hop and rock. But she hates/doesn't hate country music.

2 A day in the life of a DJ

Tip:
He, she, it – das s muss mit.

DJ Chrissie (work) in a big club in London – *The End*. "It's a great job," Chrissie (say). "I (like) all music, but hip hop is the best!" Chrissie (go) to the club every Thursday, Friday, Saturday and Sunday. She (arrive) at the club at 9.30. The club (open) at 10 o'clock. People usually (come) to the club at 10.30 or 11 o'clock. Chrissie (work) from 10 o'clock to 3 o'clock in the morning. She (play) lots of different CDs. People (love) her music. The club (close) at 3 o'clock and Chrissie (get) home at about 4 o'clock. She (not get) up early the next day. She (stay) in bed. And she (not have) lunch at lunchtime – she (have) breakfast!

3 An interview with Chrissie

Write the interview for a school radio programme.

YOU		CHRISSIE
1	Where do ... work?	In a ...
2	What music ... you like?	I ...
3	What days ... go to the club?	Every ...
4	When does ... open?	At ...
5	When ... work?	From ... to ...
6	When ... close?	At ...
7	When ... home?	...
8	When ... breakfast?	...

4 On the mobile: Put in *'m, 're, 's , are.*

MUM Hi, Asha. Where are you now?
ASHA Hi, Mum. I'm in town. I ... walking along Oxford Street.
MUM You ... walking along Oxford Street! What ... you doing in Oxford Street? Who are you with?
ASHA I'm with Lara. We ... going to Debenhams.
MUM Why ... you going to Debenhams?
ASHA Lara needs new clothes. She ... looking for T-shirts.
MUM Well, hurry up! I ... sitting at home alone!
ASHA OK, OK, Mum. We ... coming home soon!

5 In a London street: What are the people doing?

1 Sid Stone, the famous detective, (talk) on his mobile. It's very late.

2 "I (watch) two people.

3 They (wear) funny clothes.

4 They (walk) along North Street.

5 The man has a gun. He (go) to a house.

6 Oh! They (have) a party!"

6 Write Sid's sentences.

"I'm standing at the London ..."

7 What's right, a or b?

Tip: The time words can help you.

1	Lots of tourists	**a** visit **b** are visiting	London every year.
2	Today Asha's family	**a** visits **b** is visiting	Buckingham Palace.
3	The Queen usually	**a** lives **b** is living	there.
4	But sometimes she	**a** goes **b** 's going	to Windsor.
5	At the moment the Queen	**a** comes **b** is coming	in her car.
6	Now Asha's dad	**a** looks **b** is looking	for his camera.
7	"Now the Queen	**a** talks **b** is talking	to Asha and I don't have my camera!"

8 Halloween party plans

Asha is planning a Halloween party. Finish her sentences.

We have some ...
We don't have any ...

apples
bananas
pizza
cake
ice cream
crisps
orange juice
apple juice
rolls
chocolate

9 You're in London for a holiday. Write an e-mail to an English friend.

What's the name of your friend?
Where are you staying?
Who's with you?
How are you feeling?
Are you having fun?
What's London like?
What places are you visiting tomorrow?

Dear ...
the Millennium Hotel
aunt/brother/mum/sister
happy/tired/great/terrible
lots of fun/no fun
big/exciting/interesting
the London Eye/the Tower of London

SIMPLE PRESENT – PRESENT PROGRESSIVE

! Mit der einfachen Gegenwart (*simple present*) sagst du, was jemand immer wieder oder regelmäßig tut.

I You We They	live in London.

He (Luke) She (Asha) It (The food)	look**s** nice.

Diese *time words* findest du oft in Sätzen im *simple present*:

every day • every Monday • every week • every month • every year • always • usually • often • sometimes • never

I work every Saturday.
Ich arbeite jeden Samstag.

He sometimes eats chocolate.
Er isst manchmal Schokolade.

We often watch TV.
Wir schauen oft fern.

! Mit der *ing*-Form der Gegenwart (*present progressive*) sagst du, was jemand gerade tut oder plant.

I**'m** He**'s** She**'s** We**'re** You**'re** They**'re**	go**ing** to school.

Diese *time phrases* findest du oft in Sätzen im *present progressive*:

now • today • next week • at the moment • this evening

She's doing her homework now.
Sie macht jetzt ihre Hausaufgaben.
I'm having a party next week.
Ich werde nächste Woche eine Party geben.

SOME/ANY

Das Wort *some* bedeutet „etwas" *(some cake)* oder „einige" *(some apples)*.

We have some ice cream.
Wir haben etwas Eis.

We have some apples too.
Wir haben auch einige Äpfel.

Statt *some* steht im verneinten Satz *any*.

We don't have any milk.
Wir haben keine Milch.

I don't like any sports.
Ich mag keinen Sport.

EXTRA PRACTICE

1 Two films: Match the text with the right poster (A or B).

I watched a film at the cinema yesterday. It was about two police officers. They found out about a terrible plan. A man wanted to kill the Queen. The police officers didn't have any ideas. But then a woman helped them so everything was OK. It was a very good film.

2 *Titanic*: Finish the sentences. Use the simple past.

Tip:
The *List of irregular verbs* on p. 180–181 can help you.

1 I (buy) ... a DVD at the weekend.
2 The film (be) ... a love story.
3 A girl and a boy (meet) ... on a ship.
4 The ship (leave) ... England in 1912.
5 But the ship (have) ... a terrible accident.
6 The boy (die) ...
7 I (think) ... this film was very good.
8 It (win) ... lots of prizes.

3 Fiona's e-mail: Put in the words.

→ come • like • want • sell • have (2x)

To Emma From Fiona

Hi Emma,

I didn't ... a good day yesterday. Lauren and I went to the cinema but we didn't ... the film. And they didn't ... popcorn there! Then we wanted to go home. But the bus didn't ... . It was late, so we didn't ... to walk. We took a taxi, but we didn't ... any money. Mum had to pay and she wasn't happy!

Love,
Fiona

4 Fiona's week: Match Grandma's questions with Fiona's answers.

1 What did you do this week?
2 Who did you go with?
3 Did you have a good time?
4 What did you like best?

a Yes, it was great.
b I loved the dancing.
c I went with my class from school.
d I went to the Edinburgh Tattoo at the castle.

5 Fiona's questions for Callum: Write the questions.

Tip:
Did is the first word in the question OR the second word after *What, When, How*.

1 have / you / good / a / weekend / did / ?
2 go / did / the football match / you / to / ?
3 you / tickets / how / did / get / ?
4 your / win / did / team / ?
5 when / see / Cameron / you / did / ?
6 did / yesterday evening / do / you / what / ?

6 Questions and answers

a) Callum's questions for Fiona: Write the questions for the answers.

1 Did you ... early on Saturday? – No, I didn't. I got up at 11 o'clock.
2 What did you ... on Saturday afternoon? – I did some sport.
3 Did you ... at home on Saturday evening? – Yes, I did. I stayed at home and watched TV.
4 Did you ... friends on Sunday? – Yes, I did. I met Susie and Abbie.
5 When did you ... your homework? – I did it on Sunday evening!

b Read the questions in a). Write true answers for you.

Yes, I did.	I got up ...	I watched ...
No, I didn't.	I stayed ...	I went to ...
	I visited ...	I met ...
	I played ...	I did ...

EXTRA PRACTICE

7 From schoolgirl to star: Put the story in the right order: 1 c, 2 ..., 3 ..., ...

a But her father said she should try it.
b They needed an Asian girl for a new film.
c Katie Leung lived in Scotland with her father.
d When she was 16, Katie's father saw an advert for the *Harry Potter* films.
e So he took her to the audition in London.
f Katie was Asian and she was the right age but she wasn't very interested.

8 The audition: Put in the verbs.

1 More than 4,000 girls (be) ... at the audition!
2 Katie (not want) ... to wait.
3 She (want) ... to go shopping!
4 She (wait) ... for four hours for the audition.
5 Katie (feel) ... very nervous.
6 She (not think) ... that she (be) ... the right girl.
5 But Katie (have) ... two more auditions.
6 And then they (pick) ... her!

9 The films: Finish the story.

1 Katie – Cho Chang – two *Harry Potter* films. *Katie played ...*
2 Cho Chang – Harry Potter's girlfriend.
3 Harry – like – Cho Chang – very much.
4 But – she – another – boyfriend.
5 Then – boyfriend – die.
6 Later – Cho Chang – give – Harry – kiss.
7 Lots of fans – jealous – Katie.
8 But – they – love – films!

10 About you

a) Make questions.

How much	*Harry Potter* films have you seen?
How many	cinemas are there in your area?
	music do you buy or download?
	DVDs do you have at home?
	TV do you watch every day?
	money do you spend on the cinema or films every month?

b) Ask and answer the questions with a partner.

I've seen ... / I haven't seen ...
There's / There are ...
There isn't ... / There aren't ...
I buy ...
I have ...
I watch ...
I spend ...

c) Write four questions for your partner with much/many. Then ask your partner.

1 brothers and sisters/pets/computer games/... – have?
2 chocolate/fast food/healthy food/... – eat – every week?
3 water/cola/juice/... – drink – every day?
4 girls/boys/teachers/... – be – in your school?

SIMPLE PAST

! Mit der einfachen Vergangenheit (*simple past*) sagst du, was in der Vergangenheit geschah/geschehen ist. Damit kannst du Geschichten erzählen.

We watched *Titanic* at the weekend.
Wir schauten uns am Wochenende *Titanic* an.
The ship left England in 1912 and had a terrible accident.
Das Schiff verließ England 1912 und hatte einen schrecklichen Unfall.

! Diese *time phrases* verwendest du oft in Sätzen mit dem *simple past*:

last week last Saturday	**in** 1878 in August	**on** Tuesday on Saturday	**at** 3 o'clock at the weekend	**when** I was a child when I was eleven	yesterday later

! Regelmässige Verben enden auf *-ed*:

play – play**ed** • start – start**ed**

Tip:
You don't know the simple past form?
- Look at the *List of irregular verbs* on p. 180–181.
- Look for the simple past form in the *Dictionary*.

Pass auf mit der Schreibweise!

lik**e** – lik**ed** • dro**p** – dro**pp**ed • pla**n** – pla**nn**ed • cr**y** – cr**i**ed

Unregelmässige Verben haben besondere Vergangenheitsformen. Du musst sie auswendig lernen:

come – came • feel – felt • say – said • sing – sang

▸ List of irregular verbs p. 180–181.

! Mit *did* fragst du, was geschehen ist.

Mit *didn't* sagst du, was nicht geschehen ist.

We didn't like the film.

MUCH/MANY

Du benutzt *many* für Dinge, die man zählen kann, z.B. *pupils, films, magazines*.

How many pupils are in your class?
Wie viele Schüler/innen sind in deiner Klasse?

Du benutzt *much* für Dinge, die man nicht zählen kann, z.B. *time, cola, music*.

I don't have much time.
Ich habe nicht viel Zeit.

EXTRA PRACTICE

1 Match the sentences with the pictures.

A That sport can be dangerous!
B We can take this bus.
C I can speak Welsh.
D She can run fast.
E Ms Ward, can you repeat that please?
F Can I help you?

2 Finish the sentences. Use the phrases on the right.

1 Mum can speak English, but she can't ...
2 My brother is only one. He can't ...
3 It's too cold. You can't ...
4 I don't have much credit. I can't ...
5 Lisa has lots of homework so she can't ...
6 We have no money. We can't ...

a ... talk yet.
b ... buy crisps in the shop.
c ... meet her friends in town.
d ... phone my dad.
e ... swim in the river.
f ... speak French.

3 Poor Aled: Finish the dialogue.

ALED	MUM
Mum, ... I go to Porthmadog today?	– No, you ... . You're grounded!
But I ... do anything here. It's so boring!	– I have lots of work. You ... help me!
Ah, Mum! Dad ... help you!	– No, he ... . He's driving his taxi.
Well, ... Danny come to our house?	– OK. Danny ... visit you this afternoon.
Great. We ... ride our mountain boards.	– No, you ... ride your mountain boards. It's raining!

4 AND YOU? Write six sentences.

I can	drive	send	a quad	cards	English songs
I can't	play	ride	a bike	an e-mail	a text message
	sing	run	a mountain board	English	a car
	speak	write	the guitar	French	fast

5 ***Have to*: Put the two parts of the dialogues together.**

1 It's late!
2 Ms Jones, Sarah has a new mobile.
3 Aled isn't at school today.
4 We're hungry. Can we eat soon?
5 The boys want to watch a film.
6 Can you play a game with me?

a That's nice. But she has to turn it off here.
b You have to wait. The pizza isn't ready yet.
c Yes, it is. We have to hurry up.
d Sorry, I can't. I have to do my homework.
e No, it's too late. They have to go to bed.
f That's right. He has to go to hospital.

6 **Aled and Danny: Draw the table in your exercise book. Then read the text and write *Yes* or *No* in your table.**

	Aled	Danny
get up early on school days		
get up early at the weekend		
go to bed early		
help at home		
work in the holidays		

Some things are different for Aled and Danny. Some things are the same. Aled has to get up early on school days, but Danny lives near the school, so he doesn't have to get up early. The two boys don't have to get up early at the weekend. Aled's parents are strict, so he has to go to bed early. Danny's parents aren't very strict so he doesn't have to go to bed early. The two boys have to help at home. Aled and Danny have to work in the holidays. Aled has to help his parents with the mountain bikes and Danny has to help his mum in her shop.

7 **In Wales and in Germany: Look at the table. Then finish the text in your exercise book. Put in *have to/has to/doesn't have to/don't have to*.**

Exercise 6 can help you.

	Zofia	Mike
start school early	Yes	No
wear a uniform	No	Yes
go to school every afternoon	No	Yes
leave mobile at home	No	No
turn off mobile in classroom	Yes	Yes

Zofia is a pupil in Germany. Mike is a pupil in Wales. Some things are different for Zofia and Mike. Zofia ... start school early – at 8 o'clock. But Mike ... start school so early – he starts at 9 o'clock. Zofia ... wear a uniform but in Wales it's different, so Mike ... to wear a uniform.

Poor Mike – he ... go to school every afternoon – Monday to Friday. Zofia ... go to school every afternoon – only on Tuesdays and Thursdays. Mike and Zofia ... leave their mobiles at home – they can take them to school. But they ... turn them off in the classroom. It's the school rule!

8 You and your parents: Write your blog about you and your parents.

My blog:
At home I can ...
I can't ...
I have to ...
But I don't have to ...
I think my parents ... strict.

watch lots of TV • have a TV in my room • drink alcohol • invite friends • go to town at night • help at home • help in the kitchen • buy my own clothes • eat lots of fast food • buy my own CDs and magazines • drive a car • walk to school • work at weekends • work in the holidays • work in the garden • play computer games all day • go to bed early/late

9 A letter from a penfriend: Read Robbie's letter and then write an answer.

22 Newpark Road
Porthmadog GW 13 5DB
May 16th, 20...

Dear penfriend,
My name is Robbie. I live in Porthmadog in Wales. It's a small town near the sea. I live with my mum, dad and three sisters. I'm 14 now. My birthday is May 17th – that's tomorrow! My hobbies are football and mountain biking. I can speak two languages – English and Welsh. I go to school in Porthmadog. My favourite subject is maths. School is OK, but we have some problems – like text bullying.

My parents aren't very strict. I can go out at the weekend. But I have to be home at 11 o'clock. And I don't have to do many jobs at home.

Please write soon.
Best wishes,
Robbie

10 At home: What can you see in the picture? Answer all the questions.

1 Who's in the room?
– A boy ...
2 What are they doing?
– The man is ...
3 What can you see in the room?
– I can see ...
4 What are they saying?

DAD You have to pick up ...
GIRL ...
BOY ...

CAN – CAN'T

! Mit *can* sagst du, was jemand tun kann oder darf.
Mit *can't* sagst du, was jemand nicht tun kann oder nicht darf.

Aled can speak Welsh.
But he can't speak German!

You can walk and ride a bike here.
But you can't ride a motorbike or drive a car.

I You He She It We They	can can't	swim.

I can play the guitar.
Ich kann Gitarre spielen.
You can watch TV now.
Du darfst jetzt fernsehen.

The past of *can/can't*:
I could run fast when I was younger.
But I couldn't swim.

HAVE TO – DON'T HAVE TO

! Mit *have to* sagst du, was jemand tun muss.
Mit *don't have to* sagst du, was jemand nicht zu tun braucht.

I You We They	have to don't have to	wait.
He She It	has to doesn't have to	

We have to go now.
Wir müssen jetzt gehen.
You don't have to work tomorrow.
Du brauchst morgen nicht zu arbeiten.

The simple past of *have to/don't have to*:
I had to help dad yesterday.
But I didn't have to make lunch.

1 Help at home: Match the sentences with the right pictures.

- **a** I'll help you with the TV.
- **b** I'll get the charger.
- **c** I'll show you a good website.
- **d** I'll open the door for you
- **e** I'll turn off the radiator.
- **f** I'll find the DVD.

2 Problems at home: Match the sentences.

1 I'm hungry.	**a** I'll hurry up.
2 I'm tired.	**b** I'll go to bed now.
3 I'm late for school.	**c** I'll find some warm clothes.
4 I'm bored.	**d** I'll make a sandwich.
5 I'm cold.	**e** I'll watch TV.

3 An evening at home. Put in the verbs from the box.

eat • like • listen • make • show • watch

TIM I'm bored. I think I'll ... to music with Dan.
MUM Why don't we watch that new *Blackpool* DVD? It looks funny.
TIM What's that?
MUM I'll ... you the DVD. Here you are.
TIM Er, no thanks. I can see I won't ... it, Mum.
MUM I'll ... some tea and we'll ... your favourite cake.
TIM OK then, I'll ... it with you!

4 Tim's article about the future

a) Tim's article needs a title. Read the article and pick the best title.

- Bad news for computers in the future
- A great future for technology
- Lots of TVs in the future

Technology is important today. But in the future it'll be more important.

Firstly, everybody will use mobile phones. They'll be very cheap and people won't use other phones at home.

Secondly, everybody will have lots of computers. There'll be a computer in every room of your house!

Thirdly, people won't have TVs. We'll watch TV and DVDs on computers.

Technology has a great future!

b) What do you think about the future? Finish these sentences.

1 Everybody will use ... 2 ... will be very cheap. 3 People won't have ...

5 Your future

a) What will happen in your future? Write sentences.

I	'll won't	be live have	healthy. at home. a good job. happy. in this area. children.

b) Tell your friend's future. I think you'll ... / you won't ...

6 Tim's future: Tim was on *Blackpool Radio* because he won the quiz.

a) Write the questions about Tim's future.

BLACKPOOL RADIO	TIM
1 Will you ...?	– Yes, I'm sure I'll still live here.
2 Where will you ...?	– In a flat with my brother.
3 Will you ...?	– Yes, I hope I'll have a good job.
4 What will you ...?	– A teacher, I think.
5 Will you ...?	– Yes, I think I'll have children.
6 How many children ...?	– Two or three.

b) Act the interview. Read the questions and answers with a partner.

7 About Blackpool: Match the headings with the sentences.

1 c 2 ... 3 ... 4 ... 5 ...

- a How much is it?
- b Great activities and food
- c Visit us!
- d Fun all day, every day
- e Where will you find us?

1 Are you looking for things to do in Blackpool? Come to Sandcastle Waterworld, Britain's best water park!

2 Come and swim in our super pool, play on an old ship or try the world's longest water roller coaster. Or what about a salad or a hamburger in one of our cafes?

3 Sandcastle Waterworld is near Blackpool funfair, next to the sea.

4 A day at Sandcastle is £8.50 for children and £10.50 for adults.

5 The water park is open every day from 10.00 a.m. to 5.30 p.m. See you soon!

8 About the north of England: Finish the e-mail. Use *'ll* or *won't* and the verb.

Hi Markus,
I can't wait for your visit! You asked if the north of England is nice. I (tell) ... you about it. You (like) ... the people here, they're very friendly. But you (not understand) ... our English sometimes! It's different from English in the south of England.
There are lots of great places in the north, but we (not have) ... time for everything. I hope we (see) ... Manchester United, the famous football team. We (visit) ... their stadium in Manchester. And I'm sure we (go) ... to the Lake District, that's a beautiful national park near here.
I (write) ... again soon.
Tim

9 About your area: Claire, a Scottish girl that you met on holiday is coming to visit you. She has written you an e-mail. She wants to know about your part of Germany. Answer her e-mail.

Hi Claire,
You asked if ... is nice. I'll tell .... You'll like ...
There are lots of great places in .... We'll ... And I'm sure we'll ...
I ... soon.
(your name)

Tip: Look at Tim's e-mail in exercise 8.

WILL

! Wenn du voraussagen willst, was in der Zukunft geschehen wird, benutzt du *will*. Es kann um Dinge gehen, die man vermutet oder auf die man keinen Einfluss hat.

Die Kurzform von *will* ist *'ll*.

Everybody will have lots of computers.
Jeder wird viele Computer haben.
We'll watch TV on computers.
Wir werden am Computer fernsehen.

I You He She It We They	'll won't	go.

! *Will* benutzt du auch, um spontan zu sagen, was du machen wirst oder um Hilfe anzubieten.

! Wenn du voraussagen willst, was in der Zukunft **nicht** geschehen wird, benutzt du *won't (= will not)*.

People won't have TVs.
Die Menschen werden keine Fernseher haben.

! **Fragen** mit *will* werden durch die Wortstellung oder ein Fragewort angezeigt.

Everybody will use mobile phones.
=> Will everybody use mobile phones?
Wird jeder Handys benutzen?
What will happen in the future?
Was wird in der Zukunft geschehen?

Will	I you he she it we they	go?

EXTRA PRACTICE

1 Gina and Liam: Put in *I, you, he, she, we, they.*

1

If Liam sees Gina again, ...'ll be happy.

2

If Gina runs in the *Dublin Games*, ...'ll win.

3

"If I don't win in the *Dublin Games*, ...'ll be devastated!"

4

"But if you don't train, ... won't get on the team."

5

"If we have time, ...'ll have an ice cream."

6

If the Wards move to England, ...'ll get a new house.

2 The Müllers' plans: Match the sentences.

1 If the weather is nice, the Müllers will ...
2 But if it rains, they'll ...
3 "If I don't go on this boat tour, I won't ..."
4 "If you walk near the cliffs, you'll ..."
5 If Mrs Müller finds a good shop, she'll ...
6 "If we have a good holiday, we'll ..."

... see Fungi the dolphin.
... come to Ireland again next year.
... stay in Dublin.
... buy souvenirs.
... fall!
... go to the beach.

3 Athletics tips: Put in the right verbs. What are they?

Example: If you like athletics, you'll love our athletics club.

1 You'll ... lots of famous people if you ... to the *Dublin Games*.
2 A trainer will ... you if you ... to the club on Saturdays.
3 You'll ... free training if you ... our athletics club today.
4 If you ... often, you'll ... good shoes.
5 If you don't ... hard, you won't ...

meet / come
train / win
run / need
help / come
~~like / love~~
get / join

4 AND YOU? Finish these sentences.

1 If I have some money, I'll ...
2 If the weather is nice tomorrow, we'll ...
3 If I ask my mum for a new bike, she'll ...
4 My dad will be angry if I ...
5 My friends won't be happy if I ...
6 I'll be devastated if ...

Tip:
Use ideas like:
don't help/buy/don't win/ have a party/say/go to/...

5 Tips for young people

Pick *should* or *shouldn't*.

1 If you're on your skateboard, you should/shouldn't be careful.
2 If you're on a train, you should/shouldn't talk loudly on your mobile.
3 If you want to take your sister's T-shirt, you should/shouldn't ask her first.
4 If you're with other people, you should/shouldn't send text messages.
5 If there are no free seats on a bus, you should/shouldn't give your seat to an older man or woman.
6 If somebody gives you something, you should/shouldn't always say "thanks".
7 If you ask for something, you should/shouldn't forget to say "please".
8 If your parents ask you to help, you should/shouldn't do it.

6 Your tips

a) Finish these sentences and make your tips.

1 If you stand on somebody's foot, you should say ...
2 If you're a tourist in Ireland, you should visit ...
3 If you're a tourist in Germany, you should go to ...
4 If you don't understand, you should say ...
5 If you like athletics, you should join ...

b) Now write three silly tips. Example: If you don't like homework, you shouldn't do it.

7 In Ireland and Germany:

Write sentences about Germany.

1 In Ireland, if you're in a restaurant, you can't smoke. In Germany, ...
2 In Ireland, if you're 17, you can drive a car. (But you must have "L" on your car.) In our part of Germany, if ...
3 In Ireland, if you're under 13, you can't have a job. In Germany, ...
4 In Ireland, if you're 16, you can leave school. In Germany, ...
5 In Ireland, if you're under 18, you can't buy alcohol. In Germany, if ...

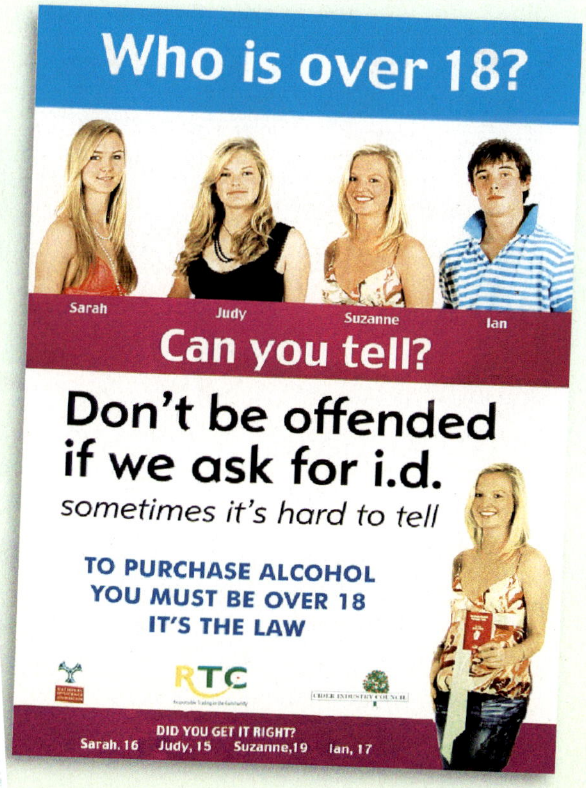

8 What should I do?

a) Read this letter to *Dublin Kidz*.

Dear Dublin Kidz,

I have a problem. There's a girl in my class and she doesn't like me. She's a bully. She often says terrible things about me to my friends. Sometimes she takes my things. I don't know what to do. If I talk to her, I'm sure she'll laugh. So should I say nothing? Please help me. What should I do?

Best wishes,

Angie (not my real name)

b) Use some of these ideas and write to Angie.

- Thanks for your letter.
- That isn't a big problem.
- If you tell your teachers, they'll help you.
- If you tell your friends, they can talk to the bully.
- Don't worry. Everything will be OK.
- You should tell your parents.
- If you talk to the bully, maybe she'll stop.
- That's a terrible problem.
- If you say nothing, nothing will change!

9 Another problem

Imagine you got this text on your mobile. Write a letter to *Dublin Kidz* about it.

Exercise 8 can help you.

10 A street in Dublin

What can you see in this picture? Use the questions and write a text.

1 Where's this scene?
2 What shops can you see?
3 What's the weather like?
4 What are the people wearing?
5 What are the children doing?
6 What's the police officer doing?
7 What's the old man doing?
8 What other things can you see?

This scene is in ...
I can see a music shop ...
The weather is ...
...

IF-SÄTZE

! Mit *if*-Sätzen sagst du, was unter bestimmten Bedingungen geschehen wird.

If I miss the bus, I'll walk to school.

If you do your homework, you can watch TV.

If you go to Ireland, you should watch a hurling game.

! *If*-Sätze bestehen aus zwei Teilen:
- einem Nebensatz (mit *if*) im *simple present*,
- einem Hauptsatz mit *will*. Statt *will* kann auch *can* oder *should* stehen.

NEBENSATZ	HAUPTSATZ	
If + simple present +	*will/'ll/won't* *can/can't* *should/shouldn't*	+ verb (infinitive)
If he runs,	he'll fall.	
If we go to London,	we'll go by plane. we can visit the London Eye.	

! Der Nebensatz (mit *if*) kann vorne oder hinten stehen:

If we go to Dingle, we can see the dolphin.
We can see the dolphin if we go to Dingle.

! Im *if*-Satz steht kein *will*.

If you take the bus, you'll be faster.
Wenn du den Bus nimmst, bist du schneller.
My father will be angry if I'm late again.
Mein Vater wird wütend sein, wenn ich wieder zu spät komme.
If you're hungry, you can have a sandwich.
Wenn du Hunger hast, kannst du ein Sandwich bekommen.
If they want tickets for the *Dublin Games*, they should buy them soon.
Wenn sie Karten für die *Dublin Games* wollen, sollten sie sie bald kaufen.

EXTRA PRACTICE*

1 Matt's day:

a) Match the sentences.

1	Yesterday Matt was tired because	**a**	he hadn't gone surfing.
2	He was hungry because	**b**	his friend had got tickets for *Lemon Jelly*.
3	And he was thirsty too because	**c**	it had been hot all day.
4	He was sad because	**d**	he hadn't had lunch.
5	But he was happy too because	**e**	a lot of people had wanted the tickets.
6	That was great news because	**f**	he had gone to bed late.

b) Your day: Finish the sentences.

1 Yesterday I was
2 I was
3 And I was

happy/bored/angry/worried/tired/devastated

because

I had lost my mobile / it had rained all day / I had bought a new CD / I had got up early / my friend had done a stupid thing / I had forgotten my homework

2 A hard day: Finish the dialogue. Use the past perfect.

Remember:
Use *had* + past participle.

MATT Hi, Moritz. How was the surfing course yesterday?
MORITZ Hard! I (~~always/think~~) *had always thought* surfing was easy!
MATT No, it's very hard when you start. I thought I (tell) ... you that.
MORITZ Well, after I (fall) ... into the water about twenty times I wasn't very happy! I didn't know why I (want) ... to try surfing!
MATT And then?
MORITZ Well, after I (try) ... lots of times, it got easier. And I didn't want to give up because you (say) ... it was great. And then suddenly I could do it – and it was great!

3 Another hard day

a) What did Matt say? Join the sentences.

1 I got up early.
2 I went to the cafe with mum.
3 I wrote the menu on the board.
4 I cleaned the tables.
5 I made the sandwiches.
6 I gave people their food.
7 I cleaned the floor.
8 I went home.

b) A class game: Make sentences about a hard day.

PUPIL 1 I got up early.
PUPIL 2 After I had got up early, I had breakfast.
PUPIL 3 After I had ...

*Unit 6 ist nur Pflichtstoff für den E-Kurs in Nordrhein-Westfalen.

4 My tattoo: Put the right words in the sentences.

→ hadn't shown • had seen • had wanted • hadn't told • hadn't hurt • had got

1

I ... a tattoo for a long time.

2

So I got a small tattoo. I was surprised because it ... too much.

3

But two days after I ... it, it became red and it started to hurt.

4

I ... my mum the tattoo, but then she saw it at the beach.

5

She was angry that I ... her about it.

6

After we ... the doctor, I felt better. No more tattoos for me!

5 Writing: Piercings

a) What Brad thinks: Read Brad's blog. Does he like piercings?

Brad's blog

Today I want to say something about piercings. My brother got a piercing in his lip at the weekend and our parents shouted and shouted. They said it looks terrible and it isn't healthy. I don't like lots of piercings in your face, but I think one piercing looks cool. It's a way to tell people something about you – like tattoos. But a piercing is better than a tattoo because when you don't want it, you just take out the ring. You have a real tattoo all your life. I don't understand our parents' problem.

b) AND YOU? Write what you think of piercings for the website. Write 60–80 words.

- **Do you know people with piercings? Where do they have them?**
- **Do you think piercings look cool or terrible?**

6 Interpreting: At a German cafe

a) Work with two other pupils. Write the dialogue together. You're in a German cafe. The English man at the next table can't speak German. You offer to help.

Remember:
Don't translate every word.
Translate the meaning.

YOU (TO TOURIST)	Can I help you?
TOURIST	Yes, please. Can you tell the waitress this knife is dirty.
YOU (TO WAITRESS)	Das Messer ...
WAITRESS	Das tut mir leid, ich werde ihm sofort ein sauberes Messer bringen.
YOU (TO TOURIST)	She ...
TOURIST	And I'd like some salt and pepper, please.
YOU (TO WAITRESS)	Könnten Sie ...
WAITRESS	Natürlich.
YOU (TO TOURIST)	...
TOURIST	Thanks for your help.
YOU (TO TOURIST)	...

b) Act your dialogue for the class.

7 Interpreting: In an English shop

a) Prepare the dialogue alone.
You're in a small English shop with your mum. Her English isn't very good. Help her.

Remember:
If you don't know a word, explain it.
Look at page 85 again for more help.

MUM	Wir brauchen Sonnen-creme.
YOU (TO ASSISTANT)	We need ...
ASSISTANT	Ah, yes. What about this? It's very good.
YOU (TO MUM)	...
MUM	Ja, das sieht gut aus.
YOU (TO ASSISTANT)	That ...
ASSISTANT	That's £8.99 please.
YOU (TO MUM)	...

b) Act the dialogue with two partners.

c) Compare your answers in your group. Then check with your teacher.

PAST PERFECT

! Wenn zwei Handlungen in der Vergangenheit passieren, steht die frühere Handlung im *past perfect*.

Matt got up.

Then Matt went down to the kitchen.

After Matt had got up, he went down to the kitchen.
Nachdem Matt aufgestanden war, ging er in die Küche hinunter.

Leni and Moritz were tired because they had spent all day at the museum.
Leni und Moritz waren müde, weil sie den ganzen Tag im Museum verbracht hatten.
Moritz had never tried surfing before he visited Newquay.
Moritz hatte das Surfen nie ausprobiert, bevor er Newquay besuchte.

! Das *past perfect* wird gebildet mit:

I You He/She/It We They	**had** **hadn't**	*Past participle* (Partizip Perfekt) talk**ed** left

! Das Partizip Perfekt von **regelmäßigen** Verben endet auf *-ed*:

talk - talk**ed** notice - notic**ed** mix - mix**ed**

! Das Partizip Perfekt von **unregelmäßigen** Verben findest du in der *List of irregular verbs* auf Seite 180–181 (vorletzte Spalte). Du musst sie auswendig lernen.
Am besten lernst du immer alle drei Formen:

leave - left - left drink - drank - drunk

Tip:
Learn verbs with the same pattern.
For example:
- buy - bought - bought
  think - thought - thought
- drive - drove - driven
  ride - rode - ridden

A CHRISTMAS CAROL by Charles Dickens

2 28

It was Christmas Eve in London, a long time ago. An old man sat in a cold office. He wasn't a very happy man. His name was Ebenezer Scrooge.

Another man sat in the office too. He worked for Mr Scrooge. He was very quiet and he worked very hard. This was Bob Cratchit.

Scrooge's old partner, Mr Marley, was dead. Now Scrooge had no friends. "Who needs people?" he thought. "Money is important, not people!"

It was very quiet in the office. Scrooge and Bob Cratchit never talked. Suddenly the door opened. "Merry Christmas, Uncle," a young man shouted. It was Fred. He was a nice young man, always happy. "Christmas! That's humbug!" Scrooge answered. "Come to our house tomorrow, Uncle. You can have Christmas dinner with us," Fred said. But Scrooge said no. So Fred left and it was quiet again in the office.

Then somebody knocked at the door. It was a young boy. He was very poor. He looked hungry. He sang a Christmas carol and then he asked Scrooge for some money for Christmas. But Scrooge said no.

At 6 o'clock Bob Cratchit went home. "Merry Christmas, Mr Scrooge," he said. "Goodbye," Scrooge answered. Then he went home too.

It was quiet and lonely in his house. Suddenly Scrooge saw something on his door. It was a face. He knew that face. It was Mr Marley, his old partner. Scrooge was frightened. Marley came into the room. He was a ghost. "What do you want?" Scrooge asked. Marley answered, "Listen to me, Scrooge. You can change your life. Three ghosts are going to visit you – the ghost of Christmas past, the ghost of Christmas present and the ghost of Christmas future." Then Marley disappeared. Scrooge was very tired and soon he fell asleep.

▸ You can find new words in the *Dictionary* (pages 151–165)

The ghost of Christmas past

2 29

In the night Scrooge woke. A small, old ghost was next to the bed. He had white hair and long arms.

"Who are you?" Scrooge asked.

"I am the ghost of Christmas past. Come with me," the ghost answered.

Scrooge and the ghost went into the country. It was a cold, sunny day. They walked along a small road and came to an old church.

"I know this church," Scrooge said.

He knew the river, the bridge, the village.

They saw some boys on ponies. They saw farmers too. Everybody was happy.

"Merry Christmas," they all shouted.

But nobody saw Scrooge and the ghost.

Then Scrooge and the ghost came to a school. They went in. There was only one small boy. He was alone. The other children were at home for Christmas. But this boy had no home. It was Scrooge when he was young. The old man – Scrooge – was very sad. He remembered the poor boy who came to his office – the boy who sang a Christmas carol. But Scrooge didn't give him any money and now he was sorry.

The ghost of Christmas past disappeared and Scrooge fell asleep again.

Reading log 1: The story so far

I like/don't like this story – so far.
I think it's/it isn't an easy story.
I think it's sad/funny/interesting/boring.
I think that Scrooge is terrible/nice/cold/unfriendly/OK.
I think Scrooge will be happy/unhappy at the end of the story.
My favourite character in the story so far is Scrooge/Bob/Mr Marley/Fred/...

Reading log 2: Write to Scrooge.

Dear Mr Scrooge,

Why don't you like Christmas? I think Christmas is ... . And I think your nephew Fred is ... . Why aren't you happy? I think that you should ... . It was sad when ... . I hope that you ... .

Best wishes, ...

The ghost of Christmas present

2◉30

Later Scrooge woke again. He saw a light in the next room and he went in.
The room was very nice – with lots of Christmas decorations and Christmas food. Another ghost was in the room.
"I'm the ghost of Christmas present," he said and smiled.

Scrooge and the ghost went into the street. It was Christmas morning and there were lots of people everywhere. Children laughed and played. The shops were open and there were lots of nice Christmas things.

The ghost took Scrooge to Bob Cratchit's house. It was a happy place. They were having Christmas dinner – turkey, vegetables and Christmas pudding. Bob Cratchit's small boy, "Tiny Tim was there too. Tim was ill and he couldn't walk.
After dinner the family sat next to the fire and talked and laughed.
"Merry Christmas to everybody – and to Mr Scrooge too," Bob said.

Scrooge was sad when he saw Tiny Tim. "Will he be OK?" he asked the ghost.
"No," the ghost answered. "He'll die if we can't change the future."
Scrooge fell asleep again and the ghost of Christmas present disappeared.

The ghost of Christmas future

2◉31

The last ghost came. But Scrooge couldn't see its face. It didn't speak.
"Are you going to take me to Christmas in the future?" Scrooge asked. But the ghost didn't answer. Scrooge was very frightened now.

Scrooge and the ghost went into the city. They saw some men. They were talking about Scrooge."He had lots of money," one man said. "But he didn't spend his money."
Everybody laughed.

Scrooge and the ghost went to a bedroom. A man was in the bed. He was dead. Scrooge couldn't see his face. He didn't want to see his face.
He was frightened.

Then they went to Bob Cratchit's house again. Everybody was there – Bob, Mrs Cratchit and the children. But where was Tiny Tim? He wasn't there! They were all very sad.

Scrooge and the ghost went to a graveyard. The ghost pointed at a grave. Scrooge didn't want to look. But the ghost pointed again. Scrooge looked and he saw two words: Ebenezer Scrooge. "Oh ghost, I've learned lots of things today. I'll change my life, I promise," he said. "I'll be good. I'll enjoy Christmas. I'll change the future ..." The ghost said nothing. It disappeared.

The end of the story

That evening, at Fred's house, everybody was eating Christmas dinner. Then somebody knocked at the door. It was Scrooge! "Merry Christmas," he said. Fred was very surprised. Scrooge was different! He was happy. He was laughing. Scrooge had Christmas dinner with the family. It was a very nice evening. After Christmas Scrooge often visited Bob Cratchit's family. He always took presents. He was like another father for Tiny Tim. And Tiny Tim didn't die.

Now Scrooge was a good man. He was friendly, nice and happy. And he loved Christmas!

Reading log 3: Write a summary of the story. These questions can help you.

- What's the name of the story?
- Who was the writer?
- Where did the story happen?
- When did it happen?
- Who was the main character?
- What was he/she like?
- What happened in the story?
- What happened at the end of the story?
- Was it a happy ending?

Reading log 4: Write some sentences about you and the story

- When did you read this story?
- How long did it take?
- Was it easy?
- Did you use a dictionary?
- Did you learn new words? What words?
- Did you like the story?
- Imagine you're a character in this story. Who do you want to be?

Tip:
You can write reading logs like this for all the stories that you read. Write your logs in a special 'Reading Log Notebook'.

THE STORY OF GELERT

2◉33

A long, long time ago there was a prince. His name was Llewelyn and he lived in Wales. He was the Prince of Wales.

Llewelyn loved hunting. He had lots of dogs. But his favourite dog was Gelert. And this dog loved Llewelyn.

Gelert often stayed in Llewelyn's house. He always looked after Llewelyn's baby boy. He was very gentle.

One day Llewelyn left the house and went hunting with his friends. Gelert stayed at the house with the baby.

It was a nice, sunny day and it was warm. Llewelyn and his friends went to the mountains on their horses. They played games, went hunting and had a picnic.

In the evening they all came back to Llewelyn's house. Everybody was happy. But something was wrong. Gelert was at the door of the house.

▸ You can find new words in the *Dictionary* (pages 151–165).

Llewelyn ran into the house. He couldn't see the baby. There was blood everywhere. Llewelyn looked at his dog.

There was blood on Gelert. Llewelyn was angry – very angry.
He took his sword and killed his dog.

Suddenly Llewelyn heard a noise. Something was under the baby's bed. He

Llewelyn picked the baby up. He was so happy to find him. And then he saw a wolf near the bed. It was dead.

Now Llewelyn knew what had happened. The wolf had come into the house and Gelert had killed it. Llewelyn was very sad.

He made a grave for his dog. Today you can visit that grave in Beddgelert – that means "Gelert's grave" in Welsh.

Reading log 1: Write a summary.

➔ There was • He had • Gelert often • One day • When he came back • He saw • Then he found • Gelert had killed • The prince was

Reading log 2: Write some sentences about you and the story.

➔ liked / didn't like • learned new words • used a dictionary • favourite picture • favourite words/phrases

POEMS BANK

Your reading log

Listen to and read the three poems.
Copy your favourite poem into your reading log and write about it.

a) Who's the poem about? What happens?

- It's about two friends. They've had a … . The writer wants to … but he doesn't want to …
- It's about a teacher. She loves … She always listens to … The pupils … . One day …
- It's about a boy. His name is … The weather is … and he's … He wants to … . But …

b) How does the poem sound?

It has a slow/fast/nice/happy … rhythm.

c) Why do you like or not like the poem?
I like it because it's funny/
it's about real life/…
I don't like it because it isn't funny/
it's stupid/it's boring …

d) Give the poem stars:
★ not very good ★★ OK
★★★ good ★★★★ great

You can make a photo collage, a comic or a rap about the poem.

I'm going to say I'm sorry

2 34

I'm going to say I'm sorry.
It's time for this quarrel to end.
I know that we both didn't mean it
and each of us misses a friend.
It isn't much fun being angry
and arguing's just the worst,
so I'm going to say I'm sorry
just as soon as you say it first!

Jeff Moss

▸ You can find new words in the *Dictionary* (pages 151–165).

My teacher loves her iPod

2◉35

My teacher loves her iPod.
It's always in her ear.
She doesn't mind it if we joke
or chat 'cause she can't hear.

If we don't pay attention,
she doesn't seem to care.
Whenever she has music on,
she wears a distant stare.

Our principal dropped by one day,
and she paid no attention.
He took away her iPod,
and he sent her to detention.

Bruce Lansky

Hot sun

2◉36

"Hot sun!
What fun!
I'll swim!"
said Tim.

"I'll get
so wet,
so cool,
in pool!"

Mom, dad,
they had
two rules
at pools.

Rule one:
Don't run.
Just go
real slow.

Rule two:
If you
splash you'll
leave pool.

But Tim,
poor him,
he got
so hot.

Oh man,
he ran!
Slip! Trip!
Backflip!

Big bomb
soaked mom
and dad.
They're mad!

Now Tim
can't swim.
No fun.
Hot sun.

Kenn Nesbitt

Unit 1 (page 17)

Partner B: You're near the London Eye. You meet Partner A. Can you help him/her? Pick the right sentences.

- Go to Westminster Bridge Road
- Go across Westminster Bridge
- You can take the tube
- Go to Westminster Tube Station
- You can take the 148 bus
- Go to Oxford Circus

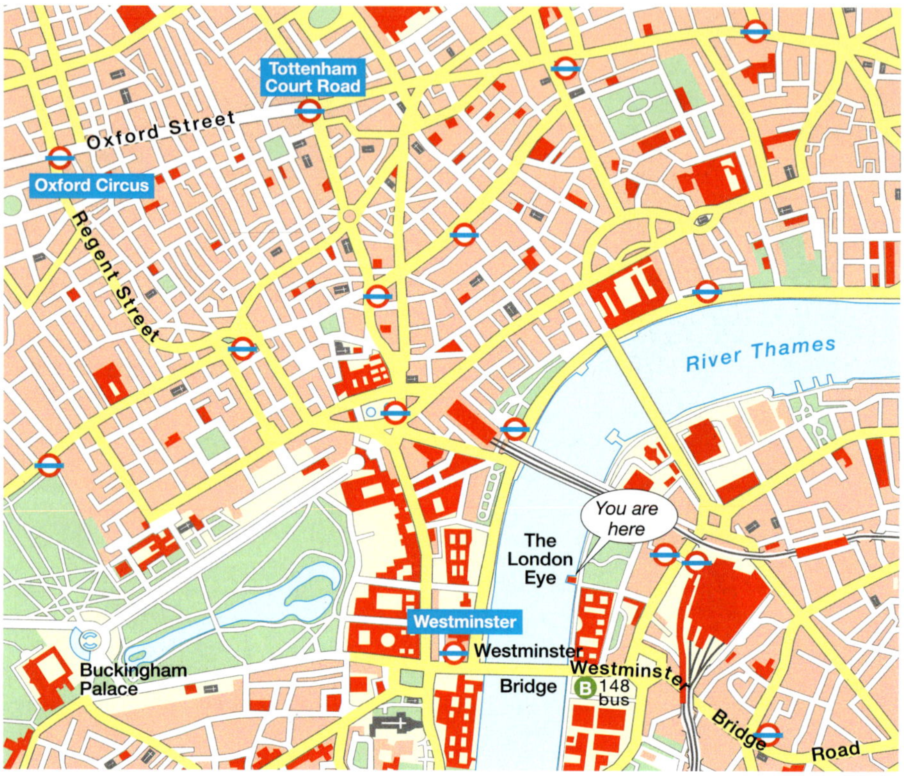

Unit 2 (page 31)

Partner B: Partner A phones you. Make an arrangement with him/her for the weekend.

Friday	Saturday	Sunday
help mum and dad in the restaurant	go to football match with dad	

A ...?

B I'm afraid, I'm ... then.

A ...?

B That's fine. Why don't we meet at the sports centre/park/... at ... o'clock?

A ...!

Unit 3 (page 45)

Partner B: Look at the adverts and answer Partner A's questions.

PARTNER A	PARTNER B
Is that a new ...?	– Yes, it is. We bought it last week/month/Saturday/... I got it for my birthday / for Christmas / from an uncle /...
It's nice/great/...	– Thanks!
Was it expensive?	– Yes, it was very expensive! / No, it was on special offer. / I don't know.
Can I look at it/try it?	– Sure! / I'm sorry, I have to go.

Unit 4 (page 59)

Partner B: You're at home. Offer Partner A a drink and a sandwich. You have tea, cola and water, cheese and ham.

B Would you like a sandwich?
A ...
B ... or ...?
A ...
B ... a drink?
A ...?
(**B** No, sorry.
A ...?)
B Sure, no problem. I'll get it.

Unit 5 (page 73)

Partner B: Do you agree with Partner A?
Say what you think. You can use these phrases:

I agree.	I don't agree!
That's true.	That isn't true!
I think you're right.	I don't think you're right!

Unit 6 (page 87)

Partner B:
You're an English tourist. You want to find a supermarket. Ask Partner A for help.

Excuse me, ...?

Partner A wants to know more about you. Answer his/her questions. Pick your answers.

Name:	Jack/Lily.
From:	Sheffield, in the north of England / Oxford in the south of England.
Staying here for:	a week / two weeks
Staying in:	a hotel / a bed and breakfast
Food:	you think it's nice / horrible
Place:	you like it here / don't like it here

WORDBANKS

Wordbank 1

Unit 1

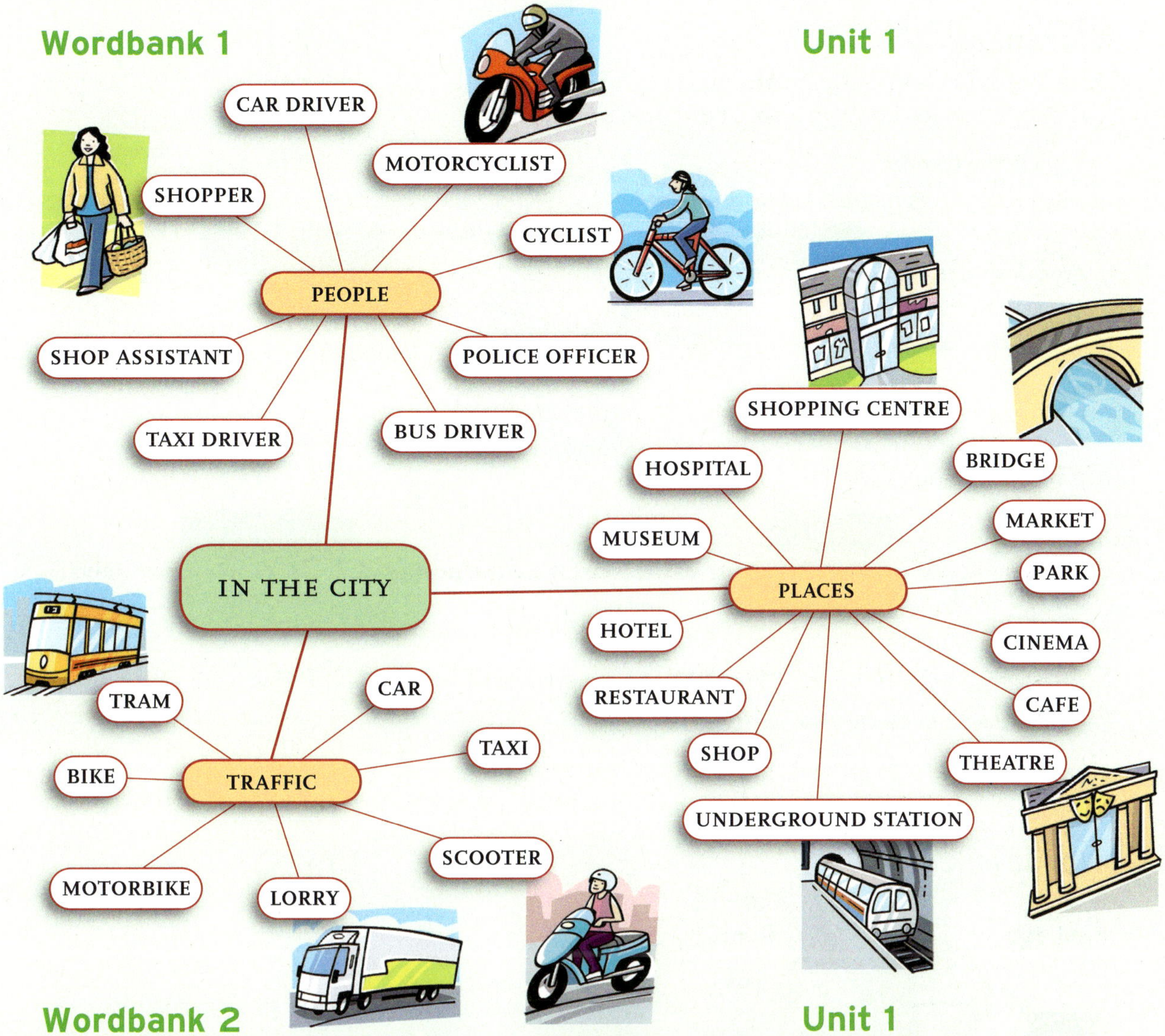

Wordbank 2

Unit 1

CLUBS

SPORTS CLUBS: badminton, basketball, canoeing, cycling, fishing, football, horse riding, jogging, judo, mountain biking, rock climbing, rugby, skiing, swimming, table tennis, tennis, walking, volleyball

aerobics

boxing

skateboarding

OTHER CLUBS: camping, computer, film, music, science

arts and crafts

camera

chess

drama

stamp

Wordbank 3 — Unit 2

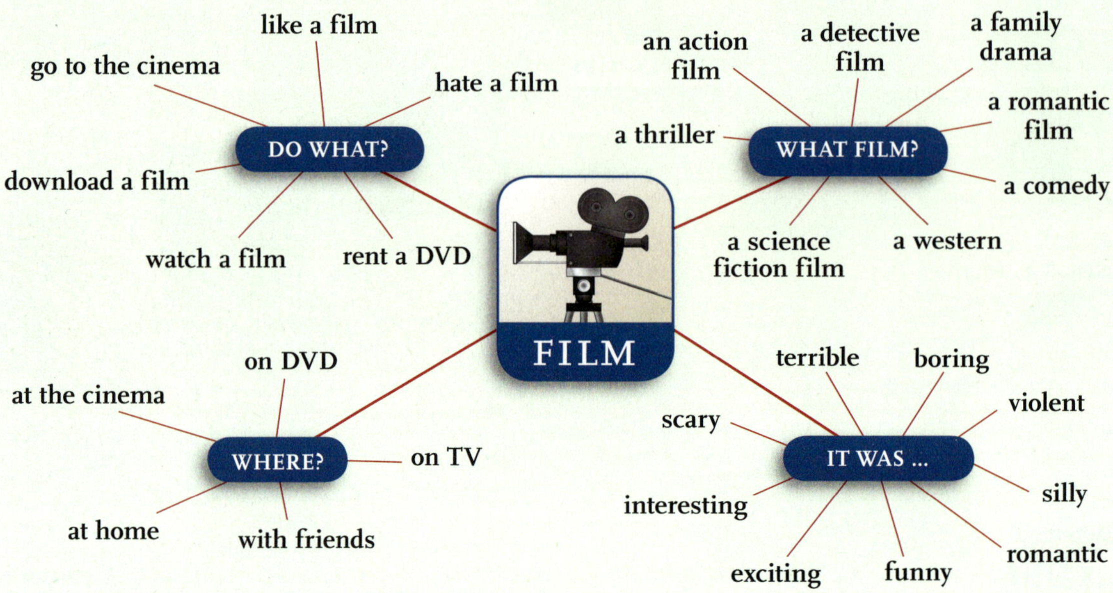

scary *gruselig, unheimlich;* violent *gewalttätig*

Wordbank 4 — Unit 2

Feelings

You

're
get
feel

angry
bored
disappointed
embarrassed
jealous
lonely
frightened
proud
sad
surprised
upset

when

a game or a film isn't interesting.
you've done something stupid.
your neighbour wins the lotto.
you have to go home alone at night.
your friend forgets your birthday.
you're alone because your friends have other plans.
you've had an accident.
you meet stupid people.
you wrote the best test in the class.
you're on holiday and you meet your class teacher.
your friend moves to another town.

bored *gelangweilt;* disappointed *enttäuscht;* proud *stolz;* surprised *überrascht;* upset *aufgeregt, aufgebracht*

Wordbank 5

Unit 3

I can speak ...

Albanian (Albanisch)
Arabic (Arabisch)
Bosnian (Bosnisch)
Chinese (Chinesisch)
Croatian (Kroatisch)
Greek (Griechisch)
Italian (Italienisch)
Kazakh (Kasachisch)
Kurdish (Kurdisch)
Macedonian (Mazedonisch)
Persian/Farsi (Persisch/Farsi)

Polish (Polnisch)
Portuguese (Portugiesisch)
Romanian (Rumänisch)
Russian (Russisch)
Serbian (Serbisch)
Spanish (Spanisch)
Thai (Thai)
Turkish (Türkisch)
Ukrainian (Ukrainisch)
Uzbek (Usbekisch)
Vietnamese (Vietnamesisch)

Wordbank 6

Unit 3

HOBBIES

- I PLAY: HANDBALL, ICE HOCKEY, VOLLEYBALL, FOOTBALL
- I LIKE: JIGSAW PUZZLES, FASHION, COMPUTER GAMES, MAKE-UP, RAP, COMICS, MOTORBIKES, ANIMALS
- I DO: KNITTING, JUGGLING, TAE KWON DO, TRAMPOLINING, KARATE, ATHLETICS, GYMNASTICS
- I GO: GO-KARTING, BOWLING, SKATING, WINDSURFING, ROWING

Wordbank 7

Unit 4

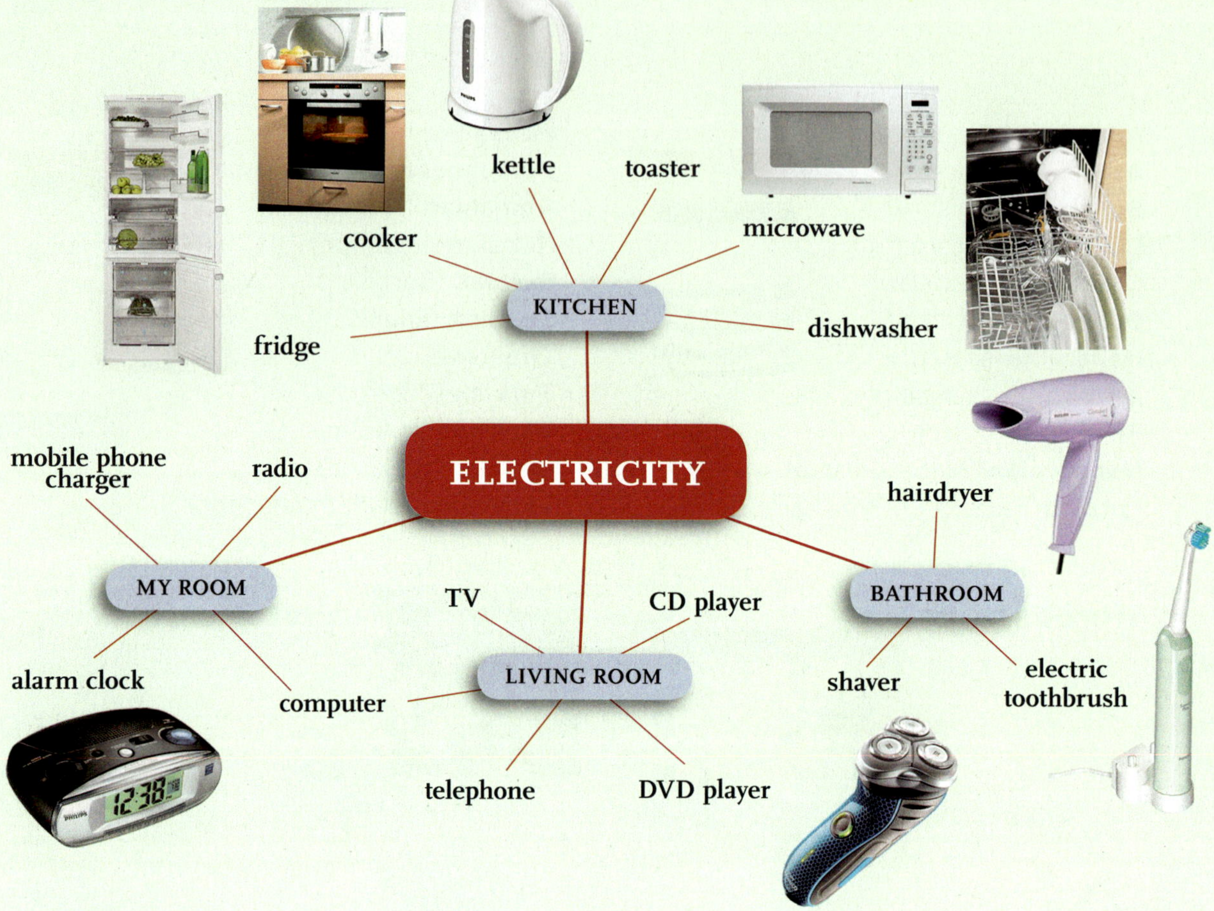

Wordbank 8

Unit 4

Sandwiches

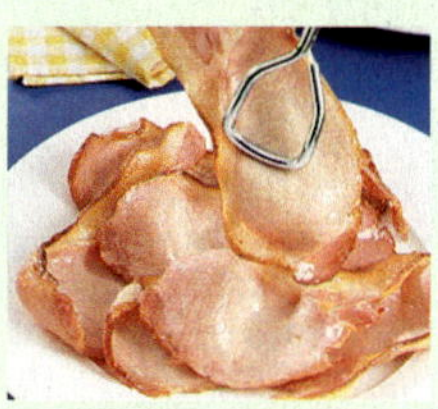
bacon

tuna

cucumber

lettuce

tomato

egg

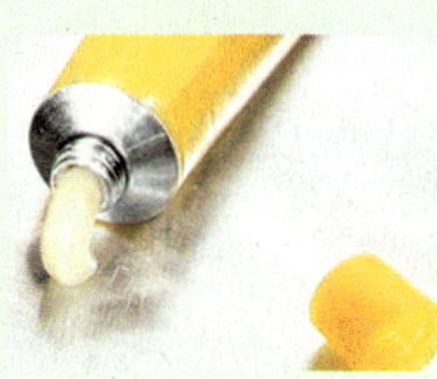
mayonnaise

butter

white bread

wholemeal bread

Wordbank 9

Unit 5

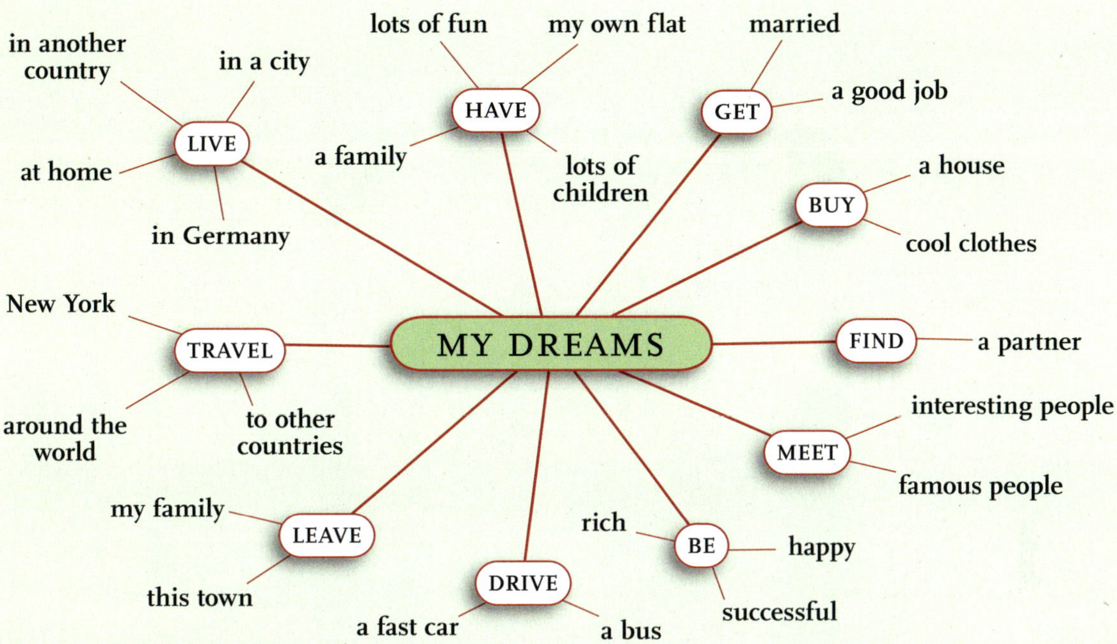

Wordbank 10

Unit 5

Athletics

long jump

pole vault

javelin

hurdles

shot-put

discus

WORDBANKS

Wordbank 11 Unit 6

Parts of the body

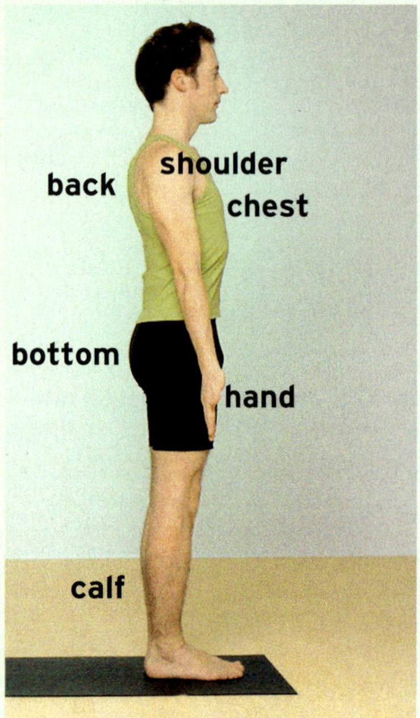

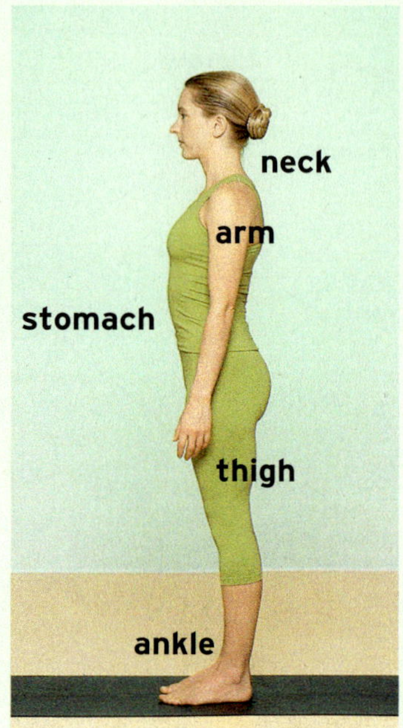

Wordbank 12 Unit 6

Tattoos

butterfly

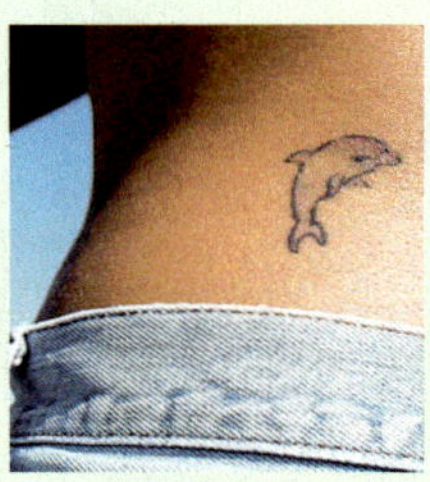
dolphin

dragon

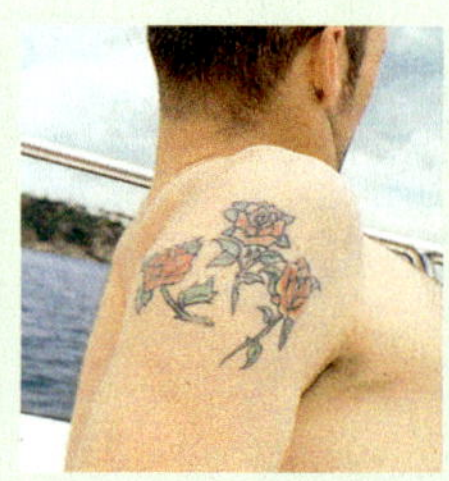
flower

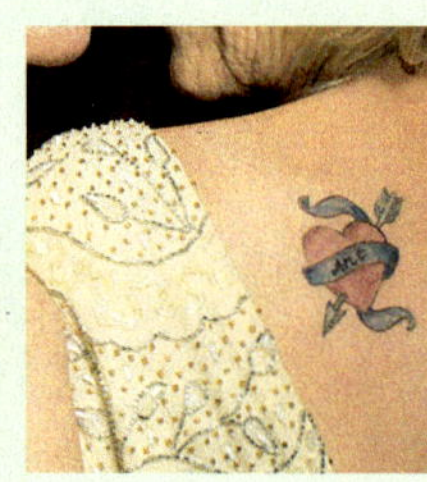
heart

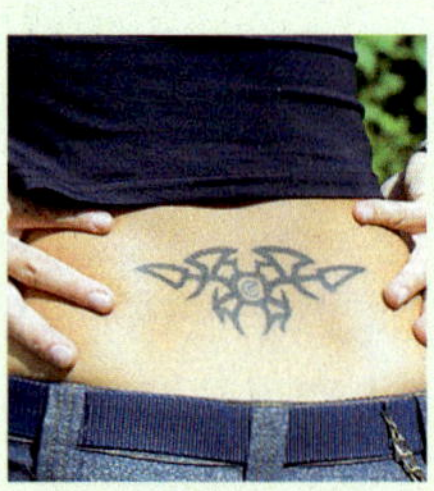
pattern

parrot

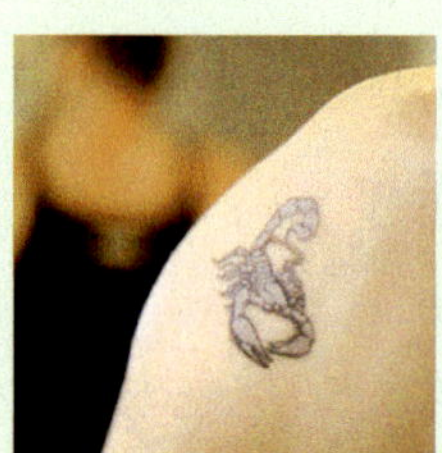
scorpion

star

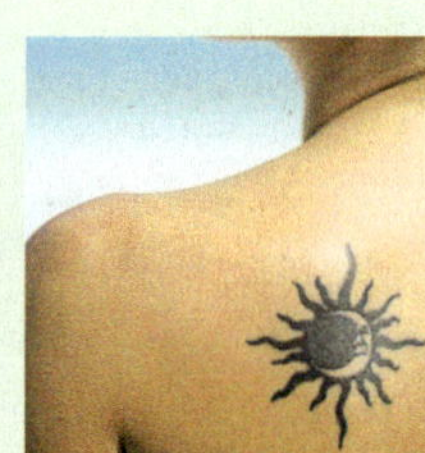
sun

Dieses Wörterverzeichnis enthält alle neuen Wörter des Buches in der Reihenfolge, in der sie im Buch zum ersten Mal vorkommen.

Do you know these words?
bad • film • frightened • happy • ideas • knew • liked • lonely • notes • played • sad • said • sent • stopped • text message • thought • told • took • went • won

Test yourself
Write the lists in your exercise book.
a) Phrases: collect ..., make ..., send a ..., watch a ...

Mit den gelben Kästen am Anfang kannst du bekannte Wörter wiederholen.

In der eckigen Klammer steht, wie die Wörter ausgesprochen werden.

Ein blauer oder roter Pfeil heißt: Schau dir den blauen oder roten Kasten rechts an.

Der graue Pfeil heißt: Schau in die rechte Spalte.

Dieses Zeichen bedeutet: Aufgepasst!

Das rote Sternchen kennzeichnet unregelmäßige Verben (vgl. unten).

In den roten Kästen stehen wichtige Hinweise.

Die blauen Kästen fassen Wörter in Gruppen zusammen. So lernst du sie besser.

Diese Zahl gibt die Seite an, auf der die Wörter zum ersten Mal vorkommen.

52 **electric** [ɪˈlektrɪk]	elektrisch	yesterday.
illuminations [ɪluːmɪˈneɪʃnz]	Festbeleuchtung	
*win: **I've won** [wʌn]	gewinnen: ich habe gewonnen	→ Sue *will* stay in London. I'll (= I will) visit her.
Will he be there? [wɪl]	Wird er da sein?	
we won't (= will not) be there [wəʊnt]	wir werden nicht da sein	→ Sam *won't* go to London.
I'm bored [bɔːd]	ich langweile mich	
free [friː]	kostenlos; frei	
million [ˈmɪljən]	Million	→ ! 2 *million* (ohne -s!)
technology [tekˈnɒlədʒi]	Technik, Technologie	
fifty **thousand** [ˈθaʊznd]	fünfzigtausend	
three **and a half** [hɑːf]	dreieinhalb	→ We'll leave in *two and a half* weeks.
on [ɒn]	an, eingeschaltet	→ The radio is *on*.
number [ˈnʌmbə]	Nummer; Zahl; Ziffer	→ Find a *number* between 1 and 9. – Five!
53 **charger** [ˈtʃɑːdʒə]	(Batterie-)Ladegerät	
radiator [ˈreɪdieɪtə]	Heizkörper	
waste [weɪst]	verschwenden	→ We shouldn't waste energy ...
energy	Energie; Kraft	

Red box: 'll – won't; I'll – I won't; you'll – you wo...; he'll – he won...; ... – ...

Blue box: a hundred; a thousand; a million

electricit... electroni...

Fette Wörter sind besonders wichtig.

Schräg gestellte Wörter gehören nicht zum Pflichtwortschatz.

love [lʌv]	Liebe	
words (of a song)	(Lied-)Text	→ I love Mel! I know the
gift [gɪft]	Geschenk	
this one's for you	dieses ist für dich	
it may be quite simple [meɪ, kwaɪt, sɪmpl]	es mag ziemlich einfach sein	

***Irregular verbs**

Infinitive form	Simple past form	Present perfect form
read [riːd]	I read [red]	I've read [red]
take [teɪk]	I took [tʊk]	I've taken [ˈteɪkən]
win [wɪn]	I won [wʌn]	I've won [wʌn]

Hier findest du die drei Formen der unregelmäßigen Verben aus der Unit.

Test yourself
1 Find the rhyme words and write them in your exercise book.
1 **my** [maɪ] – **eye**
2 **here** [hɪə] – ...
4 **trip** [trɪp] – ...
5 **dream** [driːm] – ...

Hier kannst du überprüfen, wie gut du die neuen Wörter schon beherrschst.

Here and there

6 **Britain** ['brɪtn]	Großbritannien	→ 
compare [kəm'peə]	vergleichen	→ You can't *compare* Exeter with London!
border ['bɔːdə]	Grenze	
famous ['feɪməs]	berühmt	→ This cafe is *famous* for its hamburgers.
special ['speʃl]	besondere, besonderer, besonderes	→ Tomorrow is a *special* day – remember?
beer [bɪə]	Bier	
flag [flæg]	Fahne, Flagge	
musical instrument [mjuːzɪkl'ɪnstrəmənt]	Musikinstrument	→ Do you play a *musical instrument*? – Yes, I do. I play the guitar.
produce [prə'djuːs]	herstellen, produzieren	
kilt [kɪlt]	Kilt *(Schottenrock)*	
Europe ['jʊərəp]	Europa	
capital ['kæpɪtl]	Hauptstadt	→ What's the *capital* of Ireland? – Dublin!
Turkey ['tɜːki]	Türkei	
sausage ['sɒsɪdʒ]	Wurst, Würstchen	
bread [bred]	Brot	
at the back of the book	hinten im Buch	→ We always sit *at the back of* the bus. 
7 **north** [nɔːθ]	Norden; Nord-; nördlich	
east [iːst]	Osten; Ost-; östlich	→ We live *east* of York.
south [saʊθ]	Süden; Süd-; südlich	→ I'm from *South London*.
west [west]	Westen; West-; westlich	→ The *west* of Scotland can be very lonely.

Unit 1

Lerntipp 1: Lautschrift

Englische Wörter spricht man anders aus als deutsche. Aber wie? Dafür gibt es die Lautschrift hinter dem Wort. Sie steht immer in eckigen Klammern und zeigt dir mithilfe von Symbolen, wie sich das Wort anhört. Zum Beispiel sieht der Name „Jenny" in Lautschrift so aus: ['dʒeni]
Der kleine Strich am Anfang zeigt, dass du dieses Wort auf der ersten Silbe betonen musst.

Welche Namen verbergen sich hinter diesen Lautschriftzeichen?
['ænə] ['denɪs] ['dʒuːliə] ['kevɪn] [mə'riː] [tɒm]

Am besten sprichst du alle Wörter beim Lernen immer laut aus.
(Lautschriftsymbole: S.179; Lösungen für das Namensspiel: S.181)

[uː] [aɪ] [njuː] ['haɪlaɪt]

Do you know these words?
bridge • dangerous • dirty • exciting • feel • forget • funny • important • late • letter • lonely • meet • miss • need • quiet • repeat • river • station • stay • stupid • subject • train • wear • work

Test yourself
Write the lists in your exercise book.
a) *9 Adjektive:* **dangerous, ...** ; **b)** *6 Nomen:* **bridge, ...** ; **c)** *9 Verben:* **feel, ...**

Are your answers right? Check on page 181.

Tipp:
Schau dir die Wörter in den oberen Reihen noch einmal an.

8	**scene** [si:n]	Ansicht; Szene	
	sound [saʊnd]	Geräusch	
9	**city** ['sɪti]	Stadt, Großstadt	
	traffic ['træfɪk]	Verkehr	
	underground train [ʌndəgraʊnd'treɪn]	U-Bahn-Zug	→ At an *underground station* [U-Bahnhof]
10	**title** ['taɪtl]	Titel	
	tip [tɪp]	Tipp	
	Singapore ['sɪŋəpɔ:]	Singapur	
	***send** [send]	senden, schicken	→ When can we meet? – I'll *send* you a text message.
	photo ['fəʊtəʊ]	Foto	
	Asian ['eɪʃn]	asiatisch; Asiat, Asiatin	
	aunt [ɑ:nt]	Tante	→ ! Aussprache: [ɑ:nt]
	at the moment ['məʊmənt]	zurzeit, im Moment	
	nervous ['nɜ:vəs]	nervös, ängstlich	
	I **don't** have **any** friends ['eni]	ich habe keine Freunde/Freundinnen →	
	not ... yet [jet]	noch nicht	→ Bill has*n't* arrived *yet*.
11	Who **likes** the song **best?**	Wem gefällt das Lied am besten?	→ Of all singers, I *like* Dana *best*.
	Learn about London.	Erfahre etwas über London.	→ At the museum we *learned about* trains.
	the Olympics [ə'lɪmpɪks]	die Olympischen Spiele	
	queen [kwi:n]	Königin	→

→ **some – any**
There's some chocolate on the table.
But there aren't any crisps.

Story

12	they help you **to** read	sie helfen dir zu lesen	→ It's easy *to* find new friends at this school.
	***give up** [gɪv'ʌp]	aufgeben	
	Africa ['æfrɪkə]	Afrika	→

	Asia ['eɪʃə]	Asien	
	another [ə'nʌðə]	ein anderer/anderes, eine andere	
	international [ɪntə'næʃnəl]	international	
	noticeboard ['nəʊtɪsbɔ:d]	Anschlagbrett, Schwarzes Brett	
	***have a chat** [tʃæt]	sich unterhalten	
	you **should** [ʃʊd, ʃəd]	du solltest, du müsstest →	→ We *should* go home now.
	join a club [dʒɔɪn]	einem Klub beitreten	
13	**lunchtime** ['lʌntʃtaɪm]	Mittagszeit; Mittagspause	→ Let's meet at *lunchtime*.
	start a programme	eine Sendung ins Leben rufen	
	radio ['reɪdiəʊ]	Radio	
	on the intercom ['ɪntəkɒm]	über die Sprechanlage	
	news [nju:z]	Nachricht(en); Neuigkeit(en)	→ ! That's great *news*. [= Kein Plural!]

→ **should**
I should
you should
he should
...

Skills training

16	**Asking for help**	Um Hilfe bitten	
	Excuse me, ... [ɪk'skju:z]	Entschuldigen Sie, ...	
	the tube [tju:b]	die (Londoner) U-Bahn	
	detective [dɪ'tektɪv]	Detektiv, Detektivin	
17	**queue up** [kju:'ʌp]	Schlange stehen	
	How much are the tickets?	Was kosten die Fahrkarten?	→ Excuse me, please. *How much is* this bag?
	adult ['ædʌlt]	Erwachsene, Erwachsener	
	under ['ʌndə]	unter	

	boat [bəʊt]	Boot; Schiff
	polite [pə'laɪt]	höflich
18	**quickly** ['kwɪkli]	schnell
	paragraph ['pærəgrɑːf]	Absatz
	what the book **is like**	wie das Buch ist
19	**phrase** [freɪz]	Ausdruck
	writer ['raɪtə]	Schriftsteller, Schriftstellerin
	reading week ['riːdɪŋwiːk]	Lesewoche
	sponsored ['spɒnsəd]	gesponsert

→ Ruby *quickly* finished her homework.

→ I know Robbie. – Cool! *What's* he *like?*

My friend is ...
friendly
polite
funny
interesting
nice

Look at language

20	**club** [klʌb]	Disko
	at night [naɪt]	nachts, in der Nacht
	free [friː]	frei
	ghost [gəʊst]	Geist, Gespenst
	witch [wɪtʃ]	Hexe
	dance [dɑːns]	tanzen

Clubs
computer club
football club
fan club
youth club
(night) club

The day
in the morning
at lunchtime
in the evening
at night

* Irregular verbs

Infinitive form	Simple past form	Present perfect form
give [gɪv]	I gave [geɪv]	I've given ['gɪvn]
have [hæv]	I had [hæd]	I've had [hæd]
send [send]	I sent [sent]	I've sent [sent]

Test yourself

1 What are the words? Write them in your exercise book.
1 ['sɪti] **2** ['fəʊtəʊ] **3** ['æfrɪkə] **4** [dɪ'tektɪv] **5** [klʌb] **6** [wɪtʃ]

2 Write the phrases in your exercise book and finish them with the right verbs.
... about London. • ... a chat • ... a club • ... a programme • ... for help

3 Find the partners and write them in your exercise book.
village – city • cousin – ... • at lunchtime – ... • TV – ... • child – ... • reader – ...

4 Write the sentences in your exercise book and finish them.
1 It's great ... meet my old friends again.
2 You've found your money? That's great ... !
3 ... me, please. How do we get to Westminster?
4 You've seen the new 'Ghosts!' film? Can you tell me what it's ... , please?

Are your answers right? Check on page 181.

Tipp:
Schau dir die vorangegangenen Wortlisten gut an.

Unit 2

Lerntipp 2: „Stumme" Buchstaben

Manche Buchstaben in englischen Wörtern werden gar nicht gesprochen.
Sie bleiben „stumm" und fehlen als Laut in der Lautschrift, z. B. das *w* in *who* [hu:].
Markiere diese Buchstaben beim Abschreiben, wenn du sie dir merken willst.

Die folgenden Wörter kennst du schon. Weißt du, welcher Buchstabe darin stumm bleibt?
Sprich die Wörter laut aus und schau dir die Lautschrift an.

when [wen] *friend* [frend] *park* [pɑ:k] *apple* ['æpl] *guess* [ges] *ready* ['redi] *sister* ['sɪstə]

(Lösungen S. 181)

Do you know these words?

bad • film • frightened • happy • ideas • knew • liked • lonely • notes • played • sad • said • sent • stopped • text message • thought • told • took • went • won

Test yourself

Write the lists in your exercise book.

a) Phrases: **collect ..., make ..., send a ..., watch a ...**
b) 11 verbs in the simple past: **knew, ...**
c) "I feel ... ": **bad, ..., ..., ..., ...**

Are your answers right? Check on page 181.

Tipp:
Schau dir die Wörter in den oberen Reihen noch einmal an.

22 **Scottish** ['skɒtɪʃ]	schottisch; Schotte(n), Schottin(nen)	→ Callum and Fiona are *Scottish.*
romantic [rəʊ'mæntɪk]	romantisch	
sad [sæd]	traurig	
silly ['sɪli]	dumm, albern	
24 **article** ['ɑ:tɪkl]	Artikel	
free time [fri:'taɪm]	Freizeit	
castle ['kɑ:sl]	Schloss; Burg	
actor ['æktə]	Schauspieler, Schauspielerin	
***become: I became** [bɪ'kʌm, bɪ'keɪm]	werden: ich wurde	→ Max and Kitty quickly *became* friends. ! Falscher Freund: *become* = werden (nicht: ~~bekommen~~)
file [faɪl]	Karteikarte; Akte	
age [eɪdʒ]	Alter	→ What's his *age*? – He's 21.
interest ['ɪntrəst]	Interesse	
25 **he was born ...** [bɔ:n]	er wurde ... geboren	→ When *were you born?* – *I was born* on May 2nd, 1995.
in 1971 [naɪn'ti:nsevntiwʌn]	(im Jahre) 1971	→ My family left Turkey *in 1982.*
die [daɪ]	sterben	→ ! he's dying; he died
*sing: **I sang** [sæŋ]	singen: ich sang	
they're married ['mærid]	sie sind verheiratet	→ We're a family, but my parents *aren't married.*
love [lʌv]	Liebe	
words (of a song)	(Lied-)Text	→ I love Mel! I know the *words of* all *her songs.*
gift [gɪft]	Geschenk	
this one's for you	dieses ist für dich	
it may be quite simple [meɪ, kwaɪt, sɪmpl]	es mag ziemlich einfach sein	

	now that it's done	nun, wo es fertig ist	
	you don't mind [maɪnd]	du hast nichts dagegen	
	I put down [daʊn]	ich habe aufgeschrieben	
	wonderful ['wʌndəfl]	wundervoll	
	now you're in the world	nun, wo du auf der Welt bist	
	heading ['hedɪŋ]	Rubrik; Überschrift	
	on the Internet	im Internet →	→ I found an interesting article about actors *on the Internet.*
	complete [kəm'pliːt]	vollständig	

→ **on**
on TV
on the radio
on the Internet
on the phone

Story

26	**jealous (of)** ['dʒeləs]	neidisch (auf); eifersüchtig (auf)	
	competition [kɒmpə'tɪʃn]	Wettbewerb	→ Last year I won a swimming *competition.*
	a 13-year-old girl	ein 13-jähriges Mädchen	
	Congratulations! [kəngrætʃu'leɪʃnz]	Herzlichen Glückwunsch!	→ ! *Congratulations!* [Prüfung usw.] Happy birthday! [Geburtstag]
	I'm happy for her	ich freue mich für sie	
	everything ['evriθɪŋ]	alles	
	good at	gut in	→ I'm *good at* sports.
	problem ['prɒbləm]	Problem	→ ! Aussprache: ['prɒbləm]
	cry [kraɪ]	weinen	→ ! I'm crying; I cried
	*feel: **I felt** [felt]	(sich) fühlen: ich fühlte (mich)	
27	**What's wrong?**	Ist etwas nicht in Ordnung?	
	smile [smaɪl]	lächeln	
	yeah [jeə]	ja *(besonders in wörtl. Rede)*	
	embarrassed [ɪm'bærəst]	verlegen	→ He's *embarrassed.*
	angry (with) ['æŋgri]	böse, wütend (auf)	→ She's *angry.*

He's *embarrassed.*

She's *angry.*

Training

29	**Making notes**	(Sich) Notizen machen	
	underlined [ʌndə'laɪnd]	unterstrichen	→ Find the *underlined* word!
	symbol ['sɪmbl]	Symbol	
	language ['læŋgwɪdʒ]	Sprache	→ My father speaks three *languages.*
	Scots [skɒts]	Schottisch *(engl. Dialekt)*	
	Gaelic ['gælɪk]	Gälisch *(keltische Sprache)*	

Skills training

30	**likes and dislikes** ['laɪksən'dɪslaɪks]	Vorlieben und Abneigungen	
	I can't stand them	ich kann sie nicht ausstehen	→ *I can't stand* fruit! – I love bananas, but
	I'm not keen on it [kiːn]	ich habe nicht viel dafür übrig	→ *I'm not keen on* apples.
	stress [stres]	betonen	
	underline [ʌndə'laɪn]	unterstreichen	
31	**Making arrangements** [ə'reɪndʒmənts]	Absprachen treffen	→ Let's *make an arrangement* for Saturday.
	I'm afraid ... [ə'freɪd]	Leider ...	→ Can I speak to Tim, please? – *I'm afraid* he isn't here.
33	**sound** [saʊnd]	klingen, sich anhören	→ Is everything OK? You *sound* terrible!
	carnival ['kɑːnɪvl]	Karneval	
	wedding day ['wedɪŋdeɪ]	Hochzeitstag	
	organize ['ɔːgənaɪz]	ordnen; organisieren	→ ! Aussprache: ['ɔːgənaɪz]

Look at language

34 **ill** [ɪl]	krank	→ 
grave [greɪv]	Grab	
for 14 years	14 Jahre lang	→ I lived in Scotland *for* ten years.
when [wen]	als	
statue ['stætʃu:]	Statue	→ ❗ Aussprache: ['stætʃu:]

* Irregular verbs

Infinitive form	Simple past form	Present perfect form
become [bɪ'kʌm]	I became [bɪ'keɪm]	I've become [bɪ'kʌm]
feel [fi:l]	I felt [felt]	I've felt [felt]
sing [sɪŋ]	I sang [sæŋ]	I've sung [sʌŋ]

Test yourself

1 What are the words? Write them in your exercise book.

1 ['ɑ:tɪkl] **2** ['kɑ:sl] **3** ['prɒbləm] **4** [ɪm'bærəst] **5** ['sɪmbl] **6** ['stætʃu:]

2 Write the words in your exercise book and find the third word.

1 Scotland • Scottish • Scots
2 cinema • film • ...
3 nothing • something • ...
4 ill • die • ...

Tipp: Schau dir die vorangegangenen Wortlisten gut an.

3 for – with – of? Write the sentences in your exercise book and finish them.

Sue is jealous ... Anne. Anne is happy ... Luke. Luke is angry ... Sue.

4 Write the sentences in your exercise book and finish them.

1 What's your ... ? – I'm fourteen.
2 I was ... in 1992.
3 I can speak three ... : English, German and French.
4 I lived in Poland ... three years.

Are your answers right? Check on page 181.

Unit 3

Lerntipp 3: Das Dictionary (1)

Wenn du vergessen hast, was ein Wort bedeutet oder wie es ausgesprochen wird, schlage es im **Dictionary** (S.151–165) nach.

Dort findest du auch Wendungen *(phrases)* – Einträge, die aus mehreren Wörtern bestehen, z.B. **play sports** (Sport treiben). Diese Wendung steht unter **play** und unter **sport**, damit du sie auch dann wiederfindest, wenn du einen Teil vergessen hast. Auch Wendungen mit Präpositionen sind oft doppelt aufgeführt.

Schau dir die folgenden Wendungen an. Unter welchen Einträgen findest du sie wohl im **Dictionary**?

at night (2x) **on the Internet** (2x) **What time is it?** (2x) **Learn it by heart.** (3x)

(Lösungen S.181)

Do you know these words?

bridge • cafe • car park • cinema • find • go • hotel • meet • post office • restaurant • run • school • see • shop • sports centre • swimming pool • take • think

Test yourself

Write the lists in your exercise book.

a) *Unregelmäßige Verben:* **find**, ..., ..., ..., ..., ..., ...

b) *In der Stadt:* **bridge**, ..., ..., ..., ..., ..., ..., ..., ..., ..., ...

Are your answers right? Check on page 181.

Tipp:
Schau dir die Wörter in den oberen Reihen noch einmal an.

36	**church** [tʃɜːtʃ]	Kirche	
37	**bus stop** ['bʌstɒp]	Bushaltestelle	
	tourist office ['tʊərɪstɒfɪs]	Touristeninformation, Fremdenverkehrsbüro	→ Excuse me, how do I get to the *tourist office*, please? – Sorry, I don't know. I'm not a tourist!
38	**blog** [blɒg]	Blog *(von „Weblog"; hier eine Art Online-Tagebuch)*	
	mountain ['maʊntən]	Berg	→ *in the mountains* [im Gebirge]
	in winter ['wɪntə]	im Winter	
	business ['bɪznəs]	Betrieb, Geschäft	
	Welsh [welʃ]	Walisisch; walisisch; Waliser, Waliserin(nen)	→ 'Aled' is a *Welsh* name.
	autumn ['ɔːtəm]	Herbst	
	mountain boarding ['maʊntənbɔːdɪŋ]	Mountainboardfahren	
	you ca**n't** do **anything** ['eniθɪŋ]	du kannst nichts machen	→ The test was terrible – I did*n't* know *anything*!
	a waste of time [weɪst]	Zeitverschwendung	→ I never watch TV. It's *a waste of time*.
	blogging ['blɒgɪŋ]	Bloggen *(ein Blog führen und auf andere Blogs reagieren)*	
39	**topic** ['tɒpɪk]	Thema	

Story

40	Parents **are a pain!** [peɪn]	Eltern nerven!	→ Homework *is a pain!*
	pick up [pɪk'ʌp]	abholen	→ Mum, can you *pick* me *up* after school, please? I don't want to walk home.
	he was sending	er schickte (gerade)	
	watch [wɒtʃ]	zusehen	
	he couldn't send texts ['kʊdnt]	er konnte keine SMS verschicken →	→ When I was five I *couldn't* write, but I *could* read.
	safe [seɪf]	sicher, in Sicherheit	
	they were talking	sie unterhielten sich (gerade)	
41	**cider** ['saɪdə]	Apfelwein	
	strict [strɪkt]	streng	
	I mustn't drink ['mʌsnt]	ich darf nicht trinken	→ My dad says we *mustn't* stay too long.
	alcohol ['ælkəhɒl]	Alkohol	
	that evening	an diesem Abend	
	those [ðəʊz]	diese, jene, die (da) →	
	he was in big trouble ['trʌbl]	er steckte in großen Schwierigkeiten	
	he was grounded ['graʊndɪd]	er hatte Hausarrest/Stubenarrest	

→ **I, you, he, we ...**
can / can't
could / couldn't
should / shouldn't

→ **this** bag - **that** bag
these bags - **those** bags

Revision

43	**season** ['siːzn]	Jahreszeit →	
	Christmas ['krɪsməs]	Weihnachten	
	indoors [ɪn'dɔːz]	in der Halle, drinnen	
	outdoors [aʊt'dɔːz]	im Freien, draußen	→ We often sleep *outdoors* in summer.
	translate [træns'leɪt]	übersetzen	

→ **The seasons**
spring
summer
autumn
winter

Skills training

44	**flip phone** ['flɪpfəʊn]	Klapphandy	
	credit ['kredɪt]	Guthaben	→ ! Falscher Freund: *credit* = Guthaben (nicht: ~~Kredit~~)
	ringtone ['rɪŋtəʊn]	Klingelton	
	text bullying ['tekstbʊliɪŋ]	„SMS-Terror"	
	turn on, turn off [tɜːn'ɒn, -'ɒf]	einschalten, ausschalten	→ Can I *turn on* the TV, Dad?
	***hear** [hɪə]	hören	
45	***hold** [həʊld]	halten; *(MP3-Player:)* speichern	→ Can you *hold* my dog, please? → My old MP3 player *held* only 100 songs.
	five **hundred** ['hʌndrəd]	fünfhundert	
	on special offer [speʃl'ɒfə]	im Sonderangebot	
	gear [gɪə]	Gang *(Fahrrad, Auto)*	
	mountain board ['maʊntənbɔːd]	Mountainboard *(eine Art Gelände-Skateboard)*	→  a *mountain board*
46	**poet** ['pəʊɪt]	Dichter, Dichterin →	→ This *poet* is famous for her romantic poems.
47	**summary** ['sʌməri]	Zusammenfassung	
	clean [kliːn]	sauber	
	leek [liːk]	Lauch(stange), Porree(stange)	
	beautiful ['bjuːtɪfl]	schön, wunderschön	
	if they made me say goodbye to Wales	wenn man mich zwänge, mich von Wales zu verabschieden	→ Nobody can *make me eat* leek. I hate it!
	treat [triːt]	Genuss, besonderes Vergnügen	→ The ice cream was a special *treat*. → ! great [greɪt] – treat [triːt]
	a place to meet	ein Treffpunkt	
	in the end [ɪnðɪ'end]	letztendlich, schließlich	→ I tried everything, but *in the end* I had to give up.

→ poet
writer
singer
actor

Look at language

48	**price** [praɪs]	Preis	→ ! price [praɪs] [Kaufpreis] prize [praɪz] [Gewinn]
	safety gear ['seɪftigɪə]	Sicherheitsausrüstung	
	careful ['keəfl]	vorsichtig	
	helmet ['helmɪt]	Helm	
	protector [prə'tektə]	Protektor, Schützer	→ I'm a skateboarder – of course I wear *protectors*!
	how to find us	wie man uns findet	→ I don't know *how to* play golf.
	correct [kə'rekt]	korrigieren, berichtigen	

* Irregular verbs

Infinitive form	Simple past form	Present perfect form
hear [hɪə]	I heard [hɜːd]	I've heard [hɜːd]
hold [həʊld]	I held [held]	I've held [held]

Hinweis:
Auf der nächsten Seite kannst du dich testen.

Test yourself

1 [iː]: Find the right letters and finish the words in your exercise book.
s - - son, cl - - n, l - - k, tr - - t, a place to m - - t

2 Find and write in your exercise book:
a language • a drink • a part of a bike • a vegetable

3 What are the phrases? Write them in your exercise book.
1 waste – a – time – of
2 a – pain – are – parents
3 in – he – trouble – was – big
4 to – find – us – how

4 Now make sentences and write them in your exercise book.
1 Can – up – me – pick – after – you – sport?
2 Mum – drink – mustn't – we – says – alcohol.
3 Nobody – me – can – drink – make – cider.

Are your answers right? Check on page 181.

Tipp:
Schau dir die vorangegangenen Wortlisten gut an.

Unit 4

Lerntipp 4: Das Dictionary (2)

Manche englischen Wörter haben auf Deutsch mehrere Bedeutungen. Vielleicht verstehst du manchmal einen Satz nicht sofort, weil du nicht an die anderen Bedeutungen des Wortes denkst. Dann schau einfach im **Dictionary** (S. 151–165) nach.

Tipp: Oft sind Verb und Nomen gleich, z. B. bei **dream**: **1** träumen; **2** Traum.

Kennst du die Bedeutungen folgender Wörter? (Sie stehen alle im **Dictionary**.)

help (2) **letter** (2) **open** (3) **phone** (2) **trainer** (2)

Do you know these words?
beach • computer • DVD player • eight • first • ice cream • light • mobile phone • MP3 player • one hundred • rock • second • sixty-six • sun • the sea • third • TV • water

Test yourself
Write the lists in your exercise book.
a) *Am Meer:* beach, ..., ..., ..., ..., ...
b) *„Stromverbraucher":* computer, ..., ..., ..., ..., ...
c) *Zahlen/Zählen:* eight, ..., ..., ..., ..., ...

Are your answers right? Check on page 181.

Tipp:
Schau dir die Wörter in den oberen Reihen noch einmal an.

50	**northern** ['nɔːðən]	Nord-, nördlich →	→ I'm from the *northern* part of the country.
	funfair ['fʌnfeə]	Kirmes, Jahrmarkt	
	roller coaster ['rəʊləkəʊstə]	Achterbahn	
	in the north [nɔːθ]	im Norden	
	Imagine ... [ɪ'mædʒɪn]	Stell dir/Stellt euch vor ...	
	eye [aɪ]	Auge	→ 

→ northern
eastern
southern
western

51 **tower** ['taʊə]	Turm	
pier [pɪə]	Pier, Anlegestelle	
amusement arcade [ə'mju:zməntɑ:keɪd]	Spielhalle	
electricity [ɪlek'trɪsəti]	Strom, Elektrizität	→ We didn't have any *electricity* yesterday.
52 **electric** [ɪ'lektrɪk]	elektrisch →	
illuminations [ɪlu:mɪ'neɪʃnz]	Festbeleuchtung	
***win: I've won** [wʌn]	gewinnen: ich habe gewonnen	
Will he be there? [wɪl]	Wird er da sein? →	→ Sue *will* stay in London. I*'ll* (= I will) visit her.
we won't (= will not) be there [wəʊnt]	wir werden nicht da sein →	→ Sam *won't* go to London.
I'm bored [bɔ:d]	ich langweile mich	
free [fri:]	kostenlos; frei	
million ['mɪljən]	Million	→ ! 2 *million* (ohne -s!)
technology [tek'nɒlədʒi]	Technik, Technologie	
fifty **thousand** ['θaʊznd]	fünfzigtausend →	
three **and a half** [hɑ:f]	dreieinhalb	→ We'll leave in *two and a half* weeks.
on [ɒn]	an, eingeschaltet	→ The radio is *on*.
number ['nʌmbə]	Nummer; Zahl; Ziffer	→ Find a *number* between 1 and 9. – Five!
53 **charger** ['tʃɑ:dʒə]	(Batterie-)Ladegerät	
radiator ['reɪdieɪtə]	Heizkörper	
waste [weɪst]	verschwenden	
energy ['enədʒi]	Energie; Kraft	→ We shouldn't waste *energy*.
it's charged up [tʃɑ:dʒd'ʌp]	es ist aufgeladen	
save [seɪv]	sparen →	
environment [ɪn'vaɪrənmənt]	Umwelt; Umgebung	
present [prɪ'zent]	präsentieren	→ ! [prɪ'zent] präsentieren ['preznt] Geschenk

→ electric
electrician
electricity
electronic

→ **'ll** / **won't**
I'll / I won't
you'll / you won't
he'll / he won't
... / ...

→ a hundred
a thousand
a million

→ **save ...**
waste ...
electricity
energy
money
time
water

Story

54 **dare** [deə]	Mutprobe	
wet [wet]	nass, feucht	
railings ['reɪlɪŋz]	Geländer	
down [daʊn]	hinunter/herunter, hinab/herab	
Watch me! ['wɒtʃmi:]	Pass auf!	
***he took off** his jacket [tʊk'ɒf]	er zog seine Jacke aus	→ Linda never *takes off* her cap.
55 **he was worried (about)** ['wʌrid]	er machte sich Sorgen (um)	→ *I'm worried about* my dog. He looks ill.
slip [slɪp]	ausrutschen	→ I *slipped* on the wet road and hurt my hand.
scream [skri:m]	schreien	
face [feɪs]	Gesicht	
jump [dʒʌmp]	springen	→ We all *jumped* into the cold water.
ending ['endɪŋ]	Schluss	
brave [breɪv]	mutig, tapfer	→ ! Falscher Freund: *brave* = mutig (nicht: brav)

Training

57 **short** [ʃɔ:t]	kurz; klein →	
talk [tɔ:k]	Vortrag	

→ short - long
small - big
narrow - wide

	That's why ... ['ðætswaɪ]	Deshalb ..., Darum ...	→ It rained. *That's why* I stayed at home.
	To finish, ... [tə'fɪnɪʃ]	Um zum Ende zu kommen, ...	
	Firstly, ... ['fɜːstli]	Erstens ... →	
	***read out** [riːd'aʊt]	vorlesen, ablesen	

→ firstly secondly thirdly

Skills training

58	**instructions** [ɪn'strʌkʃnz]	Gebrauchsanweisung	→ I couldn't find the *instructions* ...
	machine [mə'ʃiːn]	Maschine, Gerät	
	seashell ['siːʃel]	Muschel	
	seashore ['siːʃɔː]	Küste, Strand	
	button ['bʌtn]	Taste; Knopf	→ If you push the red *button*, the machine will stop.
59	**offer** ['ɒfə]	**1** Angebot; **2** anbieten	
	Would you like ...? [wʊd]	Möchtest du/Möchten Sie ...?	→ *Would you like* a drink? – Yes, I'd like a cola, please.
	sandwich ['sænwɪtʃ]	Sandwich *(belegtes Brot)*	→ I always take two *sandwiches* to work.
	ham [hæm]	Schinken	
	cheese [tʃiːz]	Käse	
	show [ʃəʊ]	zeigen	→ Can you *show* me where the accident happened, please?
60	**exhibition** [eksɪ'bɪʃn]	Ausstellung	
61	**158 m = 158 metres** ['miːtəz]	158 Meter	→ ! one metre ['miːtə] – two metres
	floor [flɔː]	Fußboden, Boden	
	by [baɪ]	an, in der Nähe von, neben	
	10 a.m., 10 p.m. [eɪ'em, piː'em]	zehn Uhr morgens, zehn Uhr abends	→ The shop is open from *10 a.m.* to *8 p.m.*
	address [ə'dres]	Adresse	

Look at language

→ with - without

62	**work** [wɜːk]	funktionieren	
	without [wɪ'ðaʊt]	ohne →	→ The radio doesn't work *without* batteries.

* Irregular verbs

Infinitive form	Simple past form	Present perfect form
read [riːd]	I read [red]	I've read [red]
take [teɪk]	I took [tʊk]	I've taken ['teɪkən]
win [wɪn]	I won [wʌn]	I've won [wʌn]

Test yourself

1 Find the rhyme words and write them in your exercise book.

1 **my** [maɪ] – **eye**
2 **here** [hɪə] – ...
3 **chair** [tʃeə] – ...
4 **trip** [trɪp] – ...
5 **dream** [driːm] – ...
6 **more** [mɔː] – ...

2 Odd word out: One word isn't OK. Write it in your exercise book.

1 **funfair • railings • amusement arcade • roller coaster**
2 **seashell • pier • charger • seashore**
3 **face • ham • sandwich • cheese**
4 **machine • instructions • button • dare**

Hinweis:
Auf der nächsten Seite gibt es noch mehr Aufgaben.

Test yourself (Fortsetzung von S.144)

3 Write the plural forms of these words in your exercise book.
tower – towers • face – ... • machine – ... • sandwich – ... • metre – ...

4 Make sentences from these words and write them in your exercise book.
1 Sue – from – part – is – the – of – southern – England.
2 Mark – and – half – stay – three – for – will – a – weeks.
3 Tina – about – is – her – worried – cat.
4 The – 500 – from – school – about – metres – is – here.

Are your answers right? Check on page 181.

Unit 5

Lerntipp 5: Wortgruppen

Du behältst Wörter besser, wenn du sie in Gruppen lernst. Dabei ist es ganz egal, wie du die Gruppen bildest. Hier sind einige Beispiele:

- **Gleicher Anfang:** *electric - electrician - electricity - ...*
- **Gleiches Thema:** *save - waste - electricity - ...*
- **Einheiten:** *spring - summer - autumn - ...*
- **Ähnliches:** *friendly - polite - funny - ...*
- **Gegensätze:** *save - waste; indoors - ...*

Die blauen Kästen in diesem *Vocabulary* können dir Ideen geben.

Do you know these words?
aunt • brother • cousin • daughter • fast • father • grandad • grandma • hope • like • modern • mother • parents • sister • strict • sure • think • want

Test yourself
Write the lists in your exercise book.
a) Family: aunt, ..., ..., ..., ..., ..., ..., ..., ..., ...
b) Dreams: I hope, I'd ..., I'm ..., I ..., I ...
c) Descriptions: a ... house, ... parents, a ... runner

Are your answers right? Check on page 181.

Tipp:
Schau dir die Wörter in den oberen Reihen noch einmal an.

64	**Dubliner** ['dʌblɪnə]	Dubliner, Dublinerin	→ Katie is from Dublin, so she's a *Dubliner.*
	This is me.	Dies bin ich.	
	athletics [æθ'letɪks]	Leichtathletik	
	train [treɪn]	trainieren	
65	**kid** [kɪd]	Kind, Jugendliche/Jugendlicher	→ How many children go to the art club? – Oh, there are about 15 *kids,* I think.
	mobile home [məʊbaɪl'həʊm]	(Stand-)Wohnwagen	
	shopping centre ['ʃɒpɪŋsentə]	Einkaufszentrum →	
66	**future** ['fju:tʃə]	Zukunft	
	two years **ago** [ə'gəʊ]	vor zwei Jahren	→ I met Paul a week *ago.*
	(the) high jump ['haɪdʒʌmp]	Hochsprung	→ I'm good at *the high jump.*

→ **... centre**
shopping centre
sports centre
town centre

	***come third in ...**	Dritte/Dritter werden bei ...	→ I *came second in* the class quiz!
	travel ['trævl]	reisen, fahren	→ ! I travelled
	maybe ['meɪbi]	vielleicht	→ *Maybe* I'll come first in the competition.
	traveller ['trævələ]	Landfahrer/in; Reisende/r	
	in the same place	am selben Ort	
	stay for long	lange bleiben	
	somebody ['sʌmbədi]	jemand	→ There's *somebody* at the door.
	running ['rʌnɪŋ]	Laufen	
67	**result** [rɪ'zʌlt]	Ergebnis, Folge	

→ some
somebody
something
sometimes
somewhere

Story

68	**shy** [ʃaɪ]	schüchtern	
	***get on the team**	in die Mannschaft kommen	
	gym [dʒɪm]	Turnhalle, Fitnessstudio	
	track [træk]	Bahn, Laufbahn	
	one day	eines Tages	
	worry (about) ['wʌri]	sich Sorgen machen (um)	→ Don't *worry about* us, Dad. We're OK now.
	furniture ['fɜ:nɪtʃə]	Möbel	
	***mean** [mi:n]	meinen; bedeuten	→ The word 'kid' *means* 'child' or 'teenager'.
	suburb ['sʌbɜ:b]	Vorort	
69	**The next Saturday ...**	Am nächsten Samstag ...	
	must [mʌst]	müssen	→ You *must* be careful.
	a busy road ['bɪsi]	eine viel befahrene Straße	
	they were playing	sie spielten (gerade)	
	he was watching	er beobachtete (gerade)	
	devastated ['devəsteɪtɪd]	erschüttert, am Boden zerstört	
	really ['ri:əli]	wirklich, eigentlich	→ Tell me what *really* happened!
	diary ['daɪəri]	Tagebuch	

→ **must**
I must
you must
he must
...

Revision

71	**noun** [naʊn]	Nomen	→ 'sing' is a verb, but 'singer' is a *noun*.

Skills training

72	**I agree (with you).** [ə'gri:]	Ich stimme (dir) zu. Ich bin derselben Meinung (wie du).	→ Holidays are boring. – I don't *agree*! I think holidays are fun.
	bullying ['bʊliɪŋ]	Schikanieren, Mobbing	
	true [tru:]	wahr	→ Is it *true* that you're leaving?
	bully ['bʊli]	Tyrann/in, „Mobber/in"	→ He's a *terrible* bully.
	tongue twister ['tʌŋtwɪstə]	Zungenbrecher	
	whether ['weðə]	ob	
	hot [hɒt]	heiß	
	whatever the weather [wɒt'evə]	egal, wie das Wetter ist	→ I think he looks great, *whatever* he's wearing.
73	we aren't **welcome** ['welkəm]	wir sind nicht willkommen	→ Can Tina stay at our house? – Of course. Tina is always *welcome*.
74	**Northern Ireland**	Nordirland	
75	**whale** [weɪl]	Wal	→
	cliff [klɪf]	Klippe, Felsen	

→ cold
warm
hot

→ rock
cliff
hill
mountain

Look at language

76	**hurling** ['hɜ:lɪŋ]	Hurling *(irische Sportart)*	

dolphin ['dɒlfɪn]	Delfin
high [haɪ]	hoch
Irish ['aɪrɪʃ]	irisch; Irisch; Ire(n), Irin(nen) →
Viking ['vaɪkɪŋ]	Wikinger, Wikinger-

→ The *Vikings* wore special helmets.

→ **They're …**
British
English
Irish
Scottish
Welsh

* Irregular verbs

Infinitive form	Simple past form	Present perfect form
come [kʌm]	I came [keɪm]	I've come [kʌm]
get [get]	I got [gɒt]	I've got [gɒt]
mean [mi:n]	I meant [ment]	I've meant [ment]

Test yourself

1 [eɪ]: Which 4 words have the sound [eɪ] in them? Write them in your exercise book.
devastated • high • maybe • mean • shy • train • travel • whale

2 Find and write in your exercise book:
1 a place with lots of shops
2 a part of a city
3 a word for 'very warm'
4 two sea animals
5 three sports

Tipp:
Schau dir die vorangegangenen Wortlisten gut an.

3 Find 4 words for people. Write them in your exercise book.
Dublin – Dubliner • travel – … • bullying – … • Ireland – the …

4 Make sentences from these words and write them in your exercise book.
1 in – I – third – the – came – competition.
2 know – really – happened. – I – don't – what
3 don't – agree – you. – with – I
4 you're – true – it – is – that – ill?

Are your answers right? Check on page 181.

Unit 6

Do you know these words?
agree • breakfast • cups • drinks • food • glasses • like • lunch • right • sandwiches • think • true

Test yourself
Write the lists in your exercise book.
a) *Im Café:* breakfast, …, …, …, …, …, …
b) *Meinungen äußern:* I agree, I …, I …, You're …, That's …

Are your answers right? Check on page 181.

Tipp:
Schau dir die Wörter in den oberen Reihen noch einmal an.

78 *Cornish* ['kɔ:nɪʃ]	kornisch, aus Cornwall
furthest ['fɜ:θɪst]	am weitesten (entfernt)
painting ['peɪntɪŋ]	Malen
sailing ['seɪlɪŋ]	Segeln

	sunbathing ['sʌnbeɪðɪŋ]	Sonnenbaden	
79	*tattoo* [tə'tuː]	Tätowierung, Tattoo	
	sticker ['stɪkə]	Aufkleber	
	real ['riːəl]	echt, richtig	
80	*over there* [əʊvə'ðeə]	da drüben, dort drüben	→ Penny? She's *over there.*
	Give me a break!	Hör doch auf!	
	clothes *like this* [laɪk'ðɪs]	solche Kleidung	→ I've never seen a dog *like this*!
	I hadn't thought of that.	Daran hatte ich nicht gedacht. →	
	to sell our pictures	um unsere Bilder zu verkaufen	
81	*pasty* ['pæsti]	Pastete	
	200 g = 200 grams [græmz]	200 Gramm	
	butter ['bʌtə]	Butter	
	beef [biːf]	Rindfleisch	→ I like chicken, but I don't like *beef.*
	carrot ['kærət]	Karotte, Möhre	→ 
	potato, potatoes [pə'teɪtəʊ, pə'teɪtəʊz]	Kartoffel, Kartoffeln	
	salt [sɔːlt]	Salz	
	pepper ['pepə]	Pfeffer	
	175 ml = 175 millilitres ['mɪliliːtəz]	175 Milliliter	
	flour ['flaʊə]	Mehl	
	onion ['ʌniən]	Zwiebel →	
	pastry ['peɪstri]	Teig	→ ! pastry ['peɪstri] / pasty ['pæsti]
	mix [mɪks]	mischen	
	roll out [rəʊl'aʊt]	ausrollen	
	cut [kʌt]	schneiden →	
	round a plate [raʊnd, pleɪt]	um einen Teller herum	
	time [taɪm]	Mal	→ I tried three *times*, but he didn't answer. ! three times [dreimal]
	bake [beɪk]	backen	
	220° C = 220 degrees Celsius [dɪ'griːz, 'selsiəs]	220 Grad Celsius →	
	menu ['menjuː]	Speisekarte	→ Can I see the *menu*, please?

→ I **had** thought – I **hadn't** thought
he **had** talked – he **hadn't** talked

→ think – I thought – I've/I had thought

→ **Vegetables**
carrots
leeks
onions
potatoes

→ cut – I cut – I've/I had cut

→ **100 ...s**
millilitres
grams
metres
kilometres
miles
degrees
euros
pounds

Story

82	*notice* ['nəʊtɪs]	bemerken	
	self-service [self'sɜːvɪs]	Selbstbedienung	
	cutlery ['kʌtləri]	Besteck	
	knife, knives [naɪf, naɪvz]	Messer	
	fork [fɔːk]	Gabel	
	spoon [spuːn]	Löffel →	
	busy ['bɪzi]	beschäftigt; hektisch, belebt	→ I can't come. I'm too *busy.*
	they had gone [gɒn]	sie waren gegangen →	
	paint [peɪnt]	malen	
	they made money from the tourists	sie verdienten Geld an den Touristen	
83	*A short time after* she had gone in, ...	Kurz nachdem sie hineingegangen war, ...	→ *After* I had told her the news, she started to cry.

→ **Cutlery**
knife
fork
spoon

→ go – I went – I've/I had gone

Training

85	*try on* [traɪ'ɒn]	anprobieren	→ I *tried on* as many clothes as possible!
	What size does she take? [saɪz]	Welche Größe hat sie?	
	changing room ['tʃeɪndʒɪŋruːm]	Umkleidekabine	
	mirror ['mɪrə]	Spiegel	
	a kind of book [kaɪnd]	eine Art Buch	
	flip-flop ['flɪpflɒp]	Flipflop *(eine Art Badesandale mit Zehensteg)*	→ *flip-flops*

Skills training

86	*conversation* [kɒnvə'seɪʃn]	Gespräch, Unterhaltung	
	bed and breakfast (B and B) [bedən'brekfəst, biːən'biː]	Zimmer mit Frühstück (in kleiner Frühstückspension)	→ We stayed at a great *B and B* in Chester.
87	*Helping visitors*	Gästen helfen	
	library ['laɪbrəri]	Bücherei	→ I always get my books from the *library*.
	building ['bɪldɪŋ]	Gebäude	
	You can't miss it. [mɪs]	Sie können es nicht übersehen.	
	You're welcome. [jɔː'welkəm]	Nichts zu danken; Bitte schön.	→ Thanks for your help. – *You're welcome.*
	opposite ['ɒpəzɪt]	gegenüber (vom)	→ Our house is *opposite* the shop.
88	*smuggler* ['smʌglə]	Schmuggler, Schmugglerin	
	I drove [drəʊv]	ich fuhr →	→ drive - I drove - I've/I had driven
89	*smuggling* ['smʌglɪŋ]	Schmuggel, Schmuggeln	
	do a course [kɔːs]	einen Kurs machen	

Look at language

90	*spend: they had spent* [spend, spent]	verbringen: sie hatten verbracht →	→ spend - I spent - I've/I had spent
	I had forgotten [fə'gɒtn]	ich hatte vergessen →	→ forget - I forgot - I've/I had forgotten
	under 18s [ʌndəreɪ'tiːnz]	unter 18-Jährige	
91	*past perfect* [pɑːst'pɜːfɪkt]	Vorvergangenheit	
	past participle [pɑːstpɑː'tɪsɪpl]	Partizip Perfekt	

Test yourself

1 Write the words in your exercise book and find the third word.

1 **Scottish • Welsh • Cornish**
2 **fork • spoon • ...**
3 **clothes • changing room • ...**
4 **shoes • trainers • ...**

Tipp: Schau dir die vorangegangenen Wortlisten gut an.

2 Odd word out: One word isn't OK. Write it in your exercise book.

1 **sailing • building • painting • sunbathing**
2 **sandwich • pasty • flour • cake**
3 **onion • potato • carrot • beef**
4 **fork • mix • bake • cut**

3 Find the partners and write them in your exercise book.

nearest – furthest • salt – ... • restaurant – ... • book – ... • police officer – ...

Are your answers right? Check on page 181.

Extra Practice · Unit 1

93	*gun* [gʌn]	Gewehr
94	*camera* ['kæmrə]	Kamera, Fotoapparat →

→ camera
film
photo

Extra Practice · Unit 2

96	*kill* [kɪl]	umbringen
97	*dancing* ['dɑːnsɪŋ]	Tanzen →
98	*audition* [ɔː'dɪʃn]	Vorsprechen
	kiss [kɪs]	Kuss →
	download [daʊn'ləʊd]	herunterladen
	spend on	ausgeben für

→ dance
dancing
go dancing

→ kiss
love
married

Extra Practice · Unit 3

101	*table* ['teɪbl]	Tabelle
102	*penfriend* ['penfrend]	Brieffreund, Brieffreundin →
	go out [gəʊ'aʊt]	ausgehen, weggehen

→ card
e-mail
letter
pen
penfriend

Extra Practice · Unit 4

105	*future* ['fjuːtʃə]	Zukunft
	still [stɪl]	(immer) noch
106	*visit* ['vɪzɪt]	Besuch
	stadium ['steɪdiəm]	Stadion →

→ **Football**
ball
fan
match
player
stadium
team
trainer

Extra Practice · Unit 5

109	*loudly* ['laʊdli]	laut
	stand on somebody's foot	jemandem auf den Fuß treten
	smoke [sməʊk]	rauchen
110	*real* ['riːəl]	echt, richtig →

→ right
real
really
true

Extra Practice · Unit 6

112	*he was thirsty* ['θɜːsti]	er hatte Durst →
	I had lost [lɒst]	ich hatte verloren
	clean [kliːn]	sauber machen, putzen
113	*take out* [teɪk'aʊt]	herausnehmen
	ring [rɪŋ]	Ring
114	*meaning* ['miːnɪŋ]	Bedeutung
	waitress ['weɪtrəs]	Kellnerin
115	*pattern* ['pætn]	Muster

→ Hungry? Eat!
Thirsty? Drink!
Tired? Sleep!
Sad? Laugh!
Bored? Play a game!
Lonely? Meet friends!

Alphabetische Liste der Wörter aus den Bänden 1–3 (Englisch – Deutsch)

mit Fundstellenangaben für den Lernwortschatz aus Band 3, z. B.
H&T: 6 = Here and there, S. 6 oder U2: 24 = Unit 2, S. 24

WF (wahlfrei): nicht zum Lernwortschatz gehörende Wörter
RD U1/...: Abschnitt „Reading" in Unit 1/...
→ verweist auf die Grundform eines Wortes

A

a [ə] ein, eine; **she's a bus driver** sie ist Busfahrerin; **24 hours a day** 24 Stunden am/pro Tag
about [ə'baʊt] **1** über; **The text is about ...** Der Text handelt von ...; **What about you?** Und du?/Was ist mit dir? **2** ungefähr
accident ['æksɪdənt] Unfall
across [ə'krɒs] über; hinüber, herüber
act [ækt]: **Act the dialogue.** Spielt das Gespräch nach.
action film ['ækʃnfɪlm] Actionfilm
activity [æk'tɪvəti] Beschäftigung, Aktivität
actor ['æktə] Schauspieler, Schauspielerin U2: 24
address [ə'dres] Adresse U4: 61
adult ['ædʌlt] Erwachsene/r U1: 17
advert ['ædvɜ:t] Anzeige
aerobics [eə'rəʊbɪks] Aerobic WF
afraid [ə'freɪd]: **I'm afraid ...** Leider ... U2: 31
Africa ['æfrɪkə] Afrika U1: 12
after ['ɑ:ftə] **1** nach; **after school** nach der Schule; **after a ball** hinter einem Ball her; **2** nachdem WF U6
afternoon ['ɑ:ftə'nu:n] Nachmittag; **in the afternoon** am Nachmittag, nachmittags
again [ə'gen] noch einmal, (schon) wieder
age [eɪdʒ] Alter U2: 24; **she was the right age** sie hatte das richtige Alter WF
ago [ə'gəʊ]: **a long time ago** vor langer Zeit WF; **two years ago** vor zwei Jahren U5: 66
agree [ə'gri:]: **I agree (with you).** Ich stimme (dir) zu. Ich bin derselben Meinung (wie du). U5: 72
airport ['eəpɔ:t] Flughafen; **at Exeter Airport** am Flughafen Exeter
alarm clock [ə'lɑ:mklɒk] Wecker WF
Albanian [æl'beɪniən] Albanisch WF
alcohol ['ælkəhɒl] Alkohol U3: 41
all (the) [ɔ:l] alle; **all weekend** das ganze Wochenende
alone [ə'ləʊn] allein
along [ə'lɒŋ] entlang
alphabet ['ælfəbet] Alphabet
alphabetical [ælfə'betɪkl] alphabetisch
always ['ɔ:lweɪz] immer
a.m. [eɪ'em] morgens, vormittags U4: 61
am [æm] bin; **I'm (= I am) Sarah.** Ich heiße Sarah. **I'm from London.** Ich komme aus London. **How are you? – I'm fine, thanks.** Wie geht's? – Danke, gut. **Are you ...? – Yes, I am./No, I'm not.** Bist du ...? – Ja./Nein.
amazing [ə'meɪzɪŋ] erstaunlich RD U5
amusement arcade [ə'mju:zməntɑ:keɪd] Spielhalle U4: 51
an [ən] ein, eine
and [ænd, ənd] und
angry (with) ['æŋgri] böse, wütend (auf) U2: 27
animal ['ænɪml] Tier
ankle ['æŋkl] Knöchel, Fußgelenk WF
another [ə'nʌðə] **1** noch ein, eine, einer, eins; **2** ein anderer/anderes, eine andere U1: 12
answer ['ɑ:nsə] **1** antworten, beantworten; **2** Antwort
any ['eni]: **not ... any** kein, keine U1: 10
anything ['eniθɪŋ]: **not ... anything** nichts U3: 38
anywhere ['eniweə]: **not ... anywhere** nirgendwo, nirgendwohin, nirgendwoher
apple ['æpl] Apfel
April ['eɪprəl] April
Arabic ['ærəbɪk] Arabisch WF
are [ɑ:] bist; seid; sind; **aren't (= are not)** bist/seid/sind nicht; **How are you?** Wie geht's? **What are they in German?** Wie heißen sie auf Deutsch?
area ['eəriə] Gegend
arguing ['ɑ:gju:ɪŋ] Streiten WF
arm [ɑ:m] Arm
around [ə'raʊnd]: **around the world** um die Welt WF
arrangement [ə'reɪndʒmənt] Absprache U2: 31; **make an arrangement** eine Absprache treffen U2: 31
arrive [ə'raɪv] ankommen
art [ɑ:t] Kunst
article ['ɑ:tɪkl] Artikel U2: 24
arts and crafts [ɑ:tsənd'krɑ:fts] Kunsthandwerk WF
as [æz, əz]: **as soon as** sobald WF
Asia ['eɪʃə] Asien U1: 12
Asian ['eɪʃn] asiatisch; Asiat, Asiatin U1: 10
ask [ɑ:sk] fragen; **ask a question** eine Frage stellen; **ask for** bitten um U1: 16
asking ['ɑ:skɪŋ]: **Asking for help** Um Hilfe bitten U1: 16
asleep [ə'sli:p]: **fall asleep** einschlafen WF
assistant [ə'sɪstənt]: **shop assistant** Verkäufer, Verkäuferin
at [æt, ət] bei; an; in; **at eight o'clock** um acht/zwanzig Uhr; **at Exeter Station** im Bahnhof Exeter; **at home** zu Hause, daheim; **at night** nachts, in der Nacht U1: 20; **at the moment** zurzeit, im Moment 1: 10; **at the weekend** am Wochenende; **she's at school** sie ist in der Schule; sie geht zur Schule
athletics [æθ'letɪks] Leichtathletik U5: 64
Atlantic [ət'læntɪk] Atlantik RD U5
attention [ə'tenʃn]: **pay attention** aufpassen WF
audition [ɔ:'dɪʃn] Vorsprechen WF
August ['ɔ:gəst] August; **August 20th** 20. August
aunt [ɑ:nt] Tante U1: 10
Austria ['ɒstriə] Österreich
autograph ['ɔ:təgrɑ:f] Autogramm
autumn ['ɔ:təm] Herbst U3: 38
away [ə'weɪ]: **take away** wegnehmen WF

B

baby ['beɪbi] Baby WF; **baby boy** kleiner Junge WF
back [bæk] **1** zurück; **back from school** aus der Schule zurück; **I'm back!** Ich bin wieder da! **at the back of the book** hinten im Buch H&T: 6; **2** Rücken WF
backflip ['bækflɪp] einen Salto rückwärts machen WF
bacon ['beɪkən] Speck WF
bad [bæd] schlecht; schlimm
badminton ['bædmɪntən] Badminton, Federball(spiel)
bag [bæg] (Schul-)Tasche
baggage handler ['bægɪdʒhændlə] Gepäckabfertiger/in
bake [beɪk] backen WF U6
ball [bɔ:l] Ball
banana [bə'nɑ:nə] Banane
band [bænd] Band, (Musik-)Gruppe
bank [bæŋk] Bank, Sparkasse
basketball ['bɑ:skɪtbɔ:l] Basketball
bathroom ['bɑ:θru:m] Badezimmer, Bad
be [bi:, bi] (I/he was, you were; I've been) sein
beach [bi:tʃ] Strand
beautiful ['bju:tɪfl] schön, wunderschön U3: 47
became [bɪ'keɪm] (→ become): **I became** ich wurde, ich bin geworden U2: 24
because [bɪ'kɒz] weil
become [bɪ'kʌm] (I became, I've become) werden U2: 24; **I've become** ich bin geworden U2: 139
bed [bed] Bett
bed and breakfast (B and B) [bedən'brekfəst, bi:ən'bi] Zimmer mit Frühstück *(in kleiner Frühstückspension)* WF U6
bedroom ['bedru:m] Schlafzimmer
beef [bi:f] Rindfleisch WF U6
been [bi:n, bɪn] (→ be): **I've been** ich bin gewesen
beer [bɪə] Bier H&T: 6
before [bɪ'fɔ:] bevor
behind [bɪ'haɪnd] hinter
being ['bi:ɪŋ]: **it isn't fun being angry** es macht keinen Spaß, wütend zu sein WF
Belgium ['beldʒəm] Belgien
best [best] beste, bester, bestes; am besten U1: 11; **Best wishes, ...** Viele Grüße ...
better ['betə] besser
big [bɪg] groß
bike [baɪk] Fahrrad, Rad
bird [bɜ:d] Vogel
birthday ['bɜ:θdeɪ] Geburtstag; **It's my birthday.** Ich habe Geburtstag.
black [blæk] schwarz
blog [blɒg] Blog *(von Weblog; hier eine Art Online-Tagebuch)* U3: 38
blogger ['blɒgə] Blogger, Bloggerin *(Autor/in eines Blogs)* U5: 71
blogging ['blɒgɪŋ] Bloggen *(ein Blog führen und auf andere Blogs reagieren)* U3: 38
blonde [blɒnd] blond
blood [blʌd] Blut WF
blue [blu:] blau
board [bɔ:d] **1** Tafel; **2** Board, Brett U3: 48
boat [bəʊt] Boot; Schiff U1: 17
bomb [bɒm] Bombe WF
book [bʊk] Buch; Heft
bookshop ['bʊkʃɒp] Buchladen, Buchhandlung
border ['bɔ:də] Grenze H&T: 6
bored [bɔ:d] gelangweilt U4: 52; **I'm bored** ich langweile mich U4: 52
boring ['bɔ:rɪŋ] langweilig
born [bɔ:n]: **I was born ...** ich wurde ... geboren U2: 25
borrow ['bɒrəʊ]: **borrow a pen** sich einen Füller (aus)leihen
Bosnian ['bɒzniən] Bosnisch WF
both [bəʊθ] beide WF
bottom ['bɒtəm] Hintern, Po WF
bought [bɔ:t] (→ buy): **I bought** ich kaufte, ich habe gekauft; **I've bought** ich habe gekauft
bowling ['bəʊlɪŋ] Bowling WF
box [bɒks] Kiste, Kasten
boxing ['bɒksɪŋ] Boxen WF
boy [bɔɪ] Junge
boyfriend ['bɔɪfrend] (fester) Freund WF
brave [breɪv] mutig, tapfer U4: 55
bread [bred] Brot H&T: 6
break [breɪk] Pause; **Give me a break!** Hör doch auf! WF U6
breakfast ['brekfəst] Frühstück; **have breakfast** frühstücken
bridge [brɪdʒ] Brücke
bring [brɪŋ] (I brought, I've brought) bringen
Britain ['brɪtn] Großbritannien H&T: 6
brochure ['brəʊʃə] Broschüre
brother ['brʌðə] Bruder; **brothers and sisters** Geschwister
brown [braʊn] braun
buddy ['bʌdi] „Kumpel" *(ältere/r Schüler/in, der/die jüngeren hilft)*
building ['bɪldɪŋ] Gebäude WF U6
bully ['bʊli] Tyrann, „Mobber/in" U5: 72
bullying ['bʊliɪŋ] Schikanieren, Mobbing U5: 72; **text bullying** SMS-Terror U3: 44
bus [bʌs] Bus
bus driver ['bʌsdraɪvə] Busfahrer, Busfahrerin
bus stop ['bʌstɒp] Bushaltestelle U3: 37
business ['bɪznəs] Betrieb, Geschäft(s-) U3: 38
busy ['bɪzi] beschäftigt; hektisch, belebt WF U6; **a busy road** eine viel befahrene Straße U5: 69
but [bʌt] aber
butter ['bʌtə] Butter WF U6
butterfly ['bʌtəflaɪ] Schmetterling WF
button ['bʌtn] Knopf; Taste U4: 58
buy [baɪ] (I bought, I've bought) kaufen
by [baɪ] **1** an, in der Nähe von, neben U4: 61; **2** von; durch; **by bike/bus/car/...** mit dem Rad/Bus/Auto/...; **by his arms** an den Armen; **Learn it by heart.** Lerne es auswendig.
Bye. [baɪ] Tschüs. Wiedersehen.

C

cafe ['kæfeɪ] Café
cake [keɪk] Kuchen
calf [kɑ:f] Wade WF
calling ['kɔ:lɪŋ]: **Thanks for calling.** Danke für den Anruf.
came [keɪm] (→ come): **I came** ich kam, ich bin gekommen
camera ['kæmrə] Kamera, Fotoapparat WF
camping ['kæmpɪŋ] Camping
can [kæn, kən] können, dürfen; **can't** [kɑ:nt] nicht können; **Can you ...? - Yes, I can./No, I can't.** Kannst du ...? - Ja./Nein.
canal [kə'næl] Kanal
canoe [kə'nu:] Kanu
canoeing [kə'nu:ɪŋ] Kanu fahren, Paddeln
cap [kæp] Kappe
capital ['kæpɪtl] Hauptstadt H&T: 6
car [kɑ:] Auto
card [kɑ:d] Karte

care [keə] sich interessieren WF

careful ['keəfl] vorsichtig U3: 48

carnival ['kɑ:nɪvl] Karneval U2: 33

carol ['kærəl]: **Christmas carol** Weihnachtslied WF

car park ['kɑ:pɑ:k] (großer) Parkplatz

carrot ['kærət] Karotte, Möhre WF U6

castle ['kɑ:sl] Schloss; Burg U2: 24

cat [kæt] Katze

cave [keɪv] Höhle RD U6

CD [si:'di:] CD

centre ['sentə] Zentrum; Mitte

century ['sentʃəri] Jahrhundert RD U6

chair [tʃeə] Stuhl; Sessel

chairperson ['tʃeəpɜ:sn] Vorsitzende, Vorsitzender

change [tʃeɪndʒ] (sich) ändern, (sich) verändern

changing room ['tʃeɪndʒɪŋru:m] Umkleidekabine, Anprobe WF U6

character ['kærəktə] Figur, Person WF

charged up [tʃɑ:dʒd'ʌp]: **it's charged up** es ist aufgeladen U4: 53

charger ['tʃɑ:dʒə] (Batterie-)Ladegerät U4: 53

chat [tʃæt] sich unterhalten WF; **have a chat** sich unterhalten U1: 12

cheap [tʃi:p] billig, preiswert

check [tʃek] kontrollieren, überprüfen

cheese [tʃi:z] Käse U4: 59

chess [tʃes] Schach WF

chest [tʃest] Brust WF

chicken ['tʃɪkɪn] Huhn; (Brat-)Hähnchen

child, children [tʃaɪld, 'tʃɪldrən] Kind, Kinder

Chinese [tʃaɪ'ni:z] Chinesisch WF

chips [tʃɪps] Pommes frites

chocolate ['tʃɒklət] Schokolade

Christmas ['krɪsməs] Weihnachten U3: 43

Christmas Eve [krɪsməs'i:v] Heiligabend WF

church [tʃɜ:tʃ] Kirche U3: 36

cider ['saɪdə] Apfelwein U3: 41

cinema ['sɪnəmə] Kino

city ['sɪti] Stadt, Großstadt U1: 9

class [klɑ:s] Klasse

classroom ['klɑ:sru:m] Klassenzimmer

class teacher ['klɑ:sti:tʃə] Klassenlehrer, Klassenlehrerin

clean [kli:n] **1** sauber U3: 47; **2** sauber machen, putzen WF U6

cliff [klɪf] Klippe, Felsen U5: 75

climb (a hill) [klaɪm] (auf einen Hügel) klettern

climber ['klaɪmə] Kletterer, Kletterin

close [kləʊz] zumachen, schließen

closed [kləʊzd] geschlossen, zu

clothes [kləʊðz] Kleidung, Kleider

cloud [klaʊd] Wolke

cloudy ['klaʊdi] bewölkt

club [klʌb] **1** Klub; Arbeitsgemeinschaft; Verein; **2** Disko U1: 20

coast [kəʊst] Küste RD U5

cola ['kəʊlə] Cola

cold [kəʊld] kalt

collage ['kɒlɑ:ʒ] Collage WF

collect [kə'lekt] sammeln

collection [kə'lekʃn] Sammlung RD U4

colour ['kʌlə] Farbe; **What colour is your room?** Welche Farbe hat dein Zimmer?

come [kʌm] (I came, I've come) kommen; mitkommen; **I've come** ich bin gekommen U2: 147; **come in** hereinkommen; **come first in ...** Erste/r werden bei ... U5: 66

comedy ['kɒmədi] Komödie WF

comic ['kɒmɪk] Comic WF

compare [kəm'peə] vergleichen H&T: 6

competition [kɒmpə'tɪʃn] Wettbewerb U2: 26

complain [kəm'pleɪn] sich beschweren

complete [kəm'pli:t] vollständig U2: 25

computer [kəm'pju:tə] Computer, Rechner

Congratulations! [kəngrætʃu'leɪʃnz] Herzlichen Glückwunsch! U2: 26

conversation [kɒnvə'seɪʃn] Gespräch, Unterhaltung WF U6

cook [kʊk] Koch, Köchin

cooker ['kʊkə] Herd WF

cool [ku:l] **1** cool, toll; **2** kühl WF

copy ['kɒpi] abschreiben WF

Cornish ['kɔ:nɪʃ] kornisch, aus Cornwall WF U6

correct [kə'rekt] korrigieren, berichtigen U3: 48

could [kʊd]: **I could(n't)** ich konnte (nicht) U3: 40

country ['kʌntri] Land; **country music** Countrymusik WF; **in the country** auf dem Land

courier ['kʊriə] Kurier/Kurierin, Bote/Botin

course [kɔ:s] Kurs WF U6; **do a course** einen Kurs machen WF U6; **of course** natürlich, selbstverständlich

cousin ['kʌzn] Cousin, Cousine

cow [kaʊ] Kuh

crash [kræʃ] zerschellen RD U6

crawl (in) [krɔ:l] (hinein-)kriechen

credit ['kredɪt] Guthaben U3: 44

crisps [krɪsps] Kartoffelchips

Croatian [krəʊ'eɪʃn] Kroatisch WF

cry [kraɪ] weinen U2: 26

crystal ['krɪstl] kristallklar RD U3

cucumber ['kju:kʌmbə] Gurke WF

cup [kʌp] Tasse; **a cup of tea** eine Tasse Tee

cupboard ['kʌbəd] Schrank

cut [kʌt] schneiden WF U6

cutlery ['kʌtləri] Besteck WF U6

cycling ['saɪklɪŋ] Radfahren

cyclist ['saɪklɪst] Radfahrer, Radfahrerin WF

Czech Republic [tʃekrɪ'pʌblɪk] Tschechische Republik

D

dad [dæd] Papa, Vati

dance [dɑ:ns] tanzen U1: 20

dancing ['dɑ:nsɪŋ] Tanzen WF; **go dancing** tanzen gehen

dangerous ['deɪndʒərəs] gefährlich

dare [deə] Mutprobe U4: 54

dark [dɑ:k] dunkel RD U1

date [deɪt] Datum

daughter ['dɔ:tə] Tochter

day [deɪ] Tag

dead [ded] tot WF

deal [di:l]: **deal with bags** sich um Taschen kümmern

dear [dɪə]: **Dear ...** Liebe/Lieber ...

December [dɪ'sembə] Dezember

decorations [dekə'reɪʃnz]: **Christmas decorations** Weihnachtsschmuck WF

degree [dɪ'gri:] Grad WF U6

Denmark ['denmɑ:k] Dänemark

department store [dɪ'pɑ:tməntstɔ:] Kaufhaus

description [dɪ'skrɪpʃn] Beschreibung

detective [dɪ'tektɪv] Detektiv, Detektivin U1: 16

detention [dɪ'tenʃn] Nachsitzen WF

devastated ['devəsteɪtɪd] erschüttert, am Boden zerstört U5: 69

dialogue ['daɪəlɒg] Dialog, Gespräch
diary ['daɪəri] Tagebuch; **homework diary** Hausaufgabenheft; Schülerkalender
dictionary ['dɪkʃənri] Wörterbuch; Wörterverzeichnis
did [dɪd] (→ do): **I did** ich machte, ich habe gemacht
die [daɪ] sterben U2: 25
different ['dɪfrənt] verschieden; anders; andere, anderer, anderes; **different from** anders als
dinner ['dɪnə]: **Christmas dinner** Weihnachts(fest)essen WF
dirty ['dɜ:ti] schmutzig
disappear [dɪsə'pɪə] verschwinden WF
disappointed [dɪsə'pɔɪntɪd] enttäuscht WF
discus ['dɪskəs] Diskus(werfen) WF
dishwasher ['dɪʃwɒʃə] Geschirrspülmaschine WF
dislike [dɪs'laɪk] Abneigung U2: 30
display [dɪ'spleɪ] Bildschirmdarstellung RD U4
distant ['dɪstənt] geistesabwesend WF
DJ ['di:dʒəɪ] DJ (= Discjockey)
do [du:] (he does; I did, I've done) **1** tun, machen; schaffen; **2** **I don't (= do not)/He doesn't (= does not) live here.** Ich wohne/Er wohnt nicht hier. **Do you/Does he live here? - Yes, I do./No, I don't. / Yes, he does./No, he doesn't.** Wohnst du/Wohnt er hier? - Ja./Nein. **Don't eat.** Iss nicht.
doctor ['dɒktə] Doktor RD U4
does [dʌz] → do
dog [dɒg] Hund
doing ['du:ɪŋ]: **What are you doing?** Was machst du (da)?
dolphin ['dɒlfɪn] Delfin U5: 76
done [dʌn] (→ do): **I've done** ich habe gemacht; **now that it's done** nun, wo es fertig ist WF
door [dɔ:] Tür
down [daʊn] hinunter/herunter, hinab/herab U4: 54
download [daʊn'ləʊd] herunterladen WF
dragon ['drægən] Drache WF
drama ['drɑ:mə] Schauspiel, Drama WF
drank [dræŋk] (→ drink): **I drank** ich trank, ich habe getrunken
draw [drɔ:] (I drew, I've drawn) zeichnen
dream [dri:m] **1** träumen; **2** Traum
drink [drɪŋk] **1** (I drink, I've drunk) trinken; **2** Getränk
drive [draɪv] (I drove, I've driven) fahren
driver ['draɪvə] (Auto-)Fahrer/in
drop [drɒp] fallen lassen RD U2
drop by [drɒp'baɪ] vorbeischauen WF
drove [drəʊv]: **I drove** ich fuhr, ich bin gefahren WF U6
Dubliner ['dʌblɪnə] Dubliner, Dublinerin U5: 64
DVD [di:vi:'di:] DVD
DVD player [di:vi:'di:pleɪə] DVD-Player U4: 56

E

each [i:tʃ] jede/jeder/jedes WF
ear [ɪə] Ohr WF
early ['ɜ:li] früh
east [i:st] Osten; Ost-; östlich H&T: 7
easy ['i:zi] einfach, leicht
eat [i:t] (I ate, I've eaten) essen; fressen
egg [eg] Ei WF
electric [ɪ'lektrɪk] elektrisch U4: 52
electricity [ɪlek'trɪsəti] Strom, Elektrizität U4: 51
electronic [ɪlek'trɒnɪk] elektronisch
e-mail ['i:meɪl] E-Mail
embarrassed [ɪm'bærəst] verlegen U2: 27
end [end] **1** enden WF; **2** Ende WF; **in the end** letztendlich; schließlich U3: 47
ending ['endɪŋ] Schluss U4: 55
enemy ['enəmi] Feind/in RD U4
energy ['enədʒi] Energie; Kraft U4: 53
England ['ɪŋglənd] England
English ['ɪŋglɪʃ] englisch; Englisch; Engländer, Engländerin(nen); **English teacher** Englischlehrer, Englischlehrerin
enjoy [ɪn'dʒɔɪ] genießen WF
environment [ɪn'vaɪrənmənt] Umwelt; Umgebung U4: 53
euro (€) ['jʊərəʊ] Euro
Europe ['jʊərəp] Europa H&T: 6
evening ['i:vnɪŋ] Abend; **in the evening** am Abend, abends
ever ['evə] schon einmal, jemals
every ['evri] jede, jeder, jedes
everybody ['evribɒdi] jeder, alle
everything ['evriθɪŋ] alles U2: 26
everywhere ['evriweə] überall, überallhin, überallher
example [ɪg'zɑ:mpl] Beispiel
exciting [ɪk'saɪtɪŋ] aufregend, spannend
excuse [ɪk'skju:z]: **Excuse me, ...** Entschuldigen Sie, ... U1: 16
exercise ['eksəsaɪz] Übung
exercise book ['eksəsaɪzbʊk] Schulheft
exhibition [eksɪ'bɪʃn] Ausstellung U4: 60
expensive [ɪk'spensɪv] teuer
explain [ɪk'spleɪn] erklären
eye [aɪ] Auge U4: 50

F

face [feɪs] Gesicht U4: 55; **come face to face with them** ihnen gegenüberstehen RD U4
fact [fækt]: **In fact, it was better.** Es war sogar besser.
factory ['fæktri] Fabrik
fall [fɔ:l] (I fell, I've fallen) fallen; hinfallen RD U2; **fall asleep** einschlafen WF; **fall to the ground** auf den Boden fallen
family ['fæməli] Familie
famous ['feɪməs] berühmt H&T: 6
fan [fæn] Fan, Anhänger/in
fantastic [fæn'tæstɪk] fantastisch RD U2
farm [fɑ:m] Bauernhof, Hof
farmer ['fɑ:mə] Bauer, Bäuerin
Farsi ['fɑ:si] Farsi WF
fashion ['fæʃn] Mode WF
fast [fɑ:st] schnell
fast food [fɑ:st'fu:d] Fastfood *(schnell verzehrbare Gerichte)*
father ['fɑ:ðə] Vater
favourite ['feɪvərɪt] Lieblings-; Favorit, Favoritin
February ['februəri] Februar
feed [fi:d] (I fed, I've fed) füttern, zu essen geben
feel [fi:l] (I felt, I've felt) (sich) fühlen
feet [fi:t] Füße (→ foot)
fell [fel] (→ fall): **I fell** ich fiel, ich bin gefallen
felt [felt] (→ feel): **I felt** ich fühlte (mich), ich habe (mich) gefühlt U2: 26; **I've felt** ich habe (mich) gefühlt U2: 139
festival ['festɪvl] Fest RD U5

field [fi:ld] Feld, Wiese
fight [faɪt] Kampf RD U6
file [faɪl] Karteikarte; Akte U2: 24
film [fɪlm] Film
find [faɪnd] (I found, I've found) finden; **find out** herausfinden
fine [faɪn] gut, schön; **How are you? – I'm fine, thanks.** Wie geht's? – Danke, gut.
finish ['fɪnɪʃ] aufhören (mit); beenden; **To finish, ...** Um zum Ende zu kommen, ... U4: 57
fire ['faɪə] (Kamin-)Feuer WF
first [fɜ:st] **1** erste, erster, erstes; **2** zuerst
firstly ['fɜ:stli] erstens U4: 57
fish [fɪʃ] Fisch, Fische
fish and chip shop [fɪʃən'tʃɪpʃɒp] *Schnellimbiss für Fisch und Pommes frites*
fishing ['fɪʃɪŋ] Fischen, Angeln
fit [fɪt] fit WF
flag [flæg] Fahne, Flagge H&T: 6
flat [flæt] Wohnung
flip-flop ['flɪpflɒp] Flipflop *(eine Art Badesandale mit Zehensteg)* WF U6
flip phone ['flɪpfəʊn] Klapphandy U3: 44
floor [flɔ:] (Fuß-)Boden U4: 61
flour ['flaʊə] Mehl WF U6
flower ['flaʊə] Blume WF
follow ['fɒləʊ] folgen, verfolgen
food [fu:d] Essen; Lebensmittel
foot, feet [fʊt, fi:t] Fuß, Füße; **on foot** zu Fuß
football ['fʊtbɔ:l] Fußball
for [fɔ:, fə] für; **for 14 years** 14 Jahre lang U2: 34; **for breakfast/lunch** zum Frühstück/ Mittagessen; **stay for long** lange bleiben U5: 66
forget [fə'get] (I forgot, I've forgotten) vergessen
forgotten [fə'gɒtn]: **I had forgotten** ich hatte vergessen WF U6
fork [fɔ:k] Gabel WF U6
form [fɔ:m] Form
found [faʊnd] (→ find): **I found** ich fand, ich habe gefunden; **I've found** ich habe gefunden
France [frɑ:ns] Frankreich
freak [fri:k] Freak *(jemand, der sich sehr für etwas begeistert)* U4: 62
free [fri:] **1** frei U1: 20; **2** kostenlos U4: 52; **free time** Freizeit U2: 24
French [frentʃ] französisch; Französisch; Franzose(n), Französin(nen)
Friday ['fraɪdeɪ, 'fraɪdi] Freitag
fridge [frɪdʒ] Kühlschrank WF
friend [frend] Freund, Freundin
friendly ['frendli] freundlich
frightened ['fraɪtnd]: **I'm frightened** ich habe Angst
frightening ['fraɪtnɪŋ] furchterregend RD U4
from [frɒm, frəm] aus; von; **I'm from London.** Ich komme aus London.
fruit [fru:t] Obst, Früchte
fun [fʌn] Spaß; **Have fun!** Viel Spaß! WF; **It's fun.** Es macht Spaß.
funfair ['fʌnfeə] Kirmes, Jahrmarkt U4: 50
funny ['fʌni] lustig, komisch
furniture ['fɜ:nɪtʃə] Möbel U5: 68
furthest ['fɜ:ðɪst] am weitesten (entfernt) WF U6
future ['fju:tʃə] Zukunft U5: 66

G

Gaelic ['gælɪk] Gälisch *(keltische Sprache)* U2: 29
game [geɪm] Spiel
gang [gæŋ] Gang, Bande, Clique U4: 54
garden ['gɑ:dn] Garten
gardener ['gɑ:dnə] Gärtner/in
gate [geɪt] Tor
gave [geɪv] (→ give): **I gave** ich gab, ich habe gegeben U1: 136
gear [gɪə] Gang *(Fahrrad, Auto)* U3: 45; **safety gear** Sicherheitsausrüstung U3: 48
gentle ['dʒentl] sanft WF
geography [dʒi'ɒgrəfi] Erdkunde, Geografie
German ['dʒɜ:mən] deutsch; Deutsch; Deutsche, Deutscher
Germany ['dʒɜ:məni] Deutschland
get [get] (I got, I've got) **1** bekommen; **2** holen; **3** kommen, gelangen; **4** werden WF; **get married** heiraten WF; **I have to get out of this place.** Ich muss hier raus. **get up** aufstehen
ghost [gəʊst] Geist, Gespenst U1: 20
giant ['dʒaɪənt] Riese RD U5
gift [gɪft] Geschenk WF
girl [gɜ:l] Mädchen
girlfriend ['gɜ:lfrend] (feste) Freundin
give [gɪv] (I gave, I've given) geben; **Give the book to Tim.** Gib Tim das Buch. **Give me a break!** Hör doch auf! WF U6; **give up** aufgeben U1: 12
given ['gɪvn] (→ give): **I've given** ich habe gegeben U1: 136
glass [glɑ:s] Glas, Trinkglas
go [gəʊ] (I went, I've gone) gehen; fahren; fliegen; führen; **go in** hineingehen; **go out** ausgehen, weggehen WF
going to ['gəʊɪŋtu, 'gəʊɪŋtə]: **I'm going to win** ich werde gewinnen, ich gewinne; **I'm going to be a ranger.** Ich werde Ranger. **It's going to be OK.** Es wird gut werden.
go-karting ['gəʊkɑ:tɪŋ] Gokartfahren WF
golf [gɒlf] Golf H&T: 6
gone [gɒn]: **I/they had gone** ich/sie war(en) gegangen WF U6
good [gʊd] gut; **good at** gut in U2: 26; **Good evening/morning/ night.** Gute(n) Abend/Morgen/ Nacht.
Goodbye. [gʊd'baɪ] Auf Wiedersehen.
goods [gʊdz] Waren RD U6
got [gɒt] (→ get): **I got** ich bekam, ich habe bekommen; **I've got** ich habe bekommen U2: 147
gram [græm] Gramm WF U6
grandad ['grændæd] Opa, Großvater
grandma ['grænmɑ:] Oma, Großmutter
grave [greɪv] Grab U2: 34
graveyard ['greɪvjɑ:d] Friedhof WF
great [greɪt] toll, großartig
Greek [gri:k] Griechisch WF
green [gri:n] grün
ground [graʊnd] Boden
grounded ['graʊndɪd]: **I'm grounded** ich habe Hausarrest/ Stubenarrest U3: 41
group [gru:p] Gruppe
guard [gɑ:d]: **security guard** Wachfrau, Wachmann
guess [ges] raten; erraten
guest [gest] Gast RD U2
guide [gaɪd] Führer, Führerin *(für Sehenswürdigkeiten)*
guitar [gɪ'tɑ:] Gitarre
gun [gʌn] Gewehr WF
gym [dʒɪm] Turnhalle; Fitnessstudio U5: 68
gymnastics [dʒɪm'næstɪks] Gymnastik, Turnen WF

H

had [hæd, həd] (→ have): **I had** ich hatte, ich habe gehabt; **I've had** ich habe gehabt; **the wolf had come** der Wolf war gekommen WF; **they had gone** sie waren gegangen WF U6; **what had happened** was geschehen war WF; **he had killed it** er hatte ihn getötet WF; **I had thought** ich hatte gedacht WF U6
haggis ['hægɪs] Haggis *(gefüllter Schafsmagen; schottisches Gericht)* RD U2
hair [heə] Haar, Haare
hairdresser ['heədresə] Friseur/in
hairdryer ['heədraɪə] Föhn WF
half [hɑ:f]: **half past nine** halb zehn; **three and a half** dreieinhalb U4: 52
Halloween [hæləʊ'i:n] Halloween U1: 20
ham [hæm] Schinken U4: 59
hamburger ['hæmbɜ:gə] Hamburger
hamster ['hæmstə] Hamster
hand [hænd] Hand
handball ['hændbɔ:l] Handball WF
hand signal ['hændsɪgnəl] Handzeichen
hanging ['hæŋɪŋ]: **he was hanging** er hing (gerade)
happen ['hæpən] passieren, geschehen
happy ['hæpi] glücklich, froh; **I'm happy for her** ich freue mich für sie U2: 26; **Happy birthday!** Herzlichen Glückwunsch zum Geburtstag!
hard [hɑ:d] hart; schwer
has [hæz, həz] → have
hate [heɪt] hassen, nicht ausstehen können
have [hæv, həv] (he has; I had, I've had) **1** haben; **have a chat** sich unterhalten U1: 12; **have a cola** eine Cola trinken; **have a party** eine Party geben; **have a picnic** ein Picknick machen; **have an ice cream** ein Eis essen; **have breakfast** frühstücken; **Have fun!** Viel Spaß! WF; **2 I've (= I have)/he has finished** ich habe/er hat beendet; **I haven't (= have not)/he hasn't (= has not) finished** ich habe/er hat nicht beendet; **Have you ever …? – Yes, I have./No, I haven't.** Bist/Hast du schon einmal …? – Ja./Nein.
have to ['hævtu, 'hævtə] (I had to, I've had to) müssen
he [hi:] er; **he's (= he is)** er ist; **he'll** [hi:l] er wird WF
head [hed] Kopf
heading ['hedɪŋ] Rubrik; Überschrift U2: 25
healthy ['helθi] gesund
hear [hɪə] (I heard, I've heard) hören U3: 44
heard [hɜ:d] (→ hear): **I heard** ich hörte, ich habe gehört U3: 141; **I've heard** ich habe gehört U3: 141
heart [hɑ:t] Herz WF; **Learn it by heart.** Lerne es auswendig.
held [held] (→ hold): **I held** ich hielt, ich habe gehalten U3: 141; **I've held** ich habe gehalten U3: 141
Hello. [hə'ləʊ] Hallo. (Guten) Tag.
helmet ['helmɪt] Helm U3: 48
help [help] **1** helfen; **2** Hilfe
helper ['helpə] Helfer, Helferin
helping ['helpɪŋ]: **Helping visitors** Gästen helfen WF U6
her [hɜ:] **1** ihr, ihre; **2** ihr, sie
here [hɪə] hier; hierher; **Here you are.** Hier, bitte.
Hi. [haɪ] Hallo.
high [haɪ] hoch U5: 76
high jump ['haɪdʒʌmp] Hochsprung U5: 66
hill [hɪl] Hügel, (kleiner) Berg
him [hɪm] ihm, ihn
hip hop ['hɪphɒp] Hip-Hop WF
hire ['haɪə] mieten; vermieten
his [hɪz] sein, seine
history ['hɪstri] Geschichte
hobby ['hɒbi] Hobby U3: 38
hockey ['hɒki] Hockey
hold [həʊld] (I held, I've held) halten; (MP3-Player:) speichern U3: 45
holiday(s) ['hɒlədeɪ, -z] Ferien, Urlaub; **go on holiday** in den Urlaub fahren; **she's on holiday** sie macht Urlaub, sie ist im Urlaub
home [həʊm] Heim, Zuhause; **at home** zu Hause, daheim; **go home** nach Hause gehen
home-made [həʊm'meɪd] selbst gemacht
homework ['həʊmwɜ:k] Hausaufgaben, Schularbeiten; **I do my homework.** Ich mache (meine) Hausaufgaben.
homework diary [həʊmwɜ:k'daɪəri] Hausaufgabenheft; Schülerkalender
hope [həʊp] hoffen
horror ['hɒrə] Horror U2: 28
horse [hɔ:s] Pferd
horse riding ['hɔ:sraɪdɪŋ] Reiten
hospital ['hɒspɪtl] Krankenhaus
hot [hɒt] heiß U5: 72
hotel [həʊ'tel] Hotel
hour ['aʊə] Stunde
house [haʊs] Haus; **at Tim's house** bei Tim (zu Hause); **Let's go to my house.** Gehen wir zu mir (nach Hause).
how [haʊ] wie; **how to find us** wie man uns findet U3: 48; **How much is/are …?** Was kostet/kosten …? U1: 17
humbug ['hʌmbəg] Humbug, Unsinn WF
hundred ['hʌndrəd] hundert U3: 45
hungry ['hʌŋgri] hungrig; **I'm hungry.** Ich habe Hunger.
hunting ['hʌntɪŋ] Jagen WF
hurdles ['hɜ:dlz] Hürdenlauf WF
hurling ['hɜ:lɪŋ] Hurling *(irische Sportart; ähnlich wie Hockey)* U5: 76
hurry ['hʌri]: **Hurry up!** Beeil dich!
hurt [hɜ:t] (I hurt, I've hurt) verletzen, wehtun; **I hurt my hand** ich verletzte mir die Hand, ich habe mir die Hand verletzt

I

I [aɪ] ich; **I'd like …** Ich möchte …/Ich hätte gern …; **I'd like to go/…** Ich möchte gehen/…; **I'll (= I will) go** ich werde gehen U4: 52; **I'll give you your invitations in the break.** Ich gebe euch eure Einladungen in der Pause. **I'm (= I am)** ich bin
ice cream [aɪs'kri:m] (Speise-)Eis
idea [aɪ'dɪə] Idee, Einfall
if [ɪf] wenn, falls
ill [ɪl] krank U2: 34
illuminations [ɪlu:mɪ'neɪʃnz] Festbeleuchtung U4: 52
imagine [ɪ'mædʒɪn] sich (etwas) vorstellen U4: 50
important [ɪm'pɔ:tnt] wichtig
in [ɪn] in; **in 1971** (im Jahre) 1971 U2: 25; **in April** im April; **in Fairfield Road** in der Fairfield Road; **in German** auf Deutsch; **in the**

country auf dem Land; in the morning/afternoon/evening am Morgen/Nachmittag/Abend; in the picture auf dem Bild; in the playground auf dem Schulhof; in the same place am selben Ort U5: 66; in the street auf der Straße; in the world auf der (ganzen) Welt; in winter/... im Winter/... U3: 38; come in hereinkommen; go/crawl in hineingehen, -kriechen
in fact [ɪn'fækt]: In fact, it was better. Es war sogar besser.
indoors [ɪn'dɔːz] in der Halle, drinnen U3: 43
information [ɪnfə'meɪʃn] Informationen, Informations-
inn [ɪn] Gasthaus RD U6
instead of [ɪn'stedəv] statt
instructions [ɪn'strʌkʃnz] Gebrauchsanweisung U4: 58
instrument ['ɪnstrəmənt] Instrument H&T: 6
interactive [ɪntər'æktɪv] interaktiv RD U4
intercom ['ɪntəkɒm] Sprechanlage U1: 13
interest ['ɪntrəst] Interesse U2: 24
interested (in) ['ɪntrəstɪd] interessiert (an)
interesting ['ɪntrəstɪŋ] interessant
international [ɪntə'næʃnəl] international U1: 12
Internet ['ɪntənet] Internet; on the Internet im Internet U2: 25; Internet kiosk Internet-Kiosk *(öffentlich zugängliches Internet-Terminal)* U4: 58
interpreting [ɪn'tɜːprɪtɪŋ] Dolmetschen
interview ['ɪntəvjuː] Interview WF
into ['ɪntu, 'ɪntə] in (... hinein/herein); into the street auf die Straße (hinaus)
invitation [ɪnvɪ'teɪʃn] Einladung
invite (for) [ɪn'vaɪt] einladen (zu)
Ireland ['aɪələnd] Irland
Irish ['aɪrɪʃ] irisch; Irisch; Ire(n), Irin(nen) U5: 76
is [ɪz] ist; isn't (= is not) ist nicht; It's my birthday. Ich habe Geburtstag. What colour is your room? Welche Farbe hat dein Zimmer?
it [ɪt] **1** es *(nicht bei Personen:* er, sie); **2** ihm, es *(nicht bei Personen:* ihm, ihn; ihr, sie); it's (= it is) es ist; It's Sarah. Hier spricht Sarah.

Italian [ɪ'tæliən] Italienisch WF
its [ɪts] sein, seine; ihr, ihre

J

jacket ['dʒækət] Jacke
January ['dʒænjuəri] Januar
javelin ['dʒævlɪn] Speerwerfen WF
jealous (of) [dʒeləs] neidisch (auf); eifersüchtig (auf) U2: 26
jeans [dʒiːnz] Jeans
jigsaw puzzle ['dʒɪgsɔːpʌzl] Puzzle WF
job [dʒɒb] **1** Aufgabe, Arbeit; **2** Arbeitsstelle; Beruf
jogger ['dʒɒgə] Jogger, Joggerin
jogging ['dʒɒgɪŋ] Jogging
join [dʒɔɪn]: join a club einem Klub beitreten, Mitglied in einem Klub werden U1: 12
joke [dʒəʊk] Witze machen WF
judo ['dʒuːdəʊ] Judo
juggling ['dʒʌglɪŋ] Jonglieren WF
juice [dʒuːs] Saft
July [dʒu'laɪ] Juli
jump [dʒʌmp] springen U4: 55; (the) high jump Hochsprung U5: 66; (the) long jump Weitsprung WF
June [dʒuːn] Juni
just [dʒʌst] gerade, soeben; just before kurz (be)vor

K

karate [kə'rɑːti] Karate WF
Kazakh ['kæzæk] Kasachisch WF
keen [kiːn]: I'm not keen on it ich habe nicht viel dafür übrig U2: 30
kettle ['ketl] Wasserkocher WF
kid [kɪd] Kind; Jugendliche, Jugendlicher U5: 65
kill [kɪl] umbringen WF
kilometre ['kɪləmiːtə] Kilometer
kilt [kɪlt] Kilt *(Schottenrock)* H&T: 6
kind [kaɪnd]: a kind of book eine Art Buch WF U6
king [kɪŋ] König RD U6
kiosk ['kiːɒsk]: Internet kiosk Internet-Kiosk *(öffentlich zugängliches Internet-Terminal)* U4: 58
kiss [kɪs] Kuss WF
kitchen ['kɪtʃɪn] Küche
knew [njuː] (→ know): I knew ich wusste, ich habe gewusst
knife, knives [naɪf, naɪvz] Messer WF U6

knitting ['nɪtɪŋ] Stricken WF
knock (at) [nɒk] klopfen (an) WF
know [nəʊ] (I knew, I've known) wissen, kennen
Kurdish ['kɜːdɪʃ] Kurdisch WF

L

label ['leɪbl] Schildchen, Etikett
land [lænd] **1** landen RD U6; **2** Land RD U3
language ['læŋgwɪdʒ] Sprache U2: 29; the language we speak die Sprache, die wir sprechen RD U3
laptop ['læptɒp] Laptop U3: 47
last [lɑːst] letzte, letzter, letztes
late [leɪt] spät; zu spät, verspätet; He's late (for school). Er kommt zu spät (zur Schule).
later ['leɪtə] später
laugh [lɑːf] lachen
learn [lɜːn] lernen; learn about London etwas über London erfahren U1: 11; Learn it by heart. Lerne es auswendig.
leave [liːv] (I left, I've left) verlassen, weggehen (von); leave it too late zu lange warten RD U3
leek [liːk] Lauch(stange), Porree(stange) U3: 47
left [left] links; on the left auf der linken Seite; on your left links (von Ihnen)
left [left] (→ leave): I left ich verließ, ich habe verlassen
lemonade [lemə'neɪd] (Zitronen-)Limonade
lesson ['lesn] (Unterrichts-)Stunde
let [let]: Let's finish. Lasst uns aufhören./Hören wir auf.
letter ['letə] **1** Brief; **2** Buchstabe
letterboxing ['letəbɒksɪŋ] „Letterboxing" *(eine Art Schatzsuche)*
lettuce ['letɪs] (Kopf-)Salat WF
library ['laɪbrəri] Bücherei WF U6
life [laɪf] Leben
light [laɪt] Licht, Lampe
like [laɪk] **1** mögen, gern haben; I like it. Ich mag es./Es gefällt mir. I (don't) like walking. Ich laufe (nicht) gern. I'd like ... Ich möchte .../Ich hätte gern ...; I'd like to go/... Ich möchte gehen/...; Who likes the song best? Wem gefällt das Lied am besten? U1: 11; **2** wie; clothes like this solche Kleidung WF U6;

What does she look like? Wie sieht sie aus? **what life was like** wie das Leben war RD U1; **what the book is like** wie das Buch ist U1: 18
likes and dislikes ['laɪksən'dɪslaɪks] Vorlieben und Abneigungen U2: 30
line [laɪn] Zeile
lip [lɪp] Lippe
list [lɪst] Liste
listen ['lɪsn] zuhören; **listen to** hören, sich anhören
litter ['lɪtə] Abfall
little ['lɪtl] klein RD U5
live [lɪv] wohnen, leben
living room ['lɪvɪŋru:m] Wohnzimmer
log [lɒg]: **reading log** Lesetagebuch WF
lonely ['ləʊnli] einsam
long [lɒŋ] lang; lange
long jump ['lɒŋdʒʌmp] Weitsprung WF
look [lʊk] **1** schauen, sehen; hinschauen WF; **look at** ansehen, sich ansehen; **2** aussehen; **What does she look like?** Wie sieht sie aus? **look after him** auf ihn aufpassen WF; **look for** suchen
lorry ['lɒri] Lastwagen WF
lost [lɒst]: **I had lost** ich hatte verloren WF U6
lots [lɒts]: **lots of** viele; viel
lotto ['lɒtəʊ] Lotto; **win the lotto** im Lotto gewinnen
loudly ['laʊdli] laut WF
love [lʌv] **1** lieben, sehr mögen; **2** Liebe U2: 25; **(Lots of) Love, ...** (Viele) Liebe Grüße ...
lunch [lʌntʃ] Mittagessen
lunch break ['lʌntʃbreɪk] Mittagspause
lunchtime ['lʌntʃtaɪm] Mittagszeit; Mittagspause U1: 13
Luxembourg ['lʌksəmbɜ:g] Luxemburg

M

Macedonian [mæsə'dəʊniən] Mazedonisch WF
machine [mə'ʃi:n] Maschine, Gerät U4: 58
mad [mæd]: **they're mad** sie sind sauer WF
made [meɪd] (→ make): **I made** ich machte, ich habe gemacht; **I've made** ich habe gemacht; **if they made me say goodbye** wenn man mich zwänge, mich zu verabschieden U3: 47
magazine [mægə'zi:n] Zeitschrift
main [meɪn] Haupt- WF
make [meɪk] (I made, I've made) machen, herstellen; **make an arrangement** eine Absprache treffen U2: 31; **make money from the tourists** Geld an den Touristen verdienen WF U6; **Make notes.** Mach dir Notizen. **nobody can make me eat this** keiner kann mich dazu zwingen, dies zu essen U3: 47
make-up ['meɪkʌp] Make-up WF
making ['meɪkɪŋ]: **Making notes** (Sich) Notizen machen U2: 29; **Making arrangements** Absprachen treffen U2: 31
man, men [mæn, men] Mann, Männer
many ['meni] viele
map [mæp] Landkarte, Karte
March [mɑ:tʃ] März
market ['mɑ:kɪt] Markt WF
married ['mærid] verheiratet U2: 25; **get married** heiraten WF
match [mætʃ] **1** Spiel, Wettkampf; **2 Match the words with the pictures.** Ordne den Wörtern die Bilder zu.
maths [mæθs] Mathe(matik)
May [meɪ] Mai
may [meɪ]: **it may be quite simple** es mag ziemlich einfach sein WF
maybe ['meɪbi] vielleicht U5: 66
mayonnaise [meɪə'neɪz] Mayonnaise WF
me [mi:] **1** mir, mich; **2** ich U5: 64
mean [mi:n] (I meant, I've meant) meinen; bedeuten U5: 68
meaning ['mi:nɪŋ] Bedeutung WF U6
meant [ment] (→ mean): **I meant** ich meinte, ich habe gemeint U5: 147; **I've meant** ich habe gemeint U5: 147
meet [mi:t] (I met, I've met) **1** (sich) treffen (mit); **2** kennen lernen; **Nice to meet you.** Schön, dich/Sie kennen zu lernen.
men [men] Männer (→ man)
menu ['menju:] Speisekarte WF U6
merry ['meri]: **Merry Christmas!** Frohe Weihnachten! WF
met [met] (→ meet): **I met** ich traf, ich habe getroffen
metre ['mi:tə] Meter U4: 61
microwave ['maɪkrəweɪv] Mikrowelle WF
mile [maɪl] Meile
milk [mɪlk] Milch
millilitre ['mɪlili:tə] Milliliter WF U6
million ['mɪljən] Million U4: 52
mind [maɪnd]: **you don't mind** du hast nichts dagegen WF
minute ['mɪnɪt] Minute
mirror ['mɪrə] Spiegel WF U6
miss [mɪs] vermissen; **You can't miss it.** Sie können es nicht übersehen. WF U6
missing ['mɪsɪŋ]: **the missing words** die fehlenden Wörter
mix [mɪks] mischen WF U6
mobile (phone) ['məʊbaɪl, məʊbaɪl'fəʊn] Handy, Mobiltelefon
mobile home [məʊbaɪl'həʊm] (Stand-)Wohnwagen U5: 65
modern ['mɒdn] modern
mom [mɒm] Mama *(amerik. Englisch)* WF
moment ['məʊmənt] Moment U1: 10; **at the moment** zurzeit, im Moment U1: 10
Monday ['mʌndeɪ, 'mʌndi] Montag
money ['mʌni] Geld
monster ['mɒnstə] Monster U4: 60
month [mʌnθ] Monat
moor [mɔ:] (Hoch-)Moor
more [mɔ:] mehr, weitere; **more expensive** teurer
morning ['mɔ:nɪŋ] Morgen; **in the morning** am Morgen, morgens; **Monday morning** Montagmorgen
most [məʊst] der/die/das meiste, die meisten; **most expensive** teuerste/r/s, am teuersten
mother ['mʌðə] Mutter
motorbike ['məʊtəbaɪk] Motorrad
motorcyclist ['məʊtəsaɪklɪst] Motorradfahrer/in WF
mountain ['maʊntən] Berg U3: 38; **in the mountains** im Gebirge U3: 140
mountain bike ['maʊntənbaɪk] Mountainbike
mountain biking ['maʊntənbaɪkɪŋ] Mountainbikefahren
mountain board ['maʊntənbɔ:d] Mountainboard *(eine Art Gelände-Skateboard)* U3: 45
mountain boarding ['maʊntənbɔ:dɪŋ] Mountainboardfahren U3: 38
move [mu:v] umziehen

MP3 player [empiː'θriːpleɪə] MP3-Player U3: 45
Mr ['mɪstə]: **Mr Dunn** Herr Dunn
Mrs ['mɪsɪz]: **Mrs Jones** Frau Jones
Ms [mɪz, məz]: **Ms Brown** Frau Brown
much [mʌtʃ] viel
mum [mʌm] Mama, Mutti
museum [mju'ziːəm] Museum
music ['mjuːzɪk] Musik
musical instrument [mjuːzɪkl'ɪnstrəmənt] Musikinstrument H&T: 6
must [mʌst] müssen U5: 69
mustn't ['mʌsnt] nicht dürfen U3: 41
my [maɪ] mein, meine

N

name [neɪm] Name; **What's your name?** Wie heiβt du?
narrow ['nærəʊ] schmal, eng
national park ['næʃnəl'pɑːk] Nationalpark
near [nɪə] in der Nähe (von); nah
nearest ['nɪərɪst]: **the nearest airport** der nächste Flughafen
neck [nek] Hals WF
need [niːd] brauchen
neighbour ['neɪbə] Nachbar/in
nervous ['nɜːvəs] nervös, ängstlich U1: 10
Netherlands ['neðələndz] Niederlande
network ['netwɜːk] Netz; Wortnetz, Wörternetz
never ['nevə] (noch) nie, niemals
new [njuː] neu
news [njuːz] Nachricht(en); Neuigkeit(en) U1: 13
newspaper ['njuːzpeɪpə] Zeitung
next [nekst] nächste/r/s
next to ['nekstu, 'nekstə] neben
nice [naɪs] nett; schön
night [naɪt] Nacht U1: 20; **at night** nachts, in der Nacht U1: 20
no [nəʊ] **1** nein; **2** kein, keine; **There's no such thing.** So etwas gibt es nicht.
nobody ['nəʊbədi] niemand
noise [nɔɪz] Geräusch WF
nonsense ['nɒnsns] Unsinn, Blödsinn
north [nɔːθ] Norden; Nord-; nördlich H&T: 7; **in the north** im Norden U4: 50; **north-west** Nordwesten WF U6
northern ['nɔːðən] Nord-, nördlich U4: 50
Northern Ireland ['nɔːðən'aɪələnd] Nordirland U5: 74
not [nɒt] nicht
note [nəʊt] Notiz
notebook ['nəʊtbʊk] Notizbuch WF
nothing ['nʌθɪŋ] (gar) nichts
notice ['nəʊtɪs] bemerken WF U6
noticeboard ['nəʊtɪsbɔːd] Anschlagbrett, Schwarzes Brett U1: 12
noun [naʊn] Nomen U5: 71
November [nəʊ'vembə] November
now [naʊ] nun, jetzt; **now you're in the world** jetzt, wo du auf der Welt bist WF
number ['nʌmbə] Nummer; Zahl; Ziffer U4: 52

O

o'clock [ə'klɒk]: **at eight o'clock** um acht/zwanzig Uhr
October [ɒk'təʊbə] Oktober
of [ɒv, əv] von; **a picture of my dog** ein Bild meines Hundes; **a cup of tea** eine Tasse Tee; **think of** denken an
of course [əv'kɔːs] natürlich, selbstverständlich
off [ɒf] von
offer ['ɒfə] **1** anbieten U4: 59; **2** Angebot U4: 59; **special offer** Sonderangebot U3: 45
office ['ɒfɪs] Büro WF; **tourist office** Touristeninformation, Fremdenverkehrsbüro U3: 37
officer ['ɒfɪsə]: **police officer** Polizist/in, Polizeibeamter/-beamtin
off-road ['ɒfrəʊd] abseits der Straβe, im Gelände
often ['ɒfn] oft
OK [əʊ'keɪ] okay, (schon) gut, in Ordnung; **Are you OK?** Ist alles in Ordnung bei dir? **That's OK.** Schon gut./Bitte.
old [əʊld] alt
Olympics [ə'lɪmpɪks]: **the Olympics** die Olympischen Spiele U1: 11
on [ɒn] **1** auf; **2** an, eingeschaltet U4: 52; **on August 5th** am 5. August; **on Dartmoor** in Dartmoor; **on foot** zu Fuβ; **on holiday** in/im Urlaub; **on Saturdays** samstags; **on school days** an Schultagen; **on special offer** im Sonderangebot U3: 45; **on the bus** im Bus; **on the coast** an der Küste RD U5; **on the intercom** über die Sprechanlage U1: 13; **on the Internet** im Internet U2: 25; **on the phone** am Telefon; **on the road** unterwegs; **on TV** im Fernsehen; **get on the team** in die Mannschaft kommen U5: 68
one [wʌn] ein, eine, einer, eines; **one day** eines Tages U5: 68; **this one's for you** dieses ist für dich WF
onion ['ʌniən] Zwiebel WF U6
only ['əʊnli] nur, bloβ; erst
onto ['ɒntʊ, 'ɒntə] auf (... hinauf/herauf)
open ['əʊpən] **1** öffnen, aufmachen; **2** sich öffnen, aufgehen; **3** offen, geöffnet
opposite ['ɒpəzɪt] gegenüber (vom) WF U6
or [ɔː] oder
orange ['ɒrɪndʒ] Orange
order ['ɔːdə] Reihenfolge
organize ['ɔːgənaɪz] ordnen; organisieren U2: 33
orphan ['ɔːfn] Waise RD U1
other ['ʌðə] andere, weitere
our ['aʊə] unser, unsere
out [aʊt]: **out of** ['aʊtəv] aus (... hinaus/heraus); **out of this world** nicht von dieser Welt, fantastisch RD U4; **I have to get out of this place.** Ich muss hier raus. **find out** herausfinden
outdoor activity ['aʊtdɔːræk'tɪvəti] Beschäftigung im Freien
outdoors [aʊt'dɔːz] im Freien, drauβen U3: 43
over ['əʊvə] vorbei, zu Ende, aus; **over there** [əʊvə'ðeə] da drüben, dort drüben WF U6
own [əʊn]: **your own room** dein eigenes Zimmer

P

pack [pæk] packen, einpacken
page [peɪdʒ] Seite
paid [peɪd] (→ pay): **I paid** ich zahlte, ich habe gezahlt
pain [peɪn] Schmerzen; **Parents are a pain!** Eltern nerven! U3: 40
paint [peɪnt] malen WF U6
painting ['peɪntɪŋ] Malen WF U6
parade [pə'reɪd] Parade, Umzug RD U5

paragraph ['pærəgrɑ:f] Absatz U1: 18
parent, parents ['peərənt, 'peərənts] Elternteil, Eltern
park [pɑ:k] Park
parrot ['pærət] Papagei WF
part [pɑ:t] Teil
partner ['pɑ:tnə] Partner/in
party ['pɑ:ti] Party
passage ['pæsɪdʒ] Gang, Korridor
past [pɑ:st] Vergangenheit
past [pɑ:st]: **past the house** am Haus vorbei; **five past ten** fünf nach zehn; **half past nine** halb zehn
past participle [pɑ:stpɑ:'tɪsɪpl] Partizip Perfekt WF U6
past perfect [pɑ:st'pɜ:fɪkt] Vorvergangenheit WF U6
pastry ['peɪstri] Teig WF U6
pasty ['pæsti] Pastete WF U6
pattern ['pætn] Muster WF U6
pavement ['peɪvmənt] Bürgersteig, Gehsteig
pay [peɪ] (I paid, I've paid) zahlen, bezahlen; **pay attention** aufpassen WF
pen [pen] Füller
pence (p) [pens] Pence *(britische Währung)*
pencil ['pensl] Bleistift
pencil case ['penslkeɪs] Federmäppchen, Schreibetui
penfriend ['penfrend] Brieffreund, Brieffreundin WF
people ['pi:pl] Leute, Menschen
pepper ['pepə] Pfeffer WF U6
Persian ['pɜ:ʃn] Persisch WF
pet [pet] Haustier, zahmes Tier
pet shop ['petʃɒp] Zoohandlung, Tierhandlung
phone [fəʊn] **1** anrufen, telefonieren; **phone for pizza** telefonisch Pizza bestellen RD U2; **2** Telefon; **on the phone** am Telefon
photo ['fəʊtəʊ] Foto U1: 10
phrase [freɪz] Ausdruck U1: 19
pick [pɪk] aussuchen, wählen
pick up [pɪk'ʌp] **1** aufheben, hochheben; **2** abholen U3: 40
pickpocket ['pɪkpɒkɪt] Taschendieb, Taschendiebin RD U1
picnic ['pɪknɪk] Picknick
picture ['pɪktʃə] Bild, Foto
pier [pɪə] Pier, Anlegestelle U4: 51
piercing ['pɪəsɪŋ] Piercing WF U6
pig [pɪg] Schwein
pink [pɪŋk] rosa, pink
pizza ['pi:tsə] Pizza

place [pleɪs] Ort, Stelle, Platz; **a place to meet** ein Treffpunkt U3: 47
plan [plæn] **1** planen, vorhaben; **2** Plan
plane [pleɪn] Flugzeug
planner ['plænə] Planer, Planerin
plate [pleɪt] Teller WF U6
play [pleɪ] spielen; **play sports** Sport treiben; **play the guitar** Gitarre spielen
player ['pleɪə] Spieler, Spielerin
playground ['pleɪgraʊnd] Schulhof; **in the playground** auf dem Schulhof
please [pli:z] bitte
p.m. [pi:'em] nachmittags, abends U4: 61
poem ['pəʊɪm] Gedicht
poet ['pəʊɪt] Dichter/in U3: 46
point [pɔɪnt] **1 point (at)** zeigen (auf) WF; **2** Punkt
Poland ['pəʊlənd] Polen
pole vault ['pəʊlvɔ:lt] Stabhochsprung WF
police [pə'li:s] Polizei- U2: 34
police officer [pə'li:sɒfɪsə] Polizist/in, Polizeibeamter/-beamtin
Polish ['pəʊlɪʃ] Polnisch WF
polite [pə'laɪt] höflich U1: 17
pony ['pəʊni] Pony
poor [pʊə] arm RD U1; **Poor you!** Du Arme!/Du Armer!
popcorn ['pɒpkɔ:n] Popcorn WF
popular ['pɒpjələ] beliebt
portfolio [pɔ:t'fəʊliəʊ] Portfolio U4: 61
Portuguese [pɔ:tʃʊ'gi:z] Portugiesisch WF
postcard ['pəʊstkɑ:d] Postkarte, Ansichtskarte
poster ['pəʊstə] Poster
post office ['pəʊstɒfɪs] Post(amt)
potato, potatoes [pə'teɪtəʊ, pə'teɪtəʊz] Kartoffel, Kartoffeln WF U6
pound (£) [paʊnd] Pfund *(britische Währung)*
practise ['præktɪs] üben; trainieren
present [prɪ'zent] präsentieren U4: 53
present ['preznt] **1** Geschenk; **2** Gegenwart WF; **simple present** einfache Gegenwart
present progressive [prezntprə'gresɪv] Verlaufsform der Gegenwart U1: 20
presenter [prɪ'zentə] Moderator, Moderatorin WF

price [praɪs] Preis U3: 48
prince [prɪns] Prinz WF
principal ['prɪnsəpl] Rektor/in WF
prize [praɪz] Preis, Gewinn
problem ['prɒbləm] Problem U2: 26
produce [prə'dju:s] herstellen, produzieren H&T: 6
professional [prə'feʃənl] Profi-, Berufs- WF
programme ['prəʊgræm] (Radio-, Fernseh-)Sendung
progressive [prə'gresɪv]: **present progressive** Verlaufsform der Gegenwart U1: 20
project ['prɒdʒekt] Projekt(arbeit)
promise ['prɒmɪs] versprechen WF
protector [prə'tektə] Protektor, Schützer U3: 48
proud [praʊd] stolz WF
pudding ['pʊdɪŋ]: **Christmas pudding** Plumpudding *(heiß servierte Nachspeise)* WF
pupil ['pju:pl] Schüler, Schülerin
push [pʊʃ] drücken
put [pʊt] (I put, I've put) **1** stellen; legen; (an einen Platz) tun; **I put** ich tat, ich habe getan; **put in the right order** in die richtige Reihenfolge bringen
put in [pʊt'ɪn] einfügen, hinzufügen
put down [pʊt'daʊn]: **I put down** ich habe aufgeschrieben WF

Q

quad (bike) [kwɒd, 'kwɒdbaɪk] Quad *(eine Art vierrädriges Gelände-Motorrad)*
quarrel ['kwɒrəl] Streit WF
quarter ['kwɔ:tə]: **quarter to/past one** Viertel vor/nach eins
queen [kwi:n] Königin U1: 11
question ['kwestʃən] Frage
questionnaire [kwestʃə'neə] Fragebogen
queue (up) [kju:] Schlange stehen U1: 17
quickly ['kwɪkli] schnell U1: 18
quiet ['kwaɪət] ruhig
quite [kwaɪt] ziemlich WF
quiz, quizzes [kwɪz, 'kwɪzɪz] Quiz

R

radiator ['reɪdieɪtə] Heizkörper U4: 53

radio ['reɪdiəʊ] Radio U1: 13
railings ['reɪlɪŋz] Geländer U4: 54
railway line ['reɪlweɪlaɪn] Eisenbahnstrecke, Gleis
rain [reɪn] regnen
ran [ræn] (→ run): **I ran** ich rannte, ich bin gerannt
ranger ['reɪndʒə] Ranger *(Aufseher/in in Nationalparks)*
rap [ræp] Rap(musik)
rat [ræt] Ratte
read [ri:d] (I read, I've read) lesen, vorlesen
read [red] (→ read): **I read** ich las, ich habe gelesen U4: 144; **I've read** ich habe gelesen U4: 144
read out [ri:d'aʊt] vorlesen, ablesen U4: 57
reader ['ri:də] Leser, Leserin
reading log ['ri:dɪŋlɒg] Lesetagebuch WF
reading week ['ri:dɪŋwi:k] Lesewoche U1: 19
ready ['redi] fertig, bereit
real ['ri:əl] echt, richtig WF U6
really ['ri:əli] wirklich, eigentlich U5: 69
red [red] rot
remember [rɪ'membə] sich erinnern (an)
rent [rent] mieten; ausleihen
repeat [rɪ'pi:t] nachsprechen
report [rɪ'pɔ:t] Bericht
restaurant ['restrɒnt] Restaurant
result [rɪ'zʌlt] Ergebnis, Folge U5: 67
Rhine [raɪn] Rhein
rhyme (with) [raɪm] (sich) reimen (auf)
rhythm ['rɪðəm] Rhythmus WF
rich [rɪtʃ] reich WF
ridden ['rɪdn]: **I've ridden** ich bin gefahren (→ ride)
ride [raɪd] (I rode, I've ridden): **ride a bike/mountain board** Rad/Mountainboard fahren; **ride a quad bike** (mit einem) Quad fahren
riding ['raɪdɪŋ]: **horse riding** Reiten; **quad/Trikke/... riding** Quadfahren/Trikkefahren/...
right [raɪt] **1** richtig; **You're right.** Du hast Recht. **2** rechts; **on the right** auf der rechten Seite; **on your right** rechts (von Ihnen)
ring [rɪŋ] Ring WF U6
ringtone ['rɪŋtəʊn] Klingelton U3: 44
river ['rɪvə] Fluss; **the River Exe** der Exe

road [rəʊd] Straße; **in Fairfield Road** in der Fairfield Road; **on the road** unterwegs
road safety ['rəʊdseɪfti] Verkehrssicherheit
rock [rɒk] **1** Fels, großer Stein; **2** Rock(musik) WF
rock climber ['rɒkklaɪmə] Kletterer, Kletterin
rock climbing ['rɒkklaɪmɪŋ] Klettern
roll [rəʊl] Brötchen
roll out [rəʊl'aʊt] ausrollen WF U6
roller coaster ['rəʊləkəʊstə] Achterbahn U4: 50
Romanian [ru'meɪniən] Rumänisch WF
romantic [rəʊ'mæntɪk] romantisch U2: 22
Rome [rəʊm] Rom
room [ru:m] Raum, Zimmer
round [raʊnd] um (... herum) WF U6
rowing ['rəʊɪŋ] Rudern WF
rubber ['rʌbə] Radiergummi
rugby ['rʌgbi] Rugby
rule [ru:l] Regel, Vorschrift
ruler ['ru:lə] Lineal
run [rʌn] (I ran, I've run) rennen, laufen; **streams running by** Bäche, die vorbeifließen RD U3; **the longest-running programme** die am längsten laufende Sendung RD U4
runner ['rʌnə] Läufer, Läuferin
running ['rʌnɪŋ] Laufen U5: 66
Russian ['rʌʃn] Russisch WF

S

sad [sæd] traurig U2: 22
safe [seɪf] sicher, in Sicherheit U3: 40
safety ['seɪfti]: **road safety** Verkehrssicherheit
safety gear ['seɪftigɪə] Sicherheitsausrüstung U3: 48
said [sed] (→ say): **I said** ich sagte, ich habe gesagt; **I've said** ich habe gesagt
sailing ['seɪlɪŋ] Segeln WF U6
salad ['sæləd] Salat
salt [sɔ:lt] Salz WF U6
same [seɪm]: **the same** derselbe, dieselbe, dasselbe; der/die/das gleiche
sandwich ['sænwɪtʃ] Sandwich *(belegtes Brot)* U4: 59
sang [sæŋ] (→ sing): **I sang** ich sang, ich habe gesungen U2: 25

sat [sæt] (→ sit): **I sat** ich saß, ich habe gesessen
Saturday ['sætədeɪ, 'sætədi] Samstag, Sonnabend
sausage ['sɒsɪdʒ] Wurst, Würstchen H&T: 6
save [seɪv] sparen U4: 53
saw [sɔ:] (→ see): **I saw** ich sah, ich habe gesehen
say [seɪ] (I said, I've said) sagen; **say goodbye to ...** sich von ... verabschieden U3: 47; **Say hi to ... , please.** Grüße ... , bitte. **say sorry** sich entschuldigen
scary ['skeəri] unheimlich WF
scene [si:n] Szene; Ansicht U1: 8
school [sku:l] Schule; **she's at school** sie ist in der Schule; sie geht zur Schule
school day ['sku:ldeɪ] Schultag
schoolgirl ['sku:lgɜ:l] Schulmädchen WF
science ['saɪəns] Naturwissenschaft
science fiction [saɪəns'fɪkʃn] Science-Fiction WF
scooter ['sku:tə] Motorroller WF
scorpion ['skɔ:piən] Skorpion WF
Scotland ['skɒtlənd] Schottland
Scots [skɒts] Schottisch *(engl. Dialekt)* U2: 29
Scottish ['skɒtɪʃ] schottisch; Schotte(n), Schottin(nen) U2: 22
scream [skri:m] schreien U4: 55
sea [si:] Meer
seashell ['si:ʃel] Muschel U4: 58
seashore ['si:ʃɔ:] Küste, Strand U4: 58
season ['si:zn] Jahreszeit U3: 43
security guard [sɪ'kjʊərətigɑ:d] Wachfrau, Wachmann
see [si:] (I saw, I've seen) sehen; **see the beaches** sich die Strände anschauen RD U5; **See you.** Bis dann. **See you tomorrow/...** Bis morgen/...; **..., you see.** ..., verstehst du?
seem [si:m]: **she doesn't seem to care** es scheint sie nicht zu interessieren WF
seen [si:n] (→ see): **I've seen** ich habe gesehen
self-service [self'sɜ:vɪs] Selbstbedienung WF U6
sell [sel] (I sold, I've sold) verkaufen
send [send] (I sent, I've sent) senden, schicken U1: 10
sender ['sendə] Absender, Absenderin WF

sent [sent] (→ send): **I sent** ich sendete, ich habe gesendet U1: 136; **I've sent** ich habe gesendet U1: 136
sentence ['sentəns] Satz
September [sep'tembə] September
Serbian ['sɜ:biən] Serbisch WF
share [ʃeə]: **share a room** sich ein Zimmer teilen
shaver ['ʃeɪvə] Rasierapparat WF
she [ʃi:] sie; **she's (= she is)** sie ist
sheep [ʃi:p] Schaf, Schafe
shelf, shelves [ʃelf, ʃelvz] Regal, Regale
ship [ʃɪp] Schiff
shoe [ʃu:] Schuh
shop [ʃɒp] Laden, Geschäft
shop assistant ['ʃɒpəsɪstənt] Verkäufer, Verkäuferin
shoplifter ['ʃɒplɪftə] Ladendieb/in
shopper ['ʃɒpə] Käufer, Käuferin
shopping ['ʃɒpɪŋ]: **go shopping** einkaufen gehen
shopping centre ['ʃɒpɪŋsentə] Einkaufszentrum U5: 65
short [ʃɔ:t] kurz; klein U4: 57; **a short time after ...** kurz nachdem ... WF U6
shot-put ['ʃɒtpʊt] Kugelstoßen WF
should [ʃʊd, ʃəd]: **you should** du solltest, du müsstest U1: 12
shoulder ['ʃəʊldə] Schulter WF
shout [ʃaʊt] laut rufen, schreien
show [ʃəʊ] **1** zeigen U4: 59; **2** Show
Shut up! [ʃʌt'ʌp] Halt den Mund!
shy [ʃaɪ] schüchtern U5: 68
side [saɪd] Seite
sign [saɪn] Schild; Zeichen
signal ['sɪgnəl] Zeichen, Signal
silly ['sɪli] dumm, albern U2: 22
simple [sɪmpl] einfach WF; **simple past** einfache Vergangenheit; **simple present** einfache Gegenwart
sing [sɪŋ] (I sang, I've sung) singen
Singapore ['sɪŋəpɔ:] Singapur U1: 10
singer ['sɪŋə] Sänger, Sängerin
sister ['sɪstə] Schwester; **brothers and sisters** Geschwister
sit [sɪt] (I sat, I've sat) sitzen; sich setzen
size [saɪz] Größe WF U6; **What size do you take?** Welche Größe hast du? WF U6

skateboard ['skeɪtbɔ:d] Skateboard WF
skateboarder ['skeɪtbɔ:də] Skateboarder U3: 48
skateboarding ['skeɪtbɔ:dɪŋ] Skateboardfahren WF
skater ['skeɪtə] Skater, Skaterin
skating ['skeɪtɪŋ] Inlineskates-/Rollschuhlaufen WF
skiing ['ski:ɪŋ] Skifahren
sleep [sli:p] (I slept, I've slept) schlafen
slip [slɪp] ausrutschen U4: 55
slow [sləʊ] langsam WF
small [smɔ:l] klein
smile [smaɪl] lächeln U2: 27
smoke [sməʊk] rauchen WF
smuggler ['smʌglə] Schmuggler, Schmugglerin WF U6
smuggling ['smʌglɪŋ] Schmuggel, Schmuggeln WF U6
snowboarder ['snəʊbɔ:də] Snowboarder U3: 48
so [səʊ] so; also; daher; **so far** ['səʊfɑ:] bis hierher/jetzt WF
soak [səʊk] nass machen WF
software ['sɒftweə] Software H&T: 6
Somalia [sə'mɑ:liə] Somalia
some [sʌm] **1** einige, ein paar; **2** etwas
somebody ['sʌmbədi] jemand U5: 66
something ['sʌmθɪŋ] etwas; **something different** etwas anderes
sometimes ['sʌmtaɪmz] manchmal
song [sɒŋ] Lied
soon [su:n] bald
sorry ['sɒri]: **Sorry./I'm sorry.** Tut mir leid. **I'm sorry I ...** Tut mir leid, dass ich ...
sound [saʊnd] **1** klingen, sich anhören U2: 33; **2** Geräusch U1: 8
south [saʊθ] Süden; Süd-; südlich H&T: 7; **south-east, south-west** Südosten, -westen WF U6
souvenir [su:və'nɪə] Souvenir, Andenken WF
Spain [speɪn] Spanien
Spanish ['spænɪʃ] Spanisch WF
speak (to) [spi:k] (I spoke, I've spoken) sprechen (mit)
special ['speʃl] besondere, besonderer, besonderes H&T: 6
special offer [speʃl'ɒfə] Sonderangebot U3: 45
spell [spel] buchstabieren
spend [spend] (I spent, I've spent) **1** ausgeben; **spend on** ausgeben für WF; **2** verbringen WF U6

spent [spent] (→ spend): **I spent** ich gab aus, ich habe ausgegeben; **they had spent** sie hatten verbracht WF U6
spider ['spaɪdə] Spinne
splash [splæʃ] spritzen WF
sponsored ['spɒnsəd] gesponsert U1: 19
spoon [spu:n] Löffel WF U6
sport [spɔ:t] Sport, Sportart; **play sports** Sport treiben
sports centre ['spɔ:tssentə] Sportzentrum
sporty ['spɔ:ti] sportlich
spring [sprɪŋ] Frühling
squash [skwɒʃ] Squash
stadium ['steɪdiəm] Stadion RD U3
stamp [stæmp] **1** Stempel; **2** Briefmarke WF
stand [stænd] (I stood, I've stood) stehen; **I can't stand them** ich kann sie nicht ausstehen U2: 30; **stand on somebody's foot** jemandem auf den Fuß treten WF
star [stɑ:] **1** Star *(berühmte Persönlichkeit)* U2: 25; **2** Stern WF
stare [steə] (starrer) Blick WF
start [stɑ:t] **1** anfangen, beginnen; **I started to run** ich begann zu rennen; **start a programme** eine Sendung ins Leben rufen U1: 13; **2** Start, Anfang
station ['steɪʃn] Bahnhof; **at Exeter Station** im Bahnhof Exeter
statue ['stætʃu:] Statue U2: 34
stay [steɪ] bleiben; übernachten
steal [sti:l] stehlen RD U1
step [step] Stufe
sticker ['stɪkə] Aufkleber WF U6
still [stɪl] (immer) noch WF
stomach ['stʌmək] Bauch WF
stop [stɒp] anhalten, stoppen; stehen bleiben
story ['stɔ:ri] Geschichte
stream [stri:m] Bach RD U3
street [stri:t] Straße
stress [stres] betonen U2: 30
strict [strɪkt] streng U3: 41
stupid ['stju:pɪd] dumm, blöd
subject ['sʌbdʒɪkt] (Schul-)Fach
suburb ['sʌbɜ:b] Vorort U5: 68
successful [sək'sesfl] erfolgreich WF
such [sʌtʃ]: **There's no such thing.** So etwas gibt es nicht.
suddenly ['sʌdnli] plötzlich
summary ['sʌməri] Zusammenfassung U3: 47
summer ['sʌmə] Sommer
sun [sʌn] Sonne

sunbathing ['sʌnbeɪðɪŋ] Sonnenbaden WF U6
Sunday ['sʌndeɪ, 'sʌndi] Sonntag
sung [sʌŋ] (→ sing): **I've sung** ich habe gesungen U2: 139
sunny ['sʌni] sonnig
super ['suːpə] super, toll
supermarket ['suːpəmɑːkɪt] Supermarkt
sure [ʃʊə] sicher
surfing ['sɜːfɪŋ] Surfen RD U5
surprise [sə'praɪz] Überraschung
surprised [sə'praɪzd] überrascht WF
survey ['sɜːveɪ] Umfrage, Untersuchung
swam [swæm] (→ swim): **I swam** ich schwamm, ich bin geschwommen
swim [swɪm] (I swam, I've swum) schwimmen
swimmer ['swɪmə] Schwimmer, Schwimmerin
swimming ['swɪmɪŋ] Schwimmen; **go swimming** schwimmen gehen
swimming pool ['swɪmɪŋpuːl] Schwimmbad
Switzerland ['swɪtsələnd] Schweiz
sword [sɔːd] Schwert WF
symbol ['sɪmbl] Symbol U2: 29

T

table ['teɪbl] **1** Tisch; **2** Tabelle WF; **table tennis** Tischtennis
tae kwon do [taɪkwɒn'dəʊ] Taekwondo WF
take [teɪk] (I took, I've taken) **1** (weg)nehmen; bringen; **Take a jacket.** Nimm/Bring eine Jacke mit. **take things from people** Leuten Dinge wegnehmen RD U1; **What size do you take?** Welche Größe hast du? WF U6; **2** dauern WF
take away [teɪkə'weɪ] wegnehmen WF
take off [teɪk'ɒf]: **I took off my jacket** ich zog meine Jacke aus U4: 54
take out [teɪk'aʊt] herausnehmen WF U6
taken ['teɪkən] (→ take): **I've taken** ich habe genommen
talk [tɔːk] **1 talk (to)** reden (mit), sprechen (mit), sich unterhalten (mit); **2** Vortrag U4: 57
tall [tɔːl] groß *(bei Personen)*

tattoo [tə'tuː] Tätowierung, Tattoo WF U6
tax [tæks] Steuer RD U6
taxi ['tæksi] Taxi U1: 9
tea [tiː] Tee
teach [tiːtʃ] beibringen RD U1
teacher ['tiːtʃə] Lehrer, Lehrerin
team [tiːm] Team, Mannschaft
technology [tek'nɒlədʒi] Technik, Technologie U4: 52
teen, teenager [tiːn, 'tiːneɪdʒə] Teenager U5: 66
tell (about) [tel] (I told, I've told) erzählen (von); sagen; erkennen RD U3
tennis ['tenɪs] Tennis
terrible ['terəbl] schrecklich, furchtbar
test [test] Test, Klassenarbeit, Prüfung
text [tekst] **1** Text; **2** SMS U3: 40
text bullying ['tekstbʊliɪŋ] SMS-Terror U3: 44
text message ['tekstmesɪdʒ] SMS (Textnachricht)
Thai [taɪ] Thai WF
than [ðæn, ðən]: **faster than** schneller als
thank [θæŋk]: **Thank you.** Danke (schön).
Thanks. [θæŋks] Danke.
that [ðæt] **1** das; der, die, das (da); **2** dass; **that evening** an diesem Abend U3: 41; **That's OK.** Schon gut./Bitte. **That's why ...** Deshalb ..., Darum ... U4: 57; **That's two pounds, please.** Das macht zwei Pfund, bitte. **now that it's done** nun, wo es fertig ist WF
the [ðə, ði] der, die, das; **The next day ...** Am nächsten Tag ... U5: 69
theatre ['θɪətə] Theater WF
their [ðeə] ihr, ihre
them [ðem] ihnen, sie
then [ðen] dann
there [ðeə] da, dort; dahin, dorthin; **there's (= there is)** da ist, es gibt/ist; **there are** da sind, es gibt/sind; **there was/were** da war(en), es gab/war(en)
these [ðiːz] die (hier); diese
they [ðeɪ] sie; **they're (= they are)** sie sind
thigh [θaɪ] Oberschenkel WF
thing [θɪŋ] Ding, Sache; **the right/best/... thing** das Richtige/Beste/... ; **There's no such thing.** So etwas gibt es nicht.

think [θɪŋk] (I thought, I've thought) denken, nachdenken; finden; **think of** denken an; **What do you think of ...?** Was hältst du von ...?
thirsty ['θɜːsti]: **he was thirsty** er hatte Durst WF U6
this [ðɪs] dies (hier), das (hier); diese, dieser, dieses; **this evening/...** heute Abend/...
those [ðəʊz] diese, jene, die (da) U3: 41
thought [θɔːt] (→ think): **I thought** ich dachte, ich habe gedacht; **I had thought** ich hatte gedacht WF U6
thousand ['θaʊznd] tausend U4: 52
thriller ['θrɪlə] Thriller WF
through [θruː] durch, hindurch
Thursday ['θɜːzdeɪ, 'θɜːzdi] Donnerstag
ticket ['tɪkɪt] Eintrittskarte; Fahrkarte, Flugschein
time [taɪm] **1** Zeit; Uhrzeit; **2** Mal WF U6; **it's time for it to end** es ist Zeit, dass es aufhört WF; **What time is it?** Wie spät ist es?
timetable ['taɪmteɪbl] Stundenplan
tiny ['taɪni] winzig WF
tip [tɪp] Tipp U1: 10
tired ['taɪəd] müde
title ['taɪtl] Titel U1: 10
to [tuː, tu, tə] **1** zu, nach; an; **fall to the ground** auf den Boden fallen; **go to bed** ins Bett gehen; **I've been to France.** Ich bin (schon einmal) in Frankreich gewesen. **Jamie says goodbye to Tess.** Jamie sagt Tess auf Wiedersehen. **they help you to read** sie helfen dir zu lesen U1: 12; **things to do** Sachen, die man machen kann; **To finish, ...** Um zum Ende zu kommen, ... U4: 57; **to sell our pictures** um unsere Bilder zu verkaufen WF U6; **to visit his girlfriend** um seine Freundin zu besuchen RD U5; **Welcome to London.** Willkommen in London. **2** bis; **It's five to ten.** Es ist fünf vor zehn.
toaster ['təʊstə] Toaster WF
today [tə'deɪ] heute
together [tə'geðə] zusammen
told [təʊld] (→ tell): **I told** ich erzählte, ich habe erzählt; **I've told** ich habe erzählt

tomato [tə'mɑ:təʊ] Tomate WF
tomorrow [tə'mɒrəʊ] morgen
tongue twister ['tʌŋtwɪstə] Zungenbrecher U5: 72
too [tu:] **1** auch; **2 too old** zu alt
took [tʊk] (→ take): **I took** ich nahm, ich habe genommen
toothbrush ['tu:θbrʌʃ] Zahnbürste WF
topic ['tɒpɪk] Thema U3: 39
tough [tʌf] hart, zäh, stark
tour [tʊə] Tour
tourist ['tʊərɪst] Tourist/in U3: 37
tourist office ['tʊərɪstɒfɪs] Touristeninformation, Fremdenverkehrsbüro U3: 37
towards [tə'wɔ:dz] auf ... zu, in Richtung
tower ['taʊə] Turm U4: 51
town [taʊn] Stadt
town centre ['taʊnsentə] Stadtzentrum, Stadtmitte
toy [tɔɪ] Spielzeug
track [træk] **1** Weg, Pfad; **2** Bahn, Laufbahn U5: 68
traditional [trə'dɪʃənl] traditionell RD U2
traffic ['træfɪk] Verkehr U1: 9
traffic light ['træfɪklaɪt] (Verkehrs-)Ampel
train [treɪn] **1** trainieren U5: 64; **2** Zug, Eisenbahn
trainer ['treɪnə] **1** Trainer; **2** Sportschuh
training ['treɪnɪŋ] Training WF
tram [træm] Straßenbahn
trampolining ['træmpəli:nɪŋ] Trampolinspringen WF
translate [træns'leɪt] übersetzen U3: 43
travel ['trævl] reisen, fahren U5: 66
traveller ['trævələ] Reisende/r; Landfahrer/in U5: 66
treasure hunt ['treʒəhʌnt] Schatzsuche
treat [tri:t] Genuss, besonderes Vergnügen U3: 47
trip [trɪp] **1** Ausflug, Reise; **2** stolpern WF
trouble ['trʌbl]: **I'm in big trouble** ich stecke in großen Schwierigkeiten U3: 41
true [tru:] wahr U5: 72
try [traɪ] versuchen, probieren
try on [traɪ'ɒn] anprobieren WF U6
T-shirt ['ti:ʃɜ:t] T-Shirt
tube [tju:b]: **the tube** die (Londoner) U-Bahn U1: 16
Tuesday ['tju:zdeɪ, -di] Dienstag
tuna ['tju:nə] Tunfisch WF
tunnel ['tʌnl] Tunnel
Turkey ['tɜ:ki] **1** Türkei H&T: 6; **2** Truthahn WF
Turkish ['tɜ:kɪʃ] Türkisch WF
turn [tɜ:n]: **turn left/right (into Market Street)** nach links/rechts (in die Market Street) abbiegen
turn off [tɜ:n'ɒf] ausschalten U3: 44
turn on [tɜ:n'ɒn] einschalten U3: 44
TV ['ti:'vi:] Fernsehen, Fernsehgerät

U

Ukrainian [ju:'kreɪniən] Ukrainisch WF
uncle ['ʌŋkl] Onkel WF
under ['ʌndə] unter U1: 17; **under 18s** unter 18-Jährige WF U6
underground ['ʌndəgraʊnd] unterirdisch; **underground station** U-Bahnhof U1: 135; **underground train** U-Bahn-Zug U1: 9
underline [ʌndə'laɪn] unterstreichen U2: 30
underlined [ʌndə'laɪnd] unterstrichen U2: 29
understand [ʌndə'stænd] (I understood, I've understood) verstehen
understood [ʌndə'stʊd] (→ understand): **I understood** ich verstand, ich habe verstanden
unhappy [ʌn'hæpi] unglücklich WF
uniform ['ju:nɪfɔ:m] (Schul-)Uniform
unit ['ju:nɪt] Lektion
up [ʌp]: **What's up?** Was gibt's?
upset [ʌp'set] aufgeregt, aufgebracht WF
us [ʌs] uns
use [ju:z] benutzen, verwenden
usually ['ju:ʒuəli] meistens, normalerweise, gewöhnlich
Uzbek ['ʊzbek] Usbekisch WF

V

vegetable ['vedʒtəbl] (ein) Gemüse
verb [vɜ:b] Verb, Zeitwort
verse [vɜ:s] Strophe
very ['veri] sehr
video ['vɪdiəʊ] Videofilm, Video
video clip ['vɪdiəʊklɪp] Videoausschnitt RD U4
Vietnamese [vjetnə'mi:z] Vietnamesisch WF
Viking ['vaɪkɪŋ] Wikinger, Wikinger- U5: 76
village ['vɪlɪdʒ] Dorf
violent ['vaɪələnt] gewalttätig WF
visit ['vɪzɪt] **1** besuchen; **2** Besuch WF
visitor ['vɪzɪtə] Besucher/in, Gast
volcanic [vɒl'kænɪk] vulkanisch RD U5
volleyball ['vɒlibɔ:l] Volleyball

W

wait [weɪt]: **wait (for)** warten (auf); **I can't wait for it.** Ich kann es kaum erwarten. **Let's wait and see.** Warten wir's ab.
waitress ['weɪtrəs] Kellnerin WF U6
Wales [weɪlz] Wales
walk [wɔ:k] gehen, laufen
walker ['wɔ:kə] Spaziergänger/in, Wanderer, Wanderin
walking ['wɔ:kɪŋ] Spazierengehen, Wandern
walking shoe ['wɔ:kɪŋʃu:] Wanderschuh
want [wɒnt] wollen; **want to go** gehen wollen
warm [wɔ:m] warm
was [wɒz, wəz] war; **wasn't (= was not)** war nicht; **they thought it was a good idea** sie dachten, es wäre eine gute Idee; **everybody was eating** sie aßen alle (gerade) WF; **he was hanging/running** er hing/rannte (gerade); **he was laughing** er lachte (gerade) WF; **he was sending** er schickte (gerade) U3: 40; **he was watching** er sah (gerade) zu U5: 69
waste [weɪst] verschwenden U4: 53; **a waste of time** Zeitverschwendung U3: 38
watch [wɒtʃ] **1** beobachten, sich anschauen; **2** zusehen U3: 40; **Watch me!** Pass auf! U4: 54; **watch TV** fernsehen
water ['wɔ:tə] Wasser
way [weɪ] Weg
we [wi:] wir; **we're (= we are)** wir sind
wear [weə] (I wore, I've worn) tragen, anziehen

weather ['weðə] Wetter
webcode ['webkəʊd] Webcode
website ['websaɪt] Website U1: 11
weddingday ['wedɪŋdeɪ] Hochzeitstag U2: 33
Wednesday ['wenzdeɪ, 'wenzdi] Mittwoch
week [wi:k] Woche
weekend ['wi:k'end] Wochenende
welcome ['welkəm]: **Welcome to London.** Willkommen in London. **we aren't welcome** wir sind nicht willkommen U5: 73; **You're welcome.** Nichts zu danken; Bitte schön. WF U6
well [wel] **1** gut; **2 Well, ...** Nun/Tja, ...
Welsh [welʃ] walisisch; Walisisch; Waliser, Waliserin(nen) U3: 38
went [went] (→ go): **I went** ich ging, ich bin gegangen
were [wɜ:] waren; warst; wart; **weren't (= were not)** waren/warst/wart nicht; **they were having dinner** sie waren gerade beim Essen WF; **they were playing** sie spielten (gerade) U5: 69; **they were talking** sie unterhielten sich (gerade) U3: 40
west [west] Westen; West-; westlich H&T: 7
western ['westən] Western WF
wet [wet] nass, feucht U4: 54
whale [weɪl] Wal U5: 75
what [wɒt] **1** was; **What a ...!** Was für ein/eine ...! **What about you?** Und du?/Was ist mit dir? **What are they in German?** Wie heißen sie auf Deutsch? **What fun!** Was für ein Spaß! WF; **What time is it?** Wie spät ist es? **What's that?** Was ist das? **What's your name?** Wie heißt du? **What's up?** Was gibt's? **2** welche, welcher, welches
whatever [wɒt'evə]: **whatever the weather** egal, wie das Wetter ist U5: 72
wheelchair ['wi:ltʃeə] Rollstuhl; **he's in a wheelchair** er sitzt im Rollstuhl
when [wen] **1** wann; **2** wenn; **3** als U2: 34
whenever [wen'evə] wann immer WF
where [weə] wo; wohin; **Where are you from?** Woher kommst du?
whether ['weðə] ob U5: 72
which [wɪtʃ] welche, welcher, welches
white [waɪt] weiß; **white bread** Weißbrot WF
who [hu:] wer
wholemeal ['həʊlmi:l] Vollkorn- WF
why [waɪ] warum, weshalb; **That's why ...** Deshalb/Darum ... U4: 57
wide [waɪd] breit
wild [waɪld] wild; wild lebend
will [wɪl]: **I'll (= I will) go** ich werde gehen U4: 52
win [wɪn] (I won, I've won) gewinnen
window ['wɪndəʊ] Fenster
windsurfing ['wɪndsɜ:fɪŋ] Windsurfing WF U6
winner ['wɪnə] Gewinner/Gewinnerin, Sieger/Siegerin
winter ['wɪntə] Winter U3: 38
wishes ['wɪʃɪz]: **Best wishes, ...** Viele Grüße ...
witch [wɪtʃ] Hexe U1: 20
with [wɪð] mit; bei
without [wɪ'ðaʊt] ohne U4: 62
woke [wəʊk]: **he woke** er wachte auf WF
wolf [wʊlf] Wolf WF
woman, women ['wʊmən, 'wɪmɪn] Frau, Frauen
won [wʌn] (→ win): **I won** ich gewann, ich habe gewonnen; **I've won** ich habe gewonnen U4: 52
won't [wəʊnt]: **I won't (= will not) go** ich werde nicht gehen U4: 52
wonderful ['wʌndəfl] wundervoll WF
wood [wʊd] Wald
word [wɜ:d] Wort; **words (of a song)** (Lied-)Text U2: 25
wore [wɔ:] (→ wear): **I wore** ich trug, ich habe getragen
work [wɜ:k] **1** arbeiten; funktionieren U4: 62; **2** Arbeit
worker ['wɜ:kə] Arbeiter, Arbeiterin
world [wɜ:ld] Welt; **in the world** auf der (ganzen) Welt; **out of this world** nicht von dieser Welt, fantastisch RD U4
worried ['wʌrid]: **I'm worried (about)** ich mache mir Sorgen (um), ich bin beunruhigt (wegen) U4: 55
worry (about) ['wʌri] sich Sorgen machen (um) U5: 68
worse [wɜ:s] schlechter; schlimmer
worst [wɜ:st] schlechteste/r/s; schlimmste/r/s; **it's just the worst** es ist einfach das Allerschlimmste WF
would [wʊd]: **I'd (= I would) like to go/...** Ich möchte gehen ...; **I wouldn't (= would not) like to go/...** Ich möchte nicht gehen/...; **Would you like ...?** Möchtest du/Möchten Sie ...? U4: 59
Wow! [waʊ] Wow! Wahnsinn! U2: 26
write [raɪt] (I wrote, I've written) schreiben
writer ['raɪtə] Schriftsteller, Schriftstellerin U1: 19
writing ['raɪtɪŋ]: **Writing a story/...** Eine Geschichte/... schreiben
written ['rɪtn] (→ write): **I've written** ich habe geschrieben
wrong [rɒŋ] falsch; **What's wrong?** Ist etwas nicht in Ordnung? U2: 27
wrote [rəʊt] (→ write): **I wrote** ich schrieb, ich habe geschrieben

Y

yeah [jeə] ja *(besonders in wörtl. Rede)* U2: 27
year [jɪə] Jahr; Jahrgangsstufe; **a 13-year-old girl** ein 13-jähriges Mädchen U2: 26; **What year are you in? - I'm in year 7.** In welcher Jahrgangsstufe bist du? - Ich bin in der 7. Stufe.
yellow ['jeləʊ] gelb
yes [jes] ja
yesterday ['jestədeɪ, 'jestədi] gestern
yet [jet]: **not ... yet** noch nicht U1: 10
you [ju:] **1** du; ihr; Sie; **2** dir, euch, Ihnen; dich, euch, Sie; **you're (= you are)** du bist; ihr seid; Sie sind; **I said you'd be in the shop tomorrow.** Ich habe gesagt, du wärst morgen im Laden.
young [jʌŋ] jung
your [jɔ:] dein, deine; euer, eure; Ihr, Ihre
yourself [jɔ:'self]: **a picture of yourself** ein Bild von dir
youth club ['ju:θklʌb] Jugendklub

Alphabetische Liste der Wörter aus den Bänden 1–3 (Deutsch – Englisch)

* = unregelmäßiges Verb; siehe auch *List of irregular verbs*, S.180/181

A

abbiegen: nach links/rechts (in die Market Street) abbiegen turn left/right (into Market Street)
Abend evening
abends in the evening; *(mit Uhrzeit)* p.m.
aber but
Abfall litter
abholen pick up
ablesen *read out
Abneigung dislike
Absatz paragraph
abschreiben copy
abseits der Straße off-road
Absender/in sender
Absprache arrangement; **Absprachen treffen** Making arrangements; **eine Absprache treffen** *make an arrangement
Achterbahn roller coaster
Actionfilm action film
Adresse address
Aerobic aerobics
Afrika Africa
Akte file
Aktivität activity
Albanisch Albanian
albern silly
Alkohol alcohol
alle all (the); *(jeder)* everybody
allein alone
Allerschlimmste: es ist einfach das Allerschlimmste it's just the worst
alles everything
Alphabet alphabet
alphabetisch alphabetical
als when; **schneller als** faster than
also so
alt old
Alter age; **sie hatte das richtige Alter** she was the right age
am: am 5. August on August 5th; **am Morgen/Nachmittag/Abend** in the morning/afternoon/evening; **Am nächsten Tag ...** The next day ...; **am selben Ort** in the same place; **am Telefon** on the phone; **24 Stunden am Tag** 24 hours a day
Ampel traffic light
an **1** *(bei)* at; **2** *(nach)* to; **3** *(in der Nähe von, neben)* by; **4** *(eingeschaltet)* on; **an den Armen** by his arms; **an der Küste** on the coast; **an Schultagen** on school days; **denken an** *think of
anbieten offer
Andenken souvenir
andere other; **ein anderer/anderes, eine andere** another
andere/r/s, anders (als) different (from)
(sich) ändern change
Anfang start
anfangen start
Angebot offer
Angeln fishing
Angst: ich habe Angst I'm frightened
ängstlich nervous
Anhänger/in fan
anhalten stop
anhören: sich anhören sound; **sich die CD anhören** listen to the CD
ankommen arrive
Anlegestelle pier
Anprobe changing room
anprobieren *try on
Anruf: Danke für den Anruf. Thanks for calling.
anrufen phone
anschauen: sich den Film anschauen watch the film; **sich die Strände anschauen** *see the beaches
Anschlagbrett noticeboard
ansehen: (sich) das Bild ansehen look at the picture
Ansicht scene
Ansichtskarte postcard
Antwort answer
antworten answer
Anzeige advert
anziehen *(tragen)* *wear
Apfel apple
Apfelwein cider
April April
Arabisch Arabic
Arbeit work; job
arbeiten work
Arbeiter/in worker
Arbeitsgemeinschaft *(Klub)* club
Arbeitsstelle job
arm poor; **Du Arme/r!** Poor you!
Arm arm
Art: eine Art Buch a kind of book
Artikel article
Asiat/in Asian
asiatisch Asian
Asien Asia
aßen: sie aßen alle (gerade) everybody was eating
Atlantik Atlantic
auch too
auf on; *(auf ... hinauf/herauf)* onto; **auf das Haus zu** towards the house; **auf dem Bild** in the picture; **auf dem Land** in the country; **auf dem Schulhof** in the playground; **auf den Boden fallen** *fall to the ground; **auf der (ganzen) Welt** in the world; **auf der Straße** in the street; **auf Deutsch** in German; **auf die Straße (hinaus)** into the street; **Auf Wiedersehen.** Goodbye.
Aufgabe job
aufgeben *give up
aufgebracht upset
aufgehen *(sich öffnen)* open
aufgeladen: es ist aufgeladen it's charged up
aufgeregt upset
aufgeschrieben: ich habe aufgeschrieben I put down
aufheben pick up
aufhören (mit) finish; **Hör doch auf!** Give me a break!
Aufkleber sticker
aufmachen open
aufpassen *pay attention; **auf ihn aufpassen** look after him; **Pass auf!** Watch me!
aufregend exciting
aufstehen *get up
aufwachen: er wachte auf he woke
Auge eye
August August; **20. August** August 20th
aus **1** from; *(aus ... hinaus/heraus)* out of; **2** *(zu Ende)* over; **aus der Schule zurück** back from school
Ausdruck phrase
Ausflug trip
ausgeben (für) *spend (on)
ausgehen *go out
ausleihen *(mieten)* rent
ausprobieren *try
ausrollen roll out
ausrutschen slip

ausschalten turn off
aussehen look; **Wie sieht sie aus?** What does she look like?
ausstehen: ich kann sie nicht ausstehen I hate them; I can't stand them
Ausstellung exhibition
aussuchen pick
auswendig: Lerne es auswendig. Learn it by heart.
ausziehen: ich zog meine Jacke aus I took off my jacket
Auto car
Autofahrer/in driver
Autogramm autograph

B

Baby baby
Bach stream
backen bake
Bad, Badezimmer bathroom
Badminton badminton
Bahn *(Laufbahn)* track
Bahnhof station; **im Bahnhof Exeter** at Exeter Station
bald soon
Ball ball
Banane banana
Band *(Musikgruppe)* band
Bande gang
Bank *(Sparkasse)* bank
Basketball basketball
Batterieladegerät charger
Bauch stomach
Bauer/Bäuerin farmer
Bauernhof farm
beantworten answer
bedeuten *mean
Bedeutung meaning
beeilen: Beeil dich! Hurry up!
beenden finish
beginnen start; **ich begann zu rennen** I started to run
bei **1** *(an)* at; **2** *(mit)* with; **bei Tim (zu Hause)** at Tim's house
beibringen teach
beide both
Beispiel example
beitreten: einem Klub beitreten join a club
bekommen *get
belebt busy
Belgien Belgium
beliebt popular
bemerken notice
benutzen use
beobachten watch
bereit ready
Berg mountain
Bericht report
berichtigen correct
Beruf job; **Berufs-** professional
berühmt famous
beschäftigt busy
Beschäftigung activity; *(im Freien)* outdoor activity
Beschreibung description
(sich) beschweren complain
besondere/r/s special
besser better
beste/r/s best; **am besten** best
Besteck cutlery
Besuch visit
besuchen visit
Besucher/in visitor
betonen stress
Betrieb business
Bett bed
beunruhigt: ich bin beunruhigt (wegen) I'm worried (about)
bevor before
bewölkt cloudy
bezahlen *pay
Bier beer
Bild picture
Bildschirmdarstellung display
billig cheap
bin: ich bin I'm (= I am)
bis to; **bis hierher/jetzt** so far; **Bis dann.** See you. **Bis morgen/...** See you tomorrow/...
bist: du bist you're (= you are); **Bist du schon einmal ...? - Ja./Nein.** Have you ever ...? - Yes, I have./No, I haven't.
bitte please; **Hier, bitte.** Here you are. **Bitte.** *(Schon gut.)* That's OK. **Bitte schön.** *(Nichts zu danken.)* You're welcome.
bitten um ask for
blau blue
bleiben stay
Bleistift pencil
Blick: starrer Blick stare
blöd stupid
Blödsinn nonsense
Blog blog
Bloggen blogging
Blogger/in blogger
blond blonde
bloß only
Blume flower
Blut blood
Board *(Brett)* board
Boden floor; ground; **am Boden zerstört** devastated
Bombe bomb
Boot boat
böse (auf) angry (with)
Bosnisch Bosnian
Bote/Botin courier
Bowling bowling
Boxen boxing
brauchen need
braun brown
breit wide
Brett board; **Schwarzes Brett** noticeboard
Brief letter
Brieffreund/in penfriend
Briefmarke stamp
bringen *bring; *take; **in die richtige Reihenfolge bringen** *put in the right order
Broschüre brochure
Brot bread; **belegtes Brot** sandwich
Brötchen roll
Brücke bridge
Bruder brother
Brust chest
Buch book
Bücherei library
Buchhandlung, -laden bookshop
Buchstabe letter
buchstabieren spell
Burg castle
Bürgersteig pavement
Büro office
Bus bus
Busfahrer/in bus driver
Bushaltestelle bus stop
Butter butter

C

Café cafe
Camping camping
CD CD
Chinesisch Chinese
Clique gang
Cola cola
Collage collage
Comic comic
Computer computer
cool cool
Countrymusik country music
Cousin/e cousin

D

da: da(hin) there; **da ist** there's; **da sind** there are; **da war/waren** there was/were; **da drüben** over there; **Ich bin wieder da!** I'm back!
dagegen: du hast nichts dagegen you don't mind
daheim at home

daher so
Dänemark Denmark
Danke. Thank you./Thanks.
dann then
darum that's why
das the; *(das da)* that; *(das hier)* this; **Das ist ...** That's ...
dass that; **Tut mir leid, dass ich ...** I'm sorry I ...
dasselbe the same
Datum date
dauern *take
dein/e your
Delfin dolphin
denken (an) *think (of)
der the; *(der da)* that
derselbe the same
deshalb that's why
Detektiv/in detective
deutsch; Deutsch; Deutsche/r German
Deutschland Germany
Dezember December
Dialog dialogue
dich you
Dichter/in poet
die the; *(die da; Einzahl)* that; *(die da; Mehrzahl)* those; *(die hier; Mehrzahl)* these; **die Sprache, die wir sprechen** the language we speak
Dienstag Tuesday
dies (hier) this
diese *(Mehrzahl)* these; *(diese da)* those
diese/r/s this; **an diesem Abend** that evening; **dieses ist für dich** this one's for you
dieselbe the same
Ding thing
dir you; **ein Bild von dir** a picture of yourself
Discjockey (DJ) DJ
Disko club
Diskus(werfen) (the) discus
Doktor doctor
Dolmetschen interpreting
Donnerstag Thursday
Dorf village
dort(hin) there
Drache dragon
Drama drama
draußen *(im Freien)* outdoors
drinnen *(in der Halle)* indoors
drüben: da/dort drüben over there
drücken push
du you
Dubliner/in Dubliner
dumm silly; stupid
dunkel dark
durch *(hindurch)* through
dürfen can; **nicht dürfen** mustn't
Durst: er hatte Durst he was thirsty
DVD DVD
DVD-Player DVD player

E

echt real
egal: egal, wie das Wetter ist whatever the weather
Ei egg
eifersüchtig (auf) jealous (of)
eigen: mein eigenes Zimmer my own room
eigentlich really
ein/e a; an; *(Zahl)* one
eine/r/s one; **eines Tages** one day
einfach easy; simple; **einfache Gegenwart/Vergangenheit** simple present/past
Einfall idea
einfügen *put in
eingeschaltet on
einige some
einkaufen gehen *go shopping
Einkaufszentrum shopping centre
einladen invite; **zu einem Wochenende einladen** invite for a weekend
Einladung invitation
einpacken pack
einsam lonely
einschalten turn on
einschlafen *fall asleep
Eintrittskarte ticket
Eis *(Speiseeis)* ice cream
Eisenbahn train
Eisenbahnstrecke railway line
elektrisch electric
Elektrizität electricity
elektronisch electronic
Eltern, Elternteil parents, parent
E-Mail e-mail
Ende end; **Um zum Ende zu kommen, ...** To finish, ...; **zu Ende** over
enden end
Energie energy
eng narrow
England England
Engländer/in(nen): er ist Engländer he's English
englisch; Englisch English
Englischlehrer/in English teacher
entlang along; **die Straße entlang** along the street
entschuldigen: sich entschuldigen *say sorry; **Entschuldigen Sie, ...** Excuse me, ...
enttäuscht disappointed
er he; *(nicht bei Personen)* it
Erdkunde geography
erfahren: etwas über London erfahren learn about London
erfolgreich successful
Ergebnis result
erinnern: sich erinnern (an) remember
erkennen *tell
erklären explain
erraten guess
erschüttert devastated
erst only
erstaunlich amazing
erste/r/s first
erstens firstly
Erwachsene/r adult
erwarten: Ich kann es kaum erwarten. I can't wait for it.
erzählen (von) *tell (about)
es it; **es ist/gibt** there's; **es sind/gibt** there are; **es war(en)/gab** there was/were
essen *eat; **ein Eis essen** *have an ice cream; **zu essen geben** *feed
Essen food
Etikett label
etwas something; **etwas anderes** something different; **etwas Schokolade** some chocolate
euch you
euer/eure your
Euro euro (€)
Europa Europe

F

Fabrik factory
Fach *(Schulfach)* subject
Fahne flag
fahren *go; *(ein Auto/einen Bus)* *drive; *(reisen)* travel **Mountainboard/Quad/Rad fahren** *ride a mountain board/quad/bike
Fahren: Quadfahren/Trikkefahren/... quad/Trikke/... riding
Fahrer/in driver
Fahrkarte ticket
Fahrrad bike
fallen *fall; **auf den Boden fallen** *fall to the ground; **fallen lassen** drop

falls if
falsch wrong
Familie family
Fan fan
fantastisch fantastic; out of this world
Farbe colour
Farsi Farsi
Fastfood fast food
Favorit/in favourite
Februar February
Federball(spiel) badminton
Federmäppchen pencil case
fehlend: die fehlenden Wörter the missing words
Feind/in enemy
Feld field
Fels rock
Felsen cliff
Fenster window
Ferien holiday/s
fernsehen watch TV
Fernsehen, Fernsehgerät TV
fertig ready; **nun, wo es fertig ist** now that it's done
Fest festival
Festbeleuchtung illuminations
feucht wet
Feuer fire
Farbe colour
Figur *(Person)* character
finden *find; *think
Fisch, Fische fish
Fischen fishing
fit fit
Fitnessstudio gym
Flagge flag
fliegen *go
Flipflop flip-flop
Flughafen airport; **am Flughafen Exeter** at Exeter Airport
Flugschein (plane) ticket
Flugzeug plane
Fluss river
Föhn hairdryer
Folge result
folgen follow
Form form
Foto photo; picture
Fotoapparat camera
Frage question; **eine Frage stellen** ask a question
Fragebogen questionnaire
fragen ask
Frankreich France
Franzose(n)/Französin(nen); französisch; Französisch French
Frau, Frauen woman, women; *(Anrede allgemein)* Ms; *(Anrede für verheiratete Frauen)* Mrs
Freak freak
frei free; **im Freien** outdoors; **Beschäftigung im Freien** outdoor activity
Freitag Friday
Freizeit free time
Fremdenverkehrsbüro tourist office
fressen *eat
freuen: ich freue mich für sie I'm happy for her
Freund/in friend; *(feste/r Freundin/Freund)* girlfriend/boyfriend
freundlich friendly
Friedhof graveyard
Friseur/in hairdresser
froh happy; **Frohe Weihnachten!** Merry Christmas!
Früchte fruit
früh early
Frühling spring
Frühstück breakfast
frühstücken *have breakfast
(sich) fühlen *feel
führen *go
Führer/in *(für Sehenswürdigkeiten)* guide
Füller pen
funktionieren work
für for
furchtbar terrible
furchterregend frightening
Fuß, Füße foot, feet
Fußball football
Fußboden floor
Fußgelenk ankle
füttern *feed

G

Gabel fork
Gälisch Gaelic
Gang **1** *(Bande)* gang; **2** *(Fahrrad, Auto)* gear; **3** *(Korridor)* passage
ganz: das ganze Wochenende all weekend
gar nichts nothing
Garten garden
Gärtner/in gardener
Gast guest; visitor
Gasthaus inn
Gebäude building
geben *give; **Gib Tim das Buch.** Give the book to Tim. **eine Party geben** *have a party; **Was gibt's?** What's up?
Gebirge: im Gebirge in the mountains
geboren: ich wurde ... geboren I was born ...
Gebrauchsanweisung instructions
Geburtstag birthday
gedacht: ich hatte gedacht I had thought
Gedicht poem
gefahren: ich bin gefahren I drove
gefährlich dangerous
gefallen: Es gefällt mir. I like it. **Wem gefällt das Lied am besten?** Who likes the song best?
gegangen: ich/er/sie war(en) gegangen I/he/they had gone
Gegend area
gegenüber (vom) opposite
gegenüberstehen: ihnen gegenüberstehen come face to face with them
Gegenwart present; **einfache Gegenwart** simple present
gehen *go; walk; **sie geht zur Schule** she's at school; **Wie geht's?** How are you?
Gehsteig pavement
Geist ghost
geistesabwesend distant
gekommen: der Wolf war gekommen the wolf had come
Gelände: im Gelände off-road
Geländer railings
gelangen *get
gelangweilt bored
gelb yellow
Geld money
Gemüse vegetable/s
genießen enjoy
Genuss treat
geöffnet open
Geografie geography
Gepäckabfertiger/in baggage handler
gerade just
Gerät machine
Geräusch noise; sound
gern: gern haben like; **Ich laufe (nicht) gern.** I (don't) like walking.
Geschäft business; *(Laden)* shop
geschehen happen; **was geschehen war** what had happened
Geschenk gift; present
Geschichte **1** *(Erzählung)* story; **2** *(Schulfach)* history
Geschirrspülmaschine dishwasher
geschlossen closed

Geschwister brothers and sisters
Gesicht face
Gespenst ghost
gesponsert sponsored
Gespräch conversation; dialogue
gestern yesterday
gesund healthy
getötet: er hatte ihn getötet he had killed it
Getränk drink
gewalttätig violent
Gewehr gun
Gewinn prize
gewinnen *win; im Lotto gewinnen *win the lotto
Gewinner/in winner
gewöhnlich usually
Gitarre guitar; Gitarre spielen play the guitar
Glas glass
gleich: der/die/das gleiche the same
Gleis railway line
glücklich happy
Glückwunsch: Herzlichen Glückwunsch! Congratulations! *(zum Geburtstag)* Happy birthday!
Gokartfahren go-karting
Golf golf
Grab grave
Grad degree
Gramm gram
Grenze border
Griechisch Greek
groß big; *(bei Personen)* tall
großartig great
Großbritannien Britain
Größe size; Welche Größe hast du? What size do you take?
Großmutter *(Oma)* grandma
Großstadt city
Großvater *(Opa)* grandad
grün green
Gruppe group
Grüße: Viele Grüße ... Best wishes, ...; (Viele) Liebe Grüße ... (Lots of) Love, ...
grüßen: Grüße Dawn, bitte. Say hi to Dawn, please.
Gurke cucumber
gut good; fine; *(schon gut)* OK; gut in good at; gut kennen/... know/... well; Gute(n) Abend/Morgen/Nacht. Good evening/morning/night. Guten Tag. Hello. Wie geht's? – Danke, gut. How are you? – I'm fine, thanks.
Guthaben credit
Gymnastik gymnastics

H

Haar, Haare hair
haben *have; Ich habe Geburtstag. It's my birthday. Welche Farbe hat dein Zimmer? What colour is your room? Welche Größe hast du? What size do you take?
Haggis haggis
Hähnchen *(Brathähnchen)* chicken
halb: halb zwei/... half past one/...; dreieinhalb three and a half
Halle: in der Halle indoors
Hallo. Hello./Hi.
Halloween Halloween
Hals neck
halten *hold; Halt den Mund! Shut up! Was hältst du von ...? What do you think of ...?
Hamburger hamburger
Hamster hamster
Hand hand
Handball handball
handeln: Der Text handelt von ... The text is about ...
Handy mobile (phone)
Handzeichen hand signal
hart hard; tough
Hase rabbit
hassen hate
hast: Hast du schon einmal ...? – Ja./Nein. Have you ever ...? – Yes, I have./No, I haven't.
hätte: Ich hätte gern ... I'd like ...
Haupt- main
Hauptstadt capital
Haus house; nach Hause gehen *go home; zu Hause at home; bei Tim zu Hause at Tim's house; Gehen wir zu mir nach Hause. Let's go to my house.
Hausarrest: ich habe Hausarrest I'm grounded
Hausaufgaben homework
Hausaufgabenheft homework diary
Haustier pet
Heft book
Heiligabend Christmas Eve
Heim home
heiraten *get married
heiß hot
heißen: Ich heiße Sarah. I'm Sarah. Wie heißt du? What's your name? Wie heißen sie auf Deutsch? What are they in German?
Heizkörper radiator
hektisch busy
helfen help; Gästen helfen Helping visitors
Helfer/in helper
Helm helmet
herausfinden *find out
herausnehmen *take out
Herbst autumn
Herd cooker
hereinkommen *come in
Herr *(Anrede)* Mr
herstellen *make; produce
herüber across
herunterladen download
Herz heart
herzlich: Herzlichen Glückwunsch! Congratulations! *(zum Geburtstag)* Happy birthday!
heute today; heute Morgen/... this morning/...
Hexe witch
hier(her) here; Hier, bitte. Here you are. Hier spricht Sarah. It's Sarah.
Hilfe help; Um Hilfe bitten Asking for help
hinab/herab down
hinein in; hineingehen *go in; hineinkriechen crawl in
hinfallen fall
hing: er hing (gerade) he was hanging
hinschauen look
hinten: hinten im Buch at the back of the book
hinter behind; hinter einem Ball her after a ball
Hintern bottom
hinüber across
hinunter/herunter down
hinzufügen *put in
Hip-Hop hip hop
Hobby hobby
hoch high
hochheben pick up
Hochsprung (the) high jump
Hochzeitstag wedding day
Hockey hockey
Hof *(Bauernhof)* farm
hoffen hope
höflich polite
Höhle cave
holen *get
hören *hear; *(sich anhören)* listen to
Horror horror
Hotel hotel
Hügel hill
Huhn chicken
Humbug humbug
Hund dog

hundert hundred
Hunger: Ich habe Hunger. I'm hungry.
hungrig hungry
Hurling hurling
Hürdenlauf hurdles

I

ich I; **Dies bin ich.** This is me.
Idee idea
ihm, ihn him; *(nicht bei Personen)* it
ihnen them
Ihnen you
ihr **1** *(Wer?)* you; **2** *(Wem?)* her; *(nicht bei Personen)* it
ihr/e **1** *(Einzahl)* her; *(nicht bei Personen)* its; **2** *(Mehrzahl)* their
Ihr/e your
im: im April in April; **im Bahnhof Exeter** at Exeter Station; **im Bus** on the bus; **im Fernsehen** on TV; **im Internet** on the Internet; **im Jahre 1971** in 1971; **im Norden** in the north; **im Sonderangebot** on special offer; **im Urlaub** on holiday; **im Winter** in winter
immer always; **immer noch** still
in in; at; *(in ... hinein/herein)* into; **in Dartmoor** on Dartmoor; **in den Urlaub fahren** *go on holiday; **in der Fairfield Road** in Fairfield Road; **in der Nacht** at night; **in der Schule** at school; **in die Mannschaft kommen** *get on the team; **In welcher Jahrgangsstufe bist du? - Ich bin in der 7. Stufe.** What year are you in? - I'm in year 7. **ins Bett gehen** *go to bed; **eine Sendung ins Leben rufen** start a programme; **Willkommen in London.** Welcome to London. **Ich bin (schon einmal) in ... gewesen.** I've been to ...
Informationen, Informations- information
interaktiv interactive
interessant interesting
Interesse interest
(sich) interessieren care
interessiert (an) interested (in)
international international
Internet Internet; **im Internet** on the Internet
Internet-Kiosk Internet kiosk
Interview interview
Ire(n)/Irin(nen); irisch; Irisch Irish
Irland Ireland
ist is
Italienisch Italian

J

ja yes; *(besonders in wörtl. Rede)* yeah
Jacke jacket
Jagen hunting
Jahr year; **ein 13-jähriges Mädchen** a 13-year-old girl
Jahreszeit season
Jahrgangsstufe year; **In welcher Jahrgangsstufe bist du?** What year are you in?
Jahrhundert century
Jahrmarkt funfair
Januar January
Jeans jeans
jede/r/s each; every
jeder *(alle)* everybody
jemals ever
jemand somebody
jene *(Mehrzahl)* those
jetzt now
Jogger/in jogger
Jogging jogging
Jonglieren juggling
Judo judo
Jugendklub youth club
Jugendliche/r kid
Juli July
jung young
Junge boy
Juni June

K

kalt cold
Kamera camera
Kaminfeuer fire
Kampf fight
Kanal canal
Kanu canoe; **Kanu fahren** canoeing
Kappe cap
Karate karate
Karneval carnival
Karotte carrot
Karte card; *(Landkarte)* map
Karteikarte file
Kartoffel, Kartoffeln potato, potatoes
Kartoffelchips crisps
Kasachisch Kazakh
Käse cheese
Kasten box
Katze cat
kaufen *buy
Käufer/in shopper
Kaufhaus department store
kein/e no; not ... any
Kellnerin waitress
kennen *know; **kennen lernen** *meet; **Schön, dich/Sie kennen zu lernen.** Nice to meet you.
Kilometer kilometre
Kilt *(Schottenrock)* kilt
Kind, Kinder child, children; kid, kids
Kino cinema
Kirche church
Kirmes funfair
Kiste box
Klapphandy flip phone
Klasse class
Klassenarbeit test
Klassenlehrer/in class teacher
Klassenzimmer classroom
Kleider, Kleidung clothes
klein little; short; small; **kleiner Junge** baby boy
Kletterer/Kletterin (rock) climber
klettern climb; **auf einen Hügel klettern** climb a hill
Klettern (rock) climbing
Klingelton ringtone
klingen sound
Klippe cliff
klopfen (an) knock (at)
Klub club
Knöchel ankle
Knopf button
Koch/Köchin cook
komisch funny
kommen *come; *(gelangen)* *get; **Ich komme aus London.** I'm from London. **Er kommt zu spät.** He's late.
Komödie comedy
König king
Königin queen
können can
konnte: ich konnte (nicht) I could(n't)
kontrollieren check
Kopf head
kornisch *(aus Cornwall)* Cornish
Korridor passage
korrigieren correct
kosten: Was kostet/kosten ...? How much is/are ...?
kostenlos free
Kraft energy
krank ill

Krankenhaus hospital
kriechen crawl
kristallklar crystal
Kroatisch Croatian
Küche kitchen
Kuchen cake
Kugelstoßen (the) shot-put
Kuh cow
kühl cool
Kühlschrank fridge
kümmern: sich um Taschen kümmern deal with bags
Kumpel buddy
Kunst art
Kunsthandwerk arts and crafts
Kurdisch Kurdish
Kurier/in courier
Kurs course; **einen Kurs machen** do a course
kurz short; **kurz (be)vor** just before; **kurz nachdem ...** a short time after ...
Kuss kiss
Küste coast; *(Strand)* seashore

L

lächeln smile
lachen laugh
lachte: er lachte (gerade) he was laughing
Ladegerät charger
Laden shop
Ladendieb/in shoplifter
Lampe light
Land land; country; **auf dem Land** in the country
landen land
Landfahrer/in traveller
Landkarte map
lang: 14 Jahre lang for 14 years
lang/e long; **lange bleiben** stay for long; **vor langer Zeit** a long time ago
langsam slow
langweilen: ich langweile mich I'm bored
langweilig boring
Laptop laptop
las: ich las I read
Lasst uns aufhören. Let's finish.
Lastwagen lorry
Lauch(stange) leek
Laufbahn track
laufen *run; walk; **Inlineskates-/Rollschuhlaufen** skating; **die am längsten laufende Sendung** the longest-running programme
Laufen running
Läufer/in runner
laut loudly
leben live
Leben life
Lebensmittel food
legen *put
Lehrer/in teacher
leicht easy
Leichtathletik athletics
leid: Tut mir leid. I'm sorry./Sorry.
Leider ... I'm afraid ...
leihen: sich einen Füller (aus)leihen borrow a pen
Lektion unit
lernen learn; **Lerne es auswendig.** Learn it by heart.
lesen *read
Leser/in reader
Lesetagebuch reading log
Lesewoche reading week
„Letterboxing" letterboxing
letzte/r/s last
letztendlich in the end
Leute people
Licht light
lieb: Liebe/r ... Dear ...; **(Viele) Liebe Grüße ...** (Lots of) Love, ...
Liebe love
lieben love
Lieblings- favourite
Lied song
Limonade lemonade
Lineal ruler
links left; **auf der linken Seite** on the left; **links (von Ihnen)** on your left
Lippe lip
Liste list
Löffel spoon
Lotto lotto
lustig funny
Luxemburg Luxembourg

M

machen *do; *make; **ein Picknick machen** *have a picnic; **Das macht zwei Pfund, bitte.** That's two pounds, please. **Es macht Spaß.** It's fun. **Ich mache Hausaufgaben.** I *do my homework. **Mach dir Notizen.** *Make notes. **(Sich) Notizen machen** Making notes; **sie macht Urlaub** she's on holiday; **Was machst du (da)?** What are you doing?
Mädchen girl
Mai May
Make-up make-up
Mal time
malen paint
Malen painting
Mama mum; *(amerik. Englisch)* mom
manchmal sometimes
Mann, Männer man, men
Mannschaft team
Markt market
März March
Maschine machine
Mathe(matik) maths
Mayonnaise mayonnaise
Mazedonisch Macedonian
Meer sea
Mehl flour
mehr more
Meile mile
mein/e my
meinen *mean
Meinung: Ich bin derselben Meinung (wie du). I agree (with you).
meiste/n: der/die/das meiste, die meisten most
meistens usually
Menschen people
Messer knife, knives
Meter metre
mich me
mieten rent; *(Fahrrad/Kanu/...)* hire
Mikrowelle microwave
Milch milk
Milliliter millilitre
Million million
Minute minute
mir me
mischen mix
mit with; **mit dem Rad/Bus/Auto/...** by bike/bus/car/...
mitbringen *take
Mitglied in einem Klub werden join a club
mitnehmen *take
Mittagessen lunch
Mittagspause lunch break; lunchtime
Mittagszeit lunchtime
Mittwoch Wednesday
„Mobber/in" bully
Mobbing bullying
Möbel furniture
Mobiltelefon mobile (phone)
Mode fashion
Moderator/in presenter
modern modern
mögen like; **sehr mögen** love; **Ich möchte (gehen/...)** I'd like (to go/...); **Ich möchte nicht**

gehen/... I wouldn't like to go/...; Möchtest du/Möchten Sie ...? Would you like ...? es mag ziemlich einfach sein it may be quite simple
Möhre carrot
Moment moment; im Moment at the moment
Monat month
Monster monster
Montag Monday
Moor *(Hochmoor)* moor
morgen tomorrow
Morgen morning; Montagmorgen Monday morning
morgens in the morning; *(mit Uhrzeit)* a.m.
Motorrad motorbike
Motorradfahrer/in motorcyclist
Motorroller scooter
Mountainbike mountain bike
Mountainbikefahren mountain biking
Mountainboard mountain board
Mountainboardfahren mountain boarding
MP3-Player MP3 player
müde tired
Mund: Halt den Mund! Shut up!
Muschel seashell
Museum museum
Musik music
Musikinstrument musical instrument
müssen *have to; must; du müsstest you should
Muster pattern
mutig brave
Mutprobe dare
Mutter mother
Mutti mum

N

nach **1** *(Wann?)* after; nach der Schule after school; fünf nach zehn five past ten; Viertel nach elf quarter past eleven; **2** *(zu)* to; nach Hause gehen *go home
Nachbar/in neighbour
nachdem after
nachdenken *think
Nachmittag afternoon
nachmittags in the afternoon; *(mit Uhrzeit)* p.m.
Nachricht(en) news
Nachsitzen detention
nachsprechen repeat
nächste/r/s: der nächste Flughafen the nearest airport; nächste Woche next week
Nacht night
nachts at night
Nähe: in der Nähe von by; near
Name name
nass wet; nass machen soak
Nationalpark national park
natürlich of course
Naturwissenschaft science
neben by; next to
nehmen *take
neidisch (auf) jealous (of)
nein no
nerven: Eltern nerven! Parents are a pain!
nervös nervous
nett nice
Netz network
neu new
Neuigkeit(en) news
nicht not; Iss nicht. Don't eat.
nichts nothing; not ... anything; Nichts zu danken. You're welcome.
nie never
Niederlande Netherlands
niemals never
niemand nobody
nirgendwo(-hin/-her) not ... anywhere
noch still; noch ein/e/er/s another; noch einmal again; noch nicht not ... yet; noch nie never
Nomen noun
Nord- north; northern
Norden north; im Norden in the north
Nordirland Northern Ireland
nördlich north; northern
Nordwesten north-west
normalerweise usually
Notiz note
Notizbuch notebook
November November
Nummer number
nun now; Nun, ... Well, ...
nur only

O

ob whether
Oberschenkel thigh
Obst fruit
oder or
offen open
öffnen, sich öffnen open
oft often
ohne without
Ohr ear
okay OK
Oktober October
olympisch: die Olympischen Spiele the Olympics
Oma grandma
Onkel uncle
Opa grandad
Orange orange
ordnen organize
Ordnung: in Ordnung OK; Ist alles in Ordnung bei dir? Are you OK? Ist etwas nicht in Ordnung? What's wrong?
organisieren organize
Ort place
Ost, Osten east
Österreich Austria
östlich east

P

paar: ein paar some
packen pack
Paddeln canoeing
Papa dad
Papagei parrot
Parade parade
Park park
Parkplatz car park
Partizip Perfekt past participle
Partner/in partner
Party party
passieren happen
Pastete pasty
Pause break
Pence pence (p)
Persisch Persian
Person *(Figur)* character
Pfad track
Pfeffer pepper
Pferd horse
Pfund *(brit. Währung)* pound (£)
Picknick picnic
Pier pier
Piercing piercing
pink pink
Pizza pizza
Plan plan
planen plan
Planer/in planner
Platz place
plötzlich suddenly
Plumpudding Christmas pudding
Po bottom
Polen Poland
Polizei- police

Polizeibeamter/-beamtin, Polizist/in police officer
Polnisch Polish
Pommes frites chips
Pony pony
Popcorn popcorn
Porree(stange) leek
Portfolio portfolio
Portugiesisch Portuguese
Post(amt) post office
Poster poster
Postkarte postcard
präsentieren present
Preis **1** *(Kaufpreis)* price; **2** *(Gewinn)* prize
preiswert cheap
Prinz prince
pro: 24 Stunden pro Tag 24 hours a day
probieren *try
Problem problem
produzieren produce
Profi- professional
Projekt(arbeit) project
Protektor protector
Prüfung test
Punkt point
putzen clean
Puzzle jigsaw puzzle

Q

Quad quad (bike)
Quiz quiz

R

Rad *(Fahrrad)* bike; **Rad fahren** *ride a bike
Radfahren cycling
Radfahrer/in cyclist
Radiergummi rubber
Radio radio
Ranger ranger
rannte: er rannte (gerade) he was running
Rap(musik) rap
Rasierapparat shaver
raten guess
Ratte rat
rauchen smoke
Raum room
raus: Ich muss hier raus. I have to get out of this place.
Rechner computer
Recht: Du hast Recht. You're right.
rechts right; **auf der rechten Seite** on the right; **rechts (von Ihnen)** on your right
reden (mit) talk (to)
Regal, Regale shelf, shelves
Regel rule
regnen rain
reich rich
Reihenfolge order
(sich) reimen (auf) rhyme (with)
Reise trip
reisen travel
Reisende/r traveller
Reiten horse riding
Rektor/in principal
rennen *run
Restaurant restaurant
Rhein Rhine
Rhythmus rhythm
richtig right; *(echt)* real; **das Richtige/Beste/...** the right/best/... thing
Richtung: in Richtung Haus towards the house
Riese giant
Rindfleisch beef
Ring ring
Rock(musik) rock
Rollstuhl wheelchair; **er sitzt im Rollstuhl** he's in a wheelchair
Rom Rome
romantisch romantic
rosa pink
rot red
Rubrik heading
Rücken back
Rudern rowing
rufen: laut rufen shout
Rugby rugby
ruhig quiet
Rumänisch Romanian
Russisch Russian

S

Sache thing; **Sachen, die man machen kann** things to do
Saft juice
sagen *say; *tell; **Jamie sagt Tess auf Wiedersehen.** Jamie says goodbye to Tess.
sah: er sah (gerade) zu he was watching
Salat salad; *(Kopfsalat)* lettuce
Salto: einen Salto rückwärts machen backflip
Salz salt
sammeln collect
Sammlung collection
Samstag Saturday
samstags on Saturdays
Sandwich sandwich
sanft gentle
Sänger/in singer
Satz sentence
sauber clean; **sauber machen** clean
sauer: sie sind sauer they're mad
Schach chess
Schaf, Schafe sheep
Schatzsuche treasure hunt
schauen look
Schauspiel drama
Schauspieler/in actor
scheinen: es scheint sie nicht zu interessieren she doesn't seem to care
schicken *send
schickte: er schickte (gerade) he was sending
Schiff boat; ship
Schikanieren bullying
Schild sign
Schildchen label
Schinken ham
schlafen *sleep
Schlafzimmer bedroom
Schlange stehen queue (up)
schlecht bad
schlechter worse
schlechteste/r/s worst
schließen close
schließlich in the end
schlimm bad
schlimmer worse
schlimmste/r/s worst
Schloss castle
Schluss ending
schmal narrow
Schmerzen pain
Schmetterling butterfly
Schmuggel, Schmuggeln smuggling
Schmuggler/in smuggler
schmutzig dirty
schneiden cut
schnell fast; quickly
Schnellimbiss *(für Fisch und Pommes frites)* fish and chip shop
Schokolade chocolate
schon: schon einmal ever; **Schon gut.** *(Bitte.)* That's OK. **schon wieder** again
schön beautiful; fine; nice
Schotte(n)/Schottin(nen) Scottish

Schottisch *(engl. Dialekt)* Scots
Schottland Scotland
Schrank cupboard
schrecklich terrible
schreiben *write; **Eine Geschichte/... schreiben** Writing a story/...
Schreibetui pencil case
schreien scream; shout
Schriftsteller/in writer
schüchtern shy
Schuh shoe
Schularbeiten homework
Schule school
Schüler/in pupil
Schülerkalender homework diary
Schulheft exercise book
Schulhof playground; **auf dem Schulhof** in the playground
Schulmädchen schoolgirl
Schultag school day
Schultasche bag
Schulter shoulder
Schützer protector
schwarz black
Schwein pig
Schweiz Switzerland
schwer hard
Schwert sword
Schwester sister
Schwierigkeiten: ich stecke in großen Schwierigkeiten I'm in big trouble
Schwimmbad swimming pool
schwimmen *swim; **schwimmen gehen** *go swimming
Schwimmen swimming
Schwimmer/in swimmer
Science-Fiction science fiction
Segeln sailing
sehen look; *see
sehr very
seid: ihr seid you're (= you are)
sein *be; **es macht keinen Spaß, wütend zu sein** it isn't fun being angry
sein/e his; *(nicht bei Personen)* its
Seite side; *(Buch, Heft)* page
Selbstbedienung self-service
selbst gemacht home-made
selbstverständlich of course
senden *send
Sendung *(Radio, Fernsehen)* programme
September September
Serbisch Serbian
Sessel chair
setzen: sich setzen *sit
Show show
sicher sure; *(in Sicherheit)* safe
Sicherheit: in Sicherheit safe
Sicherheitsausrüstung safety gear
sie **1** *(Wer?)* she; *(nicht bei Personen)* it; *(Mehrzahl)* they; **2** *(Wen?)* her; *(nicht bei Personen)* it; *(Mehrzahl)* them
Sie you
Sieger/in winner
Signal signal
sind are
Singapur Singapore
singen *sing
sitzen *sit; **er sitzt im Rollstuhl** he's in a wheelchair
Skateboard skateboard
Skateboarder skateboarder
Skateboardfahren skateboarding
Skater/in skater
Skifahren skiing
Skorpion scorpion
SMS text (message)
SMS-Terror text bullying
Snowboarder snowboarder
so so; **So etwas gibt es nicht.** There's no such thing.
sobald as soon as
soeben just
Software software
sogar: Es war sogar besser. In fact, it was better.
solche/r/s: solche Kleidung clothes like this
sollen: du solltest you should
Somalia Somalia
Sommer summer
Sonderangebot special offer
Sonnabend Saturday
Sonne sun
Sonnenbaden sunbathing
sonnig sunny
Sonntag Sunday
Sorgen: sich Sorgen machen (um) worry (about); **ich mache mir Sorgen (um)** I'm worried (about)
Souvenir souvenir
Spanien Spain
Spanisch Spanish
spannend exciting
sparen save
Spaß fun; **Es macht Spaß.** It's fun. **Viel Spaß!** Have fun!
spät, zu spät late; **Er kommt zu spät.** He's late. **Wie spät ist es?** What time is it?
später later
Spazierengehen walking
Spaziergänger/in walker
Speck bacon
Speerwerfen (the) javelin
speichern *(MP3-Player)* *hold
Speiseeis ice cream
Speisekarte menu
Spiegel mirror
Spiel game; *(Wettkampf)* match
spielen play; **Gitarre spielen** play the guitar; **Spielt das Gespräch nach.** Act the dialogue.
Spieler/in player
Spielhalle amusement arcade
spielten: sie spielten (gerade) they were playing
Spielzeug toy
Spinne spider
Sport, Sportart sport; **Sport treiben** play sports
sportlich sporty
Sportschuh trainer
Sportzentrum sports centre
Sprache language
Sprechanlage intercom
sprechen (mit) *speak (to); talk (to); **Hier spricht Sarah.** It's Sarah.
springen jump
spritzen splash
Squash squash
Stabhochsprung (the) pole vault
Stadion stadium
Stadt town; *(Großstadt)* city
Stadtmitte, -zentrum town centre
Star star
stark tough
Start start
statt instead of
Statue statue
stehen *stand
stehen bleiben stop
stehlen steal
Stein *(Fels)* rock
Stelle place
stellen *put
Stempel stamp
sterben die
Stern star
Steuer tax
stolpern trip
stolz proud
stoppen stop
Strand beach; *(Küste)* seashore
Straße road; street
Straßenbahn tram
Streit quarrel
Streiten arguing
streng strict
Stricken knitting
Strom electricity
Strophe verse

Stubenarrest: ich habe Stubenarrest I'm grounded
Stufe step; *(Jahrgangsstufe)* year; **Ich bin in der 7. Stufe.** I'm in year 7.
Stuhl chair
Stunde hour; *(Unterrichtsstunde)* lesson
Stundenplan timetable
suchen look for
Süd-; Süden; südlich south
Südosten south-east
Südwesten south-west
super super
Supermarkt supermarket
Surfen surfing
Symbol symbol
Szene scene

T

Tabelle table
Taekwondo tae kwon do
Tafel board
Tag day
Tagebuch diary
Tante aunt
tanzen dance; **tanzen gehen** *go dancing
Tanzen dancing
tapfer brave
Tasche bag
Taschendieb/in pickpocket
Tasse cup; **eine Tasse Tee** a cup of tea
Taste button
Tätowierung, Tattoo tattoo
tausend thousand
Taxi taxi
Team team
Technik technology
Technologie technology
Tee tea
Teenager teenager, teen
Teig pastry
Teil part
teilen: sich ein Zimmer teilen share a room
Telefon phone; **am Telefon** on the phone
telefonieren phone
telefonisch Pizza bestellen phone for pizza
Teller plate
Tennis tennis
Terror: SMS-Terror text bullying
Test test
teuer expensive
Text text; *(Liedtext)* words (of a song)
Thai Thai
Theater theatre
Thema topic
Thriller thriller
Tier animal; *(zahmes Tier, Haustier)* pet
Tierhandlung pet shop
Tipp tip
Tisch table
Tischtennis table tennis
Titel title
Tja, ... Well, ...
Toaster toaster
Tochter daughter
toll cool; great; super
Tomate tomato
Tor gate
tot dead
Tour tour
Tourist/in tourist
Touristeninformation tourist office
traditionell traditional
träumen dream
tragen *(anziehen)* *wear
Trainer trainer
trainieren train; practise
Training training
Trampolinspringen trampolining
Traum dream
traurig sad
treffen, sich treffen (mit) *meet; **eine Absprache treffen** *make an arrangement
Treffpunkt: ein Treffpunkt a place to meet
treten: jemandem auf den Fuß treten *stand on somebody's foot
trinken *drink; **eine Cola trinken** *have a cola
Truthahn turkey
Tschechische Republik Czech Republic
Tschüs. Bye.
T-Shirt T-shirt
tun *do; *(an einen Platz tun)* *put
Tunfisch tuna
Tunnel tunnel
Tür door
Türkei Turkey
Türkisch Turkish
Turm tower
Turnen gymnastics
Turnhalle gym
Tut mir leid. I'm sorry./Sorry.
Tüte bag
Tyrann bully

U

U-Bahn: die (Londoner) U-Bahn the tube
U-Bahnhof underground station
U-Bahn-Zug underground train
üben practise
über about; *(über die Straße)* across (the road); **über die Sprechanlage** on the intercom
überall(-hin/-her) everywhere
übernachten stay
überprüfen check
überrascht surprised
Überraschung surprise
Überschrift heading
übersehen: Sie können es nicht übersehen. You can't miss it.
übersetzen translate
übrig: ich habe nicht viel dafür übrig I'm not keen on it
Übung exercise
Uhr: um acht/zwanzig Uhr at eight o'clock
Uhrzeit time
Ukrainisch Ukrainian
um: um (... herum) round; **um acht/zwanzig Uhr** at eight o'clock; **um die Welt** around the world; **um seine Freundin zu besuchen** to visit his girlfriend; **um unsere Bilder zu verkaufen** to sell our pictures
umbringen kill
Umfrage survey
Umgebung environment
Umkleidekabine changing room
Umwelt environment
umziehen move
Umzug *(Parade)* parade
und and; **Und du?** What about you?
Unfall accident
ungefähr about
unglücklich unhappy
unheimlich scary
Uniform uniform
uns us
unser/e our
Unsinn nonsense
unter under; **unter 18-Jährige** under 18s
unterhalten: sich unterhalten chat; have a chat; **sich unterhalten (mit)** talk (to)
Unterhaltung conversation
unterhielten: sie unterhielten sich (gerade) they were talking
unterirdisch underground
Unterrichtsstunde lesson

unterstreichen underline
unterstrichen underlined
Untersuchung *(Umfrage)* survey
unterwegs on the road
Urlaub holiday/s; **in den Urlaub fahren** *go on holiday; **sie macht Urlaub, sie ist im Urlaub** she's on holiday
Usbekisch Uzbek

V

Vater father
Vati dad
verabschieden: sich von ... verabschieden *say goodbye to ...
(sich) verändern change
Verb verb
verbracht: sie hatten verbracht they had spent
verbringen *spend
verdienen: Geld an den Touristen verdienen *make money from the tourists
Verein club
verfolgen follow
Vergangenheit past
vergessen *forget; **ich hatte vergessen** I had forgotten
vergleichen compare
Vergnügen: besonderes Vergnügen treat
verheiratet married
verkaufen *sell
Verkäufer/in shop assistant
Verkehr traffic
Verkehrssicherheit road safety
verlassen *leave
Verlaufsform der Gegenwart present progressive
verlegen embarrassed
verletzen *hurt; **ich habe mir die Hand verletzt** I hurt my hand
verließ: ich verließ I left
verloren: ich hatte verloren I had lost
vermieten hire
vermissen miss
verschieden different
verschwenden waste
verschwinden disappear
verspätet late
versprechen promise
verstehen *understand; **..., verstehst du?** ..., you see.
versuchen *try
verwenden use
Video(film) video
Videoausschnitt video clip
viel lots of; much; **eine viel befahrene Straße** a busy road; **Viel Spaß!** Have fun!
viele lots of; many; **Viele Grüße ...** Best wishes, ...
vielleicht maybe
Viertel vor/nach eins quarter to/past one
Vietnamesisch Vietnamese
Vogel bird
Volleyball volleyball
Vollkorn- wholemeal
vollständig complete
von of; from; *(vom/von ... herab/herunter)* off; *(durch)* by; **fünf vor zehn** five to ten; **vor zwei Jahren** two years ago
vorbei *(zu Ende)* over; **am Haus vorbei** past the house
vorbeifließen: Bäche, die vorbeifließen streams running by
vorbeischauen drop by
vorhaben plan
vorlesen *read; *read out
Vorlieben und Abneigungen likes and dislikes
Vormittag morning; *(mit Uhrzeit)* a.m.
Vorort suburb
Vorschrift rule
vorsichtig careful
Vorsitzende/r chairperson
Vorsprechen audition
vorstellen: sich (etwas) vorstellen imagine
Vortrag talk
Vorvergangenheit past perfect
vulkanisch volcanic

W

Wachfrau/Wachmann security guard
Wade calf
wählen pick
Wahnsinn! Wow!
wahr true
Waise orphan
Wal whale
Wald wood
Wales Wales
Waliser/in(nen); walisisch; Walisisch Welsh
Wanderer, Wanderin walker
Wandern walking
Wanderschuh walking shoe
wann when; **wann immer** whenever
war was
wäre: sie dachten, es wäre eine gute Idee they thought it was a good idea
waren, warst, wart were; **sie waren gerade beim Essen** they were having dinner
Waren goods
warm warm
wärst: Ich habe gesagt, du wärst morgen im Laden. I said you'd be in the shop tomorrow.
warten (auf) wait (for); **Warten wir's ab.** Let's wait and see. **zu lange warten** leave it too late
warum why
was what; **Was für ein/e ...!** What a ...! **Was für ein Spaß!** What fun! **Was gibt's?** What's up? **Was ist das?** What's that? **Was ist mit dir?** What about you?
Wasser water
Wasserkocher kettle
Webcode webcode
Website website
Wecker alarm clock
Weg way; *(Pfad)* track
weggehen (von) *leave; *(ausgehen)* *go out
wegnehmen *take away; **Leuten Dinge wegnehmen** *take things from people
wehtun *hurt
Weihnachten Christmas
Weihnachts(fest)essen Christmas dinner
Weihnachtslied Christmas carol
Weihnachtsschmuck Christmas decorations
weil because
weinen cry
weiß white
Weißbrot white bread
weit: am weitesten (entfernt) furthest
weitere **1** *(mehr)* more; **2** *(andere)* other
Weitsprung (the) long jump
welche/r/s what; which; **Welche Farbe hat dein Zimmer?** What colour is your room?
Welt world; **auf der (ganzen) Welt** in the world; **nicht von dieser Welt** out of this world
wenn if; when
wer who
werden *become; *get; **ich werde gehen** I'll (= I will) go; **ich werde nicht gehen** I won't (= will not) go; **ich werde gewinnen, ich**

gewinne I'm going to win; Ich werde Ranger. I'm going to be a ranger. Erste/r werden bei ... *come first in ...; Es wird gut werden. It's going to be OK.
weshalb why
West-; Westen west
Western western
westlich west
Wettbewerb competition
Wetter weather
Wettkampf match
wichtig important
wie 1 how; Wie geht's? How are you? Wie heißen sie auf Deutsch? What are they in German? Wie heißt du? What's your name? Wie spät ist es? What time is it? wie man uns findet how to find us; 2 *(so wie)* like; wie das Buch ist what the book is like; wie das Leben war what life was like; Wie sieht sie aus? What does she look like?
wieder again; Ich bin wieder da! I'm back!
Wiedersehen. Bye.
Wiese field
Wikinger Viking
wild wild
willkommen: wir sind nicht willkommen we aren't welcome; Willkommen in London. Welcome to London.
Windsurfing windsurfing
Winter winter
winzig tiny
wir we
wirklich really
wissen *know
Witze machen joke
wo where; jetzt, wo du auf der Welt bist now you're in the world; nun, wo es fertig ist now that it's done
Woche week
Wochenende weekend
woher: Woher kommst du? Where are you from?
wohin where
wohnen live
Wohnung flat
Wohnwagen *(Standwohnwagen)* mobile home
Wohnzimmer living room
Wolf wolf
Wolke cloud
wollen want; gehen wollen want to go
Wort word
Wörterbuch, -verzeichnis dictionary
Wortnetz, Wörternetz network
Wow! Wow!
wunderschön beautiful
wundervoll wonderful
Wurst, Würstchen sausage
wütend (auf) angry (with)

Z

zäh tough
Zahl number
zahlen *pay
zahmes Tier pet
Zahnbürste toothbrush
Zeichen sign; signal
zeichnen *draw
zeigen show; zeigen (auf) point (at)
Zeile line
Zeit time; es ist Zeit, dass es aufhört it's time for it to end
Zeitschrift magazine
Zeitung newspaper
Zeitverschwendung a waste of time
Zeitwort verb
Zentrum centre
zerschellen crash
ziemlich quite
Ziffer number
Zimmer room; Zimmer mit Frühstück *(in kleiner Frühstückspension)* bed and breakfast (B and B)
Zoohandlung pet shop
zu 1 to; sie helfen dir zu lesen they help you to read; zu Fuß on foot; zu Hause at home; 2 zu alt too old; zu spät late; 3 *(geschlossen)* closed
zuerst first
Zug train
Zuhause home
zuhören listen
Zukunft future
zum: zum Frühstück/Mittagessen for breakfast/lunch
zumachen close
Zungenbrecher tongue twister
zuordnen match
zur: sie geht zur Schule she's at school; Er kommt zu spät zur Schule. He's late for school.
zurück back
zurzeit at the moment
zusammen together
Zusammenfassung summary
zusehen watch
zustimmen: Ich stimme (dir) zu. I agree (with you).
Zwiebel onion
zwingen: keiner kann mich dazu zwingen, dies zu essen nobody can make me eat this; wenn man mich zwänge if they made me

NUMBERS, SOUNDS, ABC

ENGLISH NUMBERS

1	**one** [wʌn]	1st	**first** [fɜːst]
2	**two** [tuː]	2nd	**second** ['sekənd]
3	**three** [θriː]	3rd	**third** [θɜːd]
4	**four** [fɔː]	4th	**fourth** [fɔːθ]
5	**five** [faɪv]	5th	**fifth** [fɪfθ]
6	**six** [sɪks]	6th	**sixth** [sɪksθ]
7	**seven** ['sevn]	7th	**seventh** ['sevnθ]
8	**eight** [eɪt]	8th	**eighth** [eɪtθ]
9	**nine** [naɪn]	9th	**ninth** [naɪnθ]
10	**ten** [ten]	10th	**tenth** [tenθ]
11	**eleven** [ɪ'levn]	11th	**eleventh** [ɪ'levnθ]
12	**twelve** [twelv]	12th	**twelfth** [twelfθ]
13	**thirteen** ['θɜː'tiːn]	13th	**thirteenth** ['θɜː'tiːnθ]
14	**fourteen** ['fɔː'tiːn]	14th	**fourteenth** ['fɔː'tiːnθ]
15	**fifteen** ['fɪf'tiːn]	15th	**fifteenth** ['fɪf'tiːnθ]
16	**sixteen** ['sɪks'tiːn]	16th	**sixteenth** ['sɪks'tiːnθ]
17	**seventeen** ['sevn'tiːn]	17th	**seventeenth** ['sevn'tiːnθ]
18	**eighteen** ['eɪ'tiːn]	18th	**eighteenth** ['eɪ'tiːnθ]
19	**nineteen** ['naɪn'tiːn]	19th	**nineteenth** ['naɪn'tiːnθ]
20	**twenty** ['twenti]	20th	**twentieth** ['twentiəθ]
21	**twenty-one** ['twenti'wʌn]	21st	**twenty-first** ['twenti'fɜːst]
...		...	
30	**thirty** ['θɜːti]	30th	**thirtieth** ['θɜːtiəθ]
40	**forty** ['fɔːti]	40th	**fortieth** ['fɔːtiəθ]
50	**fifty** ['fɪfti]	50th	**fiftieth** ['fɪftiəθ]
60	**sixty** ['sɪksti]	60th	**sixtieth** ['sɪkstiəθ]
70	**seventy** ['sevnti]	70th	**seventieth** ['sevntiəθ]
80	**eighty** ['eɪti]	80th	**eightieth** ['eɪtiəθ]
90	**ninety** ['naɪnti]	90th	**ninetieth** ['naɪntiəθ]
100	**a hundred** [ə'hʌndrəd] **one hundred** ['wʌn'hʌndrəd]	100th	**hundredth** ['hʌndrədθ]
101	**one hundred and one** [wʌnhʌndrədn'wʌn]	101st	**one hundred and first** [wʌnhʌndrədn'fɜːst]
...		...	
1000	**a thousand** [ə'θaʊznd] **one thousand** ['wʌn'θaʊznd]	1000th	**thousandth** ['θaʊznθ]

ENGLISH SOUNDS

[iː]	eat, see, he
[ɑː]	ask, class, car
[ɔː]	or, ball, door, four
[uː]	ruler, blue, too, two, you
[ɜː]	early, her, girl, work
[ɪ]	in, big, England
[e]	yes, bed, again, breakfast
[æ]	animal, cat, black
[ʌ]	bus, colour
[ɒ]	on, dog, what
[ʊ]	put, good
[ə]	again, sister, today
[i]	radio, video, happy
[u]	July, museum, usually
[eɪ]	eight, name, play, great
[aɪ]	I, time, right, my
[ɔɪ]	boy, toy
[əʊ]	old, no, road, yellow
[aʊ]	our, house, now
[ɪə]	near, here, we're
[eə]	airport, share, there, their
[ʊə]	poor, you're, sure
[b]	bike, table, verb
[p]	pen, pupil, shop
[d]	day, window, good
[t]	ten, matter, at
[k]	kitchen, car, back, book
[g]	go, again, bag
[ŋ]	wrong, morning, bank
[l]	like, old, small
[r]	ruler, friend, sorry
[v]	very, seven, have
[w]	we, where, quarter
[s]	six, poster, yes
[z]	present, quiz, his, please
[ʃ]	she, station, English
[tʃ]	child, teacher, match
[dʒ]	job, German, orange
[ʒ]	usually
[j]	yes, you, young
[θ]	thing, bathroom, month
[ð]	the, father, with

[iː] [ɑː] [ɔː]

THE ENGLISH ALPHABET

a	[eɪ]	n	[en]
b	[biː]	o	[əʊ]
c	[siː]	p	[piː]
d	[diː]	q	[kjuː]
e	[iː]	r	[ɑː]
f	[ef]	s	[es]
g	[dʒiː]	t	[tiː]
h	[eɪtʃ]	u	[juː]
i	[aɪ]	v	[viː]
j	[dʒeɪ]	w	['dʌbljuː]
k	[keɪ]	x	[eks]
l	[el]	y	[waɪ]
m	[em]	z	[zed]

IRREGULAR VERBS

Infinitive form (Grundform)	**Simple past form** (Einfache Vergangenheit)	**Present perfect form** (Vollendete Gegenwart)	
be	I was, you were, she was	I've been	sein
have	I had	I've had	haben
do	I did	I've done [dʌn]	tun, machen
become	I became	I've become	werden
bring	I brought	I've brought	bringen
buy	I bought	I've bought	kaufen
come	I came	I've come	kommen
deal	I dealt [delt]	I've dealt [delt]	sich kümmern
draw	I drew	I've drawn	zeichnen
drink	I drank	I've drunk	trinken
drive	I drove	I've driven ['drɪvn]	fahren
eat	I ate [et]	I've eaten	essen
fall	I fell	I've fallen	fallen
feed	I fed	I've fed	füttern
feel	I felt	I've felt	sich fühlen
find	I found	I've found	finden
forget	I forgot	I've forgotten	vergessen
get	I got	I've got	bekommen; holen
give	I gave	I've given	geben
go	I went	I've gone [gɒn]	gehen; fahren
hear	I heard [hɜːd]	I've heard [hɜːd]	hören
hold	I held	I've held	halten
hurt	I hurt	I've hurt	verletzen
know	I knew	I've known	wissen; kennen
leave	I left	I've left	verlassen
make	I made	I've made	machen
mean	I meant [ment]	I've meant [ment]	meinen; bedeuten
meet	I met	I've met	treffen; kennen lernen
pay	I paid	I've paid	zahlen, bezahlen
put	I put	I've put	stellen, legen, tun
read	I read [red]	I've read [red]	lesen, vorlesen
ride	I rode	I've ridden	(Rad/Quad) fahren
run	I ran	I've run	rennen
say	I said [sed]	I've said [sed]	sagen
see	I saw	I've seen	sehen
sell	I sold	I've sold	verkaufen
send	I sent	I've sent	senden
sing	I sang	I've sung	singen
sit	I sat	I've sat	sitzen; sich setzen
sleep	I slept	I've slept	schlafen
speak	I spoke	I've spoken	sprechen
spend	I spent	I've spent	ausgeben
stand	I stood	I've stood	stehen
swim	I swam	I've swum	schwimmen
take	I took	I've taken	nehmen; bringen
tell	I told	I've told	erzählen; sagen

Infinitive form (Grundform)	Simple past form (Einfache Vergangenheit)	Present perfect form (Vollendete Gegenwart)	
think	I thought	I've thought	(nach)denken; finden
understand	I understood	I've understood	verstehen
wear	I wore	I've worn	tragen, anziehen
win	I won	I've won	gewinnen
write	I wrote	I've written	schreiben

Lösungen (S.6 und S.134–149)

S.6: 1 Scotland, Wales; 2 England; 3 Ireland; 4 Scotland; 5 Wales; 6 Scotland; 7 England; 8 Ireland; 9 Wales; 10 Scotland

S.134: **Lerntipp** Anna; Dennis; Julia; Kevin; Marie; Tom

Test yourself a) dangerous, dirty, exciting, funny, important, late, lonely, quiet, stupid; b) bridge, letter, river, station, subject, train; c) feel, forget, meet, miss, need, repeat, stay, wear, work

S.136: **Test yourself 1:** 1 city; 2 photo; 3 Africa; 4 detective; 5 club; 6 witch; **2:** Find out, have, join, start, Asking; **3:** city, aunt, at night, radio, adult, writer; **4:** 1 to; 2 news; 3 Excuse; 4 like

S.137: **Lerntipp** h; i; r; e; u; a; r

Test yourself a) ideas, notes, text message, film; b) knew, liked, played, said, sent, stopped, thought, told, took, went, won; c) bad, frightened, happy, lonely, sad

S.139: **Test yourself 1:** 1 article; 2 castle; 3 problem; 4 embarrassed; 5 symbol; 6 statue; **2:** 1 Scots, 2 actor; 3 everything; 4 grave; **3:** of; for; with; **4:** 1 age; 2 born; languages; for

Lerntipp at/night; on/Internet; what/time; learn/by/heart

S.140: **Test yourself** a) find, go, meet, run, see, take, think; b) bridge, cafe, car park, cinema, hotel, post office, restaurant, school, shop, sports centre, swimming pool

S.142: **Test yourself 1:** season, clean, leek, treat, meet; **2:** Welsh, cider, gear, leek; **3:** 1 a waste of time; 2 parents are a pain; 3 he was in big trouble; 4 how to find us; **4:** 1 Can you pick me up after sport? 2 Mum says we mustn't drink alcohol. 3 Nobody can make me drink cider.

Test yourself a) beach, ice cream, rock, sun, the sea, water; b) computer, DVD player, light, mobile phone, MP3 player, TV; c) eight, first, one hundred, second, sixty-six, third

S.144/145: **Test yourself 1:** 1 eye; 2 pier; 3 dare; 4 slip; 5 scream; 6 floor; **2:** 1 railings; 2 charger; 3 face; 4 dare; **3:** towers, faces, machines, sandwiches, metres; **4:** 1 Sue is from the southern part of England. 2 Mark will stay for three and a half weeks. 3 Tina is worried about her cat. 4 The school is about 500 metres from here.

Test yourself a) aunt, brother, cousin, daughter, father, grandad, grandma, mother, parents, sister; b) hope, like, sure, think, want; c) modern, strict, fast

S.147: **Test yourself 1:** devastated, maybe, train, whale; **2:** 1 shopping centre; 2 suburb; 3 hot; 4 whale, dolphin; 5 high jump, running, hurling ; **3:** Dubliner, traveller, bully, Irish; **4:** 1 I came third in the competition. 2 I don't know what really happened. 3 I don't agree with you. 4 Is it true that you're ill?

Test yourself a) breakfast, cups, drinks, food, glasses, lunch, sandwiches; b) agree, like, think, right, true

S.149: **Test yourself 1:** 1 Cornish; 2 knife; 3 mirror; 4 flip-flops; **2:** 1 building; 2 flour; 3 beef; 4 fork; **3:** furthest, pepper, menu, library, smuggler

Girls/Women

Angie ['ændʒi]
Asha ['æʃə]
Chrissie ['krɪsi]
Ciara ['kɪərə]
Claire [kleə]
Emma ['emə]
Fiona [fi'əʊnə]
Gina ['dʒi:nə]
Holly ['hɒli]
Lara ['lɑ:rə]
Lauren ['lɔ:rən]
Lily ['lɪli]
Lucy ['lu:si]
Martina [mɑ:'ti:nə]
Pauline ['pɔ:li:n]
Per Li [pɜ:'li:]
Rose [rəʊz]
Sarah ['seərə]
Sue [su:]

Boys/Men

Aled ['æled]
Brad [bræd]
Callum ['kæləm]
Cameron ['kæmərən]
Dan [dæn]
Danny ['dæni]
Fred [fred]
Harry ['hæri]
Jack [dʒæk]
Jake [dʒeɪk]
Jamie ['dʒeɪmi]
John [dʒɒn]
Leo ['li:əʊ]
Liam ['li:əm]
Luke [lu:k]
Matt [mæt]
Mike [maɪk]
Robbie ['rɒbi]
Ryan ['raɪən]
Shane [ʃeɪn]
Sid [sɪd]
Tyler ['taɪlə]

Families

Gray [greɪ]
Humphries ['hʌmpfriz]
Jones [dʒəʊnz]
Marley ['mɑ:li]
Nixon ['nɪksən]
O'Brien [əʊ'braɪən]
Roberts ['rɒbəts]
Stone [stəʊn]
Thomas ['tɒməs]
Ward [wɔ:d]

Places

Bangor ['bæŋgə]
Beddgelert [beð'gelət]
Birmingham ['bɜ:mɪŋəm]
Blackpool ['blækpu:l]
Brick Lane ['brɪk'leɪn]
Buckingham Palace [bʌkɪŋəm'pæləs]
Bunratty Castle [bʌn'ræti'kɑ:sl]
Caernarfon [kə'nɑ:vən]
Central Promenade [sentrəlprɒmə'nɑ:d]
Cliffs of Moher [klɪfsəv'məʊhə]
Cornwall ['kɔ:nwəl]
Crieff [kri:f]
Dingle ['dɪŋgl]
Dublin ['dʌblɪn]
Edinburgh ['edɪnbərə]
Giant's Causeway [dʒaɪənts'kɔ:zweɪ]
Holyrood Park ['hɒliru:d'pɑ:k]
Kings Road ['kɪŋz'rəʊd]
Lake District ['leɪkdɪstrɪkt]
Launceston ['lɔ:ntstən]
Limerick ['lɪmərɪk]
Lizard Point [lɪzəd'pɔɪnt]
London ['lʌndən]
Manchester ['mæntʃɪstə]
Mark Street ['mɑ:kstri:t]
Millennium Bridge [mɪ'leniəmbrɪdʒ]
Newquay ['nju:ki]
Oxford Circus [ɒksfəd'sɜ:kəs]
Piccadilly Circus [pɪkədɪli'sɜ:kəs]
Porthmadog [pɔθ'mædɒg]
Raleigh Road [rɔ:li'rəʊd]
Ridley Road Market [rɪdlirəʊd'mɑ:kɪt]
Sandcastle Waterworld [sændkɑ:sl'wɑ:təwɜ:ld]
Sheffield ['ʃefi:ld]
Snowdon ['snəʊdən]
Truro ['trʊərəʊ]
Upper Thames Street [ʌpə'temzstri:t]
Westminster ['westmɪnstə]
Weston Road [westən'rəʊd]
Windsor ['wɪndzə]

Other names

Auld Lang Syne [ɔ:ldlæŋ'saɪn]
Bobby ['bɒbi]
Bob Cratchit ['bɒb'krætʃɪt]
Braveheart ['breɪvhɑ:t]
Charles Dickens ['tʃɑ:lz'dɪkɪnz]
Cho Chang ['tʃəʊ'tʃæŋ]
Debenhams ['debənəmz]
Disney ['dɪzni]
Doctor Who ['dɒktə'hu:]
Ebenezer Scrooge [ebəni:zə'skru:dʒ]
Ewan McGregor ['ju:ənmə'gregə]
Fagin ['feɪgɪn]
Fungi ['fʌŋgi]
Gelert ['gelət]
Harry Potter ['hæri'pɒtə]
Highland Games [haɪlənd'geɪmz]
Ian Rider ['i:ən'raɪdə]
Katie Leung ['keɪtili'ʌŋ]
Lemon Jelly ['lemən'dʒeli]
Llewelyn [lu:'elɪn]
Loch Ness [lɒk'nes]
Madness ['mædnəs]
Manchester United ['mæntʃɪstəju'naɪtɪd]
Oliver Twist ['ɒlɪvə'twɪst]
Robert Burns ['rɒbət'bɜ:nz]
Roger Hodgson ['rɒdʒə'hɒdʒsən]
Saint Patrick's Day [sənt'pætrɪksdeɪ]
Star Wars ['stɑ:wɔ:z]
Stormbreaker ['stɔ:mbreɪkə]
The Hootz [ðə'hu:tz]
The Waifs [ðə'weɪfs]
Titanic [taɪ'tænɪk]

Bildquellen

Inhalt ActionPlus (S.76 F / Slide File; S.106 / Neale Haynes; S.131 long jump & shot-put / Neil Tingle); Alamy, Oxford (S.6 o / Ian Shaw; S.11.2 / Jon Arnold; S.8B / Photofusion Picture Library; E / Brian Horisk; S.8F / Imagesource; S.9D & S.89 o-li / Ian Macpherson; S.9H / Michael Booth; S.10 li / Henry Westheim Photography; S.11.2 / Jenny Matthews; S.31 / M. Timothy O'Keefe; S.45 o / Dick Makin; S.46.4 / isifa Image Service s.r.o; S.48 protectors / Photolibrary, mountainboarders / Jeff Morgan; S.50a / Peter T Lovatt, S.50b / Rolf Richardson, S.50c / Barry Lewis; S.51d / Tim Gartside, S.51e / Alex Segre, S.51f / Alex Segre, S.51g / Andy Myatt; S.52 u / Photolibrary Wales; S.56.2 / William Nicklin; S.58.1 / Mark Dyball, S.58.2 / Len Grant Photography, S.58.3 / Richard Levine; S.61 Tower / Worldwide Picture Library; S.74.2 / Andrew Holt; S.79A / fstop2; S.81 pasty / WR Publishing; S.84 o / David Young-Wolff; S.88o / Visual arts Library (London); S.105 / Image Source; S.109 li / Adrian Muttitt; S.112 / PhotoStockFile; S.127 arts / VStock, stamp / Andrew Palmer; S.130 micro-wave / D. Hurst; S.132 flower / Plainpicture GmbH & Co. KG, parrot / tbkmedia.de); Alimdi.net (S.16 Mi / Thomas Ruffer); Avenue Images, Hamburg (S.11.5 & 6 / Corbis; S.16 re / Comstock; S.33.1 / Image Stock, S.33.4 / Purestock; S.43.3 & 4 / Comstock; S.46.3 / Digital Vision; S.48 skateboarder / Digital Vision, snowboarder / Corbis; S.96B / Index Stock; S.127 aerobics / Purestock, camera & chess / IT Stock Free, drama / Digital Vision; S.130 butter / Comstock; S.132 dolphin / Thinkstock, scorpion / Photoalto, star / BrandXPictures); BBC (S.60; S.104); Blackpool Tower (S.61 glass floor); BluEarth (S.125 mountainboard); BritainonView (S.37); Caro (S.33.3 / Oberhaeuser); Jacky Chapman (S.10 re; S.17 o; S.93, S.94); Cinetext Bildarchiv, Frankfurt (S.18 u / Tobis; S.96 u); Conrad Electronic, Hirschau (S.45 mountain board); Corbis, Düsseldorf (S.11.3 / Jose Fuste Raga; S.11.4 Martin Jones; S.43.2 / Brigitte Sporrer / Zefa; S.46.2 / Stuart Westmorland; S.89u-li / Tim Thompson; S.132 heart / ABM / zefa); Corel Library (S.19; S.74 Hintergrund; S.127 boxing; S.129 Flaggen, fashion, ice-hockey, jigsaw; S.130 cucumber, lettuce, tomato, egg, white bread, wholemeal bread; S.131 hurdles, javelin, pole vault); DEFD, Hamburg (S.18 o); Disney (S.34 DVD); DK Images (S.132 woman / Tim Ridley, man / Graham Atkins-Hughes); Eltinger.de (S.6 Autos); Frank Donoghue (S.76B & D; S.109 re); Epic Scotland (S.24 o-re; S.97 o); Gareth Evans, Berlin (S.80 re); F1 Online (S.76A); Fabfoodpix.com (S.130 bacon); Face to Face, Hamburg (S.132 pattern); Murdoch Ferguson, Scotland (S.24 o-li, Mi, u; S.27; S.38 u; S.97 u); Freefoto.com (S.11.1; S.16 li / Ian Britton); Getty Images, München (S.17 u / Doug Menuez / Photodisc Green; S.25 / M.J. Kim; S.29 / Christopher Furlong; S.74.1 / Timothy A. Clary / AFP); Ingram Publishing, Cheshire (S.48 helmet; S.57 guitar, teddybear); Inmagine (S.52o / Digital Vision); Interfoto (S.98 / NG Collection); The Irish Image Collection (S.74.3 / Richard Cummins); Keystone, Hamburg (S.6 Love Parade / Jochen Zick); Kobal Collection; London (S.22 o / Icon / Ladd Co / Paramount / Richard Blanshard, S.22 u / Icon Ladd Co / Paramount; S.23 Mi / Polygram / Alex Bailey); Siegfried Kuttig, Lüneburg (S.76C); Joerg Lantelme, Kassel (S.6 beer); Matton Images, Karlsruhe (S.46.1 / Digital Vision; sun / Ingram Publishing); Mauritius, Mittenwald (S.33.2 / Age); MGM Home Entertainment Dist. Corp. (S.23 o & u / 1996 Orion Pictures Corporation); Miele, Gütersloh (S.130 cooker, dishwasher, fridge); Axel Mosler, Dortmund (S.6 flag); Nokia (S.26; S.44B; S.45 phone; S.125 phone); Philips (S.125 DVD player; S.130 kettle, hairdryer, toothbrush, shaver, clock); Photofusion, London (S.132 butterfly / Paul Baldesare); Photolibrary Wales (S.36; S.38 o; S.39; S.43.1; S.43 u; S.56.5; S.89 o-li & o-re); Photothek.net (S.6 football fans / Liesa Johannssen); Schapowalow, Hamburg (S.6 Brot / N.Brueggemann; S.8A / Huber); Science and Society Picture Library, London (S.62o); Shutterstock (S.38 Mi / Vladimir Ivanovich Danilov; S.44a / Anastasiya Igolkina; S.44e / Arteki; S.45 DVD player / Pedro Diaz; S.56.1 / Dainis Deric; S.56.3 / Aleksander J; S.56.4 / WizData Inc.; S.57 ring / Jackie Foster, football / Tiplyashin Anatoly; S.62 Mi / Galina Barskaya, S.62 u / Lisa F. Young; S.79D / Anita; S.81 butter / Tomasz Trojanowski, carrot / Teo Boon Keng Alvin, beef / Denis Pepim, salt and pepper / Oscar Schnell, potatoes / steveq, water / Ljupco Smokovski, flour / Anita Patterson Peppers, onion / LockStockBob; S.84 glass / Mads Abildgaard, salt and pepper / J.Gatherum, knife / Rafa Irusta, cup / Tomasz Trojanowski, spoon & fork / Rafa Irusta, plate / adv; S.86 / Dan Tataru; S.88u / Stephen Aaron Rees; S.102 / Galina Barskaya; S.127 skateboarding / Tihis; S.128 camera / Black Ink Designers Corp, smileys / Linda Bucklin; S.129 juggling / Kenneth S. Thorkildsen, trampoline / John Lumb, rowing / Paul Yates, knitting / WhiteShadePhotos; S.131 discus / Jim Parkin); Siemens (S.44c & d; S.110); Derek Speirs, Dublin (S.64-69); Stills Online, Hamburg (S.45 bike; S.57 jacket, handbag); Stockfood.de, München (S.6 cake / Klaus Stemmler; S.130 tuna / FoodPhotogr. Eising, mayonnaise / Studio R. Schmitz); Ullstein, Berlin (S.132 dragon / Caro / Riedmiller); Vario-Press, Bonn (S.9G / Bernhard Classen; S.96A / Design Pics); Viking Tours, Dublin (S.76E); Visum, Hamburg (S.9C / Martin Leissl); Jordan Weeks, Cornwall (S.79B & C; S.80 café; S.87); Susan Wright, Edinburgh (S.89 castle)
Umschlag Matthew Ford, Richmond

Lied- und Textquellen

S.25: *Your song: It's a little bit,* T: John, Elton / Taupin, Bernie © 1970 Dick James Music Ltd. Für D/A/CH: Universal Music Publ. GmbH, Berlin; S.122: *I'm going to say I'm sorry* by Jeffrey Moss. © Year by Festival Attractions, Inc. Reprinted from *The Other Side of the Door* with permission from International Creative Management, Inc.; S.123: *My Teacher Loves Her iPod* © 2006 by Bruce Lansky. Reprinted from *My Teacher's in Detention* with permission from Meadowbrook Press; S.123: *Hot Sun* © 2006 Kenn Nesbitt. All Rights Reserved. Reprinted by permission of the author.

New Highlight
Band 3

Im Auftrage des Verlages herausgegeben von
Frank Donoghue, Nenagh, Irland

Erarbeitet von
Frank Donoghue, Nenagh, Irland • Rebecca Robb Benne, Otterup, Dänemark

Verlagsredaktion
Susanne Döpper (Projektleitung) • Silvia Wiedemann (verantwortliche Redakteurin)
Christine Maxwell

Anhang
Redaktionsbüro Birgit Herrmann, Aachen

Beratende Mitwirkung
Hans Bebermeier, Bielefeld • Dr. Johannes Berning, Münster • Hartmut Bondzio, Bielefeld
Annette Bondzio-Abbit, Bielefeld • Gisela Feldmann, Haltern • Joachim Grötzinger, Stuttgart
Prof. Dr. Liesel Hermes, Karlsruhe • Ingrid-Barbara Hoffmann, Böblingen • Dagmar Höffner, Ingelheim
Barbara Hohkamp, Stuttgart • Petra Klein, Runkel • Martina Kriebel, Brigachtal
Inge Kronisch, Flensburg • Geraldine Lewington-Happe, Paderborn • Christa Lüdemann, Hannover
Dr. Michaela Sambanis, Karlsruhe • Karin Steimle-Rohde, Karlsruhe • Konstanze Stöckermann-Borst, Leimen
Ellen Wiegard-Kaiser, Bielefeld • Herbert Willms, Herford • Gunhild Wolf, Unna

Illustration/Grafik
Adrian Barclay, Bristol • John Batten, London • Carlos Borrell, Berlin • Andy Peters, Norfolk
Tanja Székessy, Berlin

Umschlaggestaltung
Leonardi.Wollein, Berlin

Layoutkonzept
Christoph Schall

Layout und technische Umsetzung
Klein & Halm Grafikdesign, Berlin

www.cornelsen.de

1. Auflage, 1. Druck 2007

Alle Drucke dieser Auflage sind inhaltlich unverändert und können im Unterricht nebeneinander verwendet werden.

Druck: CS-Druck CornelsenStürtz, Berlin

ISBN 978-3-464-34456-9 – broschiert
ISBN 978-3-464-34345-6 – gebunden

Inhalt gedruckt auf säurefreiem Papier aus nachhaltiger Forstwirtschaft.